THE LAST TESTAMENT

GOD

(WITH DAVID JAVERBAUM)

SIMON & SCHUSTER PAPERBACKS

NEW YORK LONDON TORONTO SYDNEY NEW DELHI

Simon & Schuster Paperbacks
A Division of Simon & Schuster, Inc.
1230 Avenue of the Americas
New York, NY 10020

First Simon & Schuster paperback edition October 2012

SIMON & SCHUSTER PAPERBACKS and colophon
are registered trademarks of Simon & Schuster, Inc.

For information about special discounts for bulk purchases,
please contact Simon & Schuster Special Sales at
1-866-506-1949 or business@simonandschuster.com.

The Simon & Schuster Speakers Bureau can bring authors
to your live event. For more information or to book an event,
contact the Simon & Schuster Speakers Bureau at
1-866-248-3049 or visit our website at www.simonspeakers.com.

Designed by Ruth Lee-Mui

Manufactured in the United States of America

1   3   5   7   9   10   8   6   4   2

The Library of Congress has cataloged the hardcover edition as follows:
Javerbaum, David.
The last testament / God (with David Javerbaum).
—1st Simon & Schuster hardcover ed.
    p.   cm.
1. Religion—Humor.   2. God—Humor.   I. Title.
PN6231.R4J38 2011
818'.607—dc23   2011021981

ISBN 978-1-4516-4018-2
ISBN 978-1-4516-4019-9 (pbk)
ISBN 978-1-4516-4024-3 (ebook)

To anyone who's ever been told

"THOU SHALT NOT" . . .

and obeyed.

100 "TOP TWEETS"
from
@THETWEETOFGOD

#CHRISTIANITY

God @TheTweetOfGod
The Bible is 100% accurate. Especially when thrown at close range. #truth

---

God @TheTweetOfGod
My favorite part of the story of Genesis is the way they regrouped after Peter Gabriel left.

God @TheTweetOfGod
First Ireland had no Christianity. Then it had one Christianity. Then it had two. Mo' Christianities, mo' problems.

God @TheTweetOfGod
Matthew 28, John 20. Luke 24, Mark 21. That means Matthew and Luke will meet in the finals.

God @TheTweetOfGod
The difference between Bible prophecy and a Magic 8-Ball is no one uses "Reply hazy, ask again later" as an excuse to kill people.

God @TheTweetOfGod
@humanity This Lent I'm giving up caring.

God @TheTweetOfGod
It's a shame a figure as obviously phony as the Easter Bunny keeps people from appreciating the story of God's son who rose from the dead.

God @TheTweetOfGod
"YOU WANNA PIECE OF ME?!?"—Jesus, at the first communion. #everyonesacomedian

---

God @TheTweetOfGod
Hanukkah commemorates an ancient crisis of oil dependency in the Mideast with religious overtones. How far we've come.

God @TheTweetOfGod
Remember, on the first Christmas people bought a total of three gifts. And they were last-minute. And two of them sucked.

God @TheTweetOfGod
Those seeking last-minute Christmas gifts should knoweth that Wal-Mart has great deals on trampled human corpses.

#APOCRYPHA

God @TheTweetOfGod
It's not that he likes big butts; it's that he cannot lie. THAT'S why Sir Mix-a-Lot deserved his knighthood.

God @TheTweetOfGod
The Inuit have over 50 words for "visiting ethnolinguist."

God @TheTweetOfGod
No. You cannot get a what-what. Now stop asking.

God @TheTweetOfGod
If everyone actually did unto others as they would have others do unto them, there would be a global oral-sex daisy-chain within 15 minutes.

God @TheTweetOfGod
The Milky Way is a hard place to be if you're galactose-intolerant.

God @TheTweetOfGod
The new CEO of Apple is gay. Which, ironically, is pretty PC. #RIPSTEVEJOBS #SEEYOUSOON

God @TheTweetOfGod
Marijuana is a gateway drug to really good marijuana.

God @TheTweetOfGod

"Ontario Legalizes Brothels." Or as they will soon be known, Tim Whoreton's

---

God @TheTweetOfGod

If you went to the doctor and the doctor said, "No more monkeys jumping on the bed!", consider getting a second opinion.

God @TheTweetOfGod

"Why is everything so expensive?" Because it's everything. Try shopping for individual items. They tend to be cheaper.

God @TheTweetOfGod

@aliciasilverstone Vegetarianism would be much easier if animals grew on trees.

God @TheTweetOfGod

Show me a "social media consultant" and I'll show you a twentysomething with ill-defined career plans and an iPhone.

God @TheTweetOfGod

MISSING: One particle. Mass 125 GeV. Responds to name "Higgs." Somewhat small. If found, please return to Owner. Reward: Nobel Prize.

God @TheTweetOfGod

The New 10 Plagues: 1.Spam 2.Smog 3.Starbucks 4.Kardashians 5.Hipsters 6. Talk radio 7. Sequels 8. Meth 9. CO_2 10. Chocoholism

---

#RIGHTEOUS

God @TheTweetOfGod

I support the separation of church and hate.

God @TheTweetOfGod

Yes, I'm pro-life. But if you're familiar with my work you know I'm not exactly anti-death either.

God @TheTweetOfGod
If hell existed, it would be filled mainly with people who kept telling other people they were going there. @westborobaptist @patrobertson @joelosteen #hinthintnudgenudge

God @TheTweetOfGod
Those who are passionately pro-life tend not to have one.

God @TheTweetOfGod
Every positive role religion plays in society also falls under the category of "good manners."

God @TheTweetOfGod
"Pope Warns Against 'Superficial Glitter'." Dude, LOOK AT WHAT YOU'RE WEARING.

God @TheTweetOfGod
People, don't fight over whether to say "Merry Christmas" or "Happy Holidays." ANY empty platitude devoid of sincerity is fine by Me.

God @TheTweetOfGod
The Christian right hates Halloween. Not because it's pagan, but because it involves handing out free food.

God @TheTweetOfGod
Up and down would both be good directions for Rush Limbaugh to shut. #seewhatIdidthere

God @TheTweetOfGod
The great thing about praying for a victim is that it's so much easier than helping him.

God @TheTweetOfGod
"You CAN Pray the Gay Away." Listen, @anncoulter, if people could pray unwanted things away, I'd have reduced thee to cinders years ago.

God @TheTweetOfGod
The difference between organized religion and organized crime is the former is far deadlier, more profitable, and safer from prosecution.

God @TheTweetOfGod
"I'll pray for you" is an evangelical's way of saying "Fuck you."

God @TheTweetOfGod
"Scientology" is a combination of "scient-," meaning "science," and "-ology," meaning "science." And it just gets stupider from there.

God @TheTweetOfGod
Praying the gay away is about as effective as sodomizing the religion away.

God @TheTweetOfGod
"Study: Homophobes Often Secret Homosexuals."
Three reactions: 1. Duh. 2. DUH. 3. DUUUUUUUUUUUUUUUHHHHHHHHHH.

God @TheTweetOfGod
The last people legitimately on a mission from Me were named Jake and Elwood.

God @TheTweetOfGod
Those who speak out against birth control are the ones whose parents needed it most of all. #Iwastheoriginalplannedparenthood

#SPORTS

God @TheTweetOfGod
#Tebow is proof that either I definitely exist, or I definitely don't.

God @TheTweetOfGod
It's baseball's opening day, and you know what that means—only five more months 'til football!

God @TheTweetOfGod
Shoot me up at the ballgame! Shoot me up with the clear! Buy me some steroids and HCG's! I don't care if my balls look like peas!

God @TheTweetOfGod
All things considered it would be fairer to say that @peytonmanning released the #Colts.

God @TheTweetOfGod
Is anyone else concerned that the new champion of American college football is some shadowy group called al-Abama? #soundsliketerrorists

God @TheTweetOfGod
"Lebron Dislocates Ring Finger." Good thing he'll never have to wear a ring on it.

God @TheTweetOfGod
Can anyone explain cricket to Me? I can't figure the rules out.

#WISDOM

God @TheTweetOfGod
Fool me once, shame on you. Fool me twice, fuck you.

God @TheTweetOfGod
They say patience is a virtue. They also say he who hesitates is lost. You see my point: They don't know what the fuck they're saying.

God @TheTweetOfGod
Those who do not study the past are doomed to RT it. Pls RT!

God @TheTweetOfGod
If stupid people and evil people fought to the death, the winner would be everyone else.

God @TheTweetOfGod
Insomnia stands between you and your dreams.

God @TheTweetOfGod
Closed-mindedness makes you incapable of learning. Open-mindedness makes you intellectually vulnerable. Be ajar-minded.

God @TheTweetOfGod

If a tree falls in the forest and no one hears it, that's #tragedy. If it falls on a guy, that's #comedy. And if he's deaf, that's #irony.

God @TheTweetOfGod

Everything happens for no reason.

God @TheTweetOfGod

Do not go outside during a hurricane, unless you're a reporter whose job is to show what happens to morons who go outside during hurricanes.

God @TheTweetOfGod

The thing you are currently stressing over at work is stupid. This is always true, for everyone.

God @TheTweetOfGod

Don't despair. It's always been this bad. You've just gotten better at noticing it.

God @TheTweetOfGod

"It's funny because it's true" + "the truth hurts" = it's funny because it hurts. And that's what comedy is.

God @TheTweetOfGod

Don't let anyone call you an "underachiever." If they knew you, they'd know how amazing it is that you've managed to accomplish anything.

God @TheTweetOfGod

Love is blind. Justice is blind. Hate and injustice have great eyesight. Hence, history.

God @TheTweetOfGod

Remember: other people may be more talented or hard-working or attractive than you, but deep down they're probably, like, sad or something.

God @TheTweetOfGod

Yes, other people are annoying. But to everyone else in the world, you are other people.

God @TheTweetOfGod
It's very important to be able to laugh at yourself, because you're an idiot.

#AMERICA

God @TheTweetOfGod
The United States' motto should be "America: We Put Cheese on Things."

God @TheTweetOfGod
The problem with government "of the people, by the people and for the people" is obvious to anyone who's ever dealt with people.

God @TheTweetOfGod
As a rule the more someone says they love America, the more Americans they hate.

God @TheTweetOfGod
@SarahPalinUSA "Tea party" used to denote children serving an imaginary solution to stuffing-headed friends in a make-believe world. And it still does.

God @TheTweetOfGod
Same-sex marriage should not be allowed in Alabama, but only because neither should opposite-sex marriage, or having children, or living.

God @TheTweetOfGod
I fucking hate Sarah Palin.

#GODHEAD

God @TheTweetOfGod
I made you in My image. The thing is, I'm an asshole.

God @TheTweetOfGod
People, I cannot instantaneously "damn it" just because thou art mad at "it." There's a procedure. Filleth out the paperwork.

God @TheTweetOfGod
RT if you're carbon-based and proud!

God @TheTweetOfGod
I giveth, and I taketh away. Why? Because I recycleth.

God @TheTweetOfGod
Me: "So nice to have the whole family here for Thanksgiving dinner." Jesus: "Yup, it's a lot better than my 'Last Supper'." Me: [rolls eyes]

God @TheTweetOfGod
@JayZ I've got 99,000,000,000,000,000 grains of sand and a beach ain't one.

God @TheTweetOfGod
You know why I don't give gifts on Christmas? Because I gave you an awesome one 2,000 years ago, and you returned it broken.

God @TheTweetOfGod
Got Jesus the new #AirJordans for his birthday. I hope he likes them! They were custom-made by My elves. And by "elves" I mean Chinese kids.

God @TheTweetOfGod
Jesus is so happy in his new Air Jordans! He says it feels like he's walking on water all over again.

God @TheTweetOfGod
If you RT this you can skip church. If you planned to anyway you can masturbate. If you planned to anyway you can masturbate in church.

#MOREWISDOM

God @TheTweetOfGod

Only he who has walked through the deepest valley knows how other valleys of lesser depth are relatively more walk-through-able, valley-wise.

God @TheTweetOfGod

Dress for the job you want, not the job you have. In many cases this will mean showing up to the interview in a pirate suit.

God @TheTweetOfGod

Artificial intelligence can never take the place of natural stupidity.

God @TheTweetOfGod

Two roads diverged in a wood, and I, I took the one less traveled by. And now I'm being devoured by wolves. #fuckrobertfrost

---

God @TheTweetOfGod

Being misunderstood doesn't make you a genius.

God @TheTweetOfGod

Genius is a) looking at the world in a whole new way while—and this is much rarer—b) not being batshit insane.

God @TheTweetOfGod

Is life fair? Short answer: No. Long answer: Noooooooooooooooooooooo.

God @TheTweetOfGod

The first person who says you're a jerk is just threatened by your talent. But the hundredth person who says it is probably on to something.

God @TheTweetOfGod

You can kill time as much as you like, but sooner or later it will return the favor.

God @TheTweetOfGod

It's too bad the meaning of life is 141 characters long.

#NIGH

God @TheTweetOfGod
Sometimes I love you so much I just want to kill you all and bring you up here and give you a hug.

God @TheTweetOfGod
Most New Year's resolutions are soon forgotten until next New Year's, and I'm no exception. But I mean it: THIS is the year I kill you all.

God @TheTweetOfGod
@Twitter goes overcapacity and everyone panics. Meanwhile the whole planet is overcapacity and you're all skipping along toward that oblivion.

God @TheTweetOfGod
Attention: Will the owners of a blue planet with plate tectonics please attend to your vehicle. It is overheating.

God @TheTweetOfGod
100 years ago ice sank a ship and you're still talking about it. Meanwhile ice is sinking ENTIRE COASTLINES but mum's the word on that one.

God @TheTweetOfGod
Worry less about how I might end the world and more about how you might make it less worthy of ending.

God @TheTweetOfGod
SPOILER ALERT!: Everybody dies.

TABLET OF CONTENTS

PROLOGUE

1 n the beginning, I took a lunch with Daniel Greenberg of the Levine Greenberg Literary Agency.

2 For the future of print was without hope, and void; and darkness had fallen upon the face of the entire publishing industry.

3 So one day Daniel, my agent, whom I have been with forever; by which I do not mean literally "forever," as I started out unrepresented, but a good 25 years or so;

4 Anyway, Daniel got us a table at Balthazar; for he knows someone there.

5 So we met, and exchanged pleasantries, and sat down, and caught up; and in time I coyly came around to asking him why he wanted to see me, although I knew, and he knew that I knew, and I knew that he knew that I knew; but lo, this is how the game is played.

6 And then, over a *frisée aux lardons* that they were not serving in heaven then, but they are *now*, he spoke unto me:

7 "O Lᴏʀᴅ our God, King of the Universe, here's what I'm thinking.

8 Thy previous books have sold an impressive six billion copies;

9 They form the basis of three great religions, and five crappy ones;

10 They have been translated into 2,453 languages, including that of a fictional race of TV aliens wearing shoe polish;

11 They can be found in every synagogue, church, mosque, and Comfort Inn in the world;

12 And most importantly, they have done for faith, and ethics, and morality, what *The Bartender's Bible* hath done for bartending.

13 But lo, it has been nigh on 14 centuries since thy last book—"

14 "Forget not *The Book of Mormon*," I interrupted.

¹⁵ "Thy last *serious* book," he continued; "and now a pestilence has befallen our tribe; books go unread; bookstores go unpatronized; libraries remain Dork Central;

¹⁶ And while digitalization presents an opportunity, it is also a challenge; the paradigm is shifting; I don't know if thou dost follow the trades, but content-wise—"

¹⁷ "*I follow everything!*" I bellowed, using the reverb voice and thunder-rumbling sound that I am wont to employ on such occasions.

¹⁸ "Forgive me, LORD," said Daniel; "I shall rend my garment and grovel in thy sight later.

¹⁹ I mean only to say, that if I were to approach major publishing houses with a proposal for God's last testament, it would make a pretty strong pitch."

²⁰ "But of what shall it be composed?" I asked, pressing my fork into the poached egg, then idly watching its liberated amber yolk ooze seductively over the farm-fresh chicory.

²¹ "For I have already imparted all my wisdom, and bestowed all my law, and revealed all my truth;

²² And also I confess to being sore afraid, that I may not have another book in me";

²³ And at this I sighed, and turned away, and did earnestly wonder if I still "had it."

²⁴ And Daniel said, "Surely this is not the same confident, All-Powerful God who parted the Red Sea, and bore his son through a virgin mother, and . . . and . . . well, I've never read the Koran, but I'm sure thou didst some amazing things in there also.

²⁵ Besides, the book *I* envision is not like unto those.

²⁶ For in the book I envision, thou wouldst revisit thy greatest hits—the Old and New Testaments, and the Koran if thou insistest—but in a manner more in keeping with the modern custom;

²⁷ Meaning, that thou shalt 'open up' about their events; and 'share' thy feelings; and 'dish' about the various public figures therein, thus creating a 'telleth-all.'

²⁸ (That's not a bad title, by the way.)

²⁹ Then thou shalt continue the tale by describing thy activities and where-abouts over the past one thousand four hundred years; a period I suspect many of thy devotees have a few questions about.

³⁰ And then thou shalt finish with a sneak peek into the future, with per-haps a brief glimpse of what lies in store for the end of the world; which, again, I think may be of some interest to thy hardcore fans.

³¹ But checketh it out, for here is the best part: Interspersed throughout shall be a series of short essays on matters of contemporary interest; such as natural disasters, and America, and celebrities, and regional athletic contests, and whatever other bits of frivolity thou conceivest;

³² The better to cater to the sensibilities of the modern reader, whose capac-ity for following unbroken written narrative hath dwindled to the size of a piece of Jonathan Franzen's neck-stubble.

³³ My point, G-Man"—and here Daniel reached across the table and grabbed the hem of my garment in a way few ten-percenters have ever done without an insta-smiting—

³⁴ "Is that I love thee as a deity, and worship thee as an author; so I would have thee find new favor among men, by coming down off thy pedestal and humanizing thyself,

³⁵ That thou might once again top the best-seller list, only this time in the modern era:

³⁶ An era in which, I would remind thee, royalties can be properly ac-counted for."

³⁷ Then he fell silent; and long I pondered.

³⁸ Yea, long I pondered; until slowly the ancient desire to spread my word among man that he may glorify me, began to stir in my spirit once more.

³⁹ And the waiter came and separated Daniel's check from mine; and Daniel picked up both checks; for he saw that that would be good.

AGAINESIS

CHAPTER 1

 ¹ n the beginning, God created the heavens and the earth."

² Yea; that takes me back.

³ Back to the first day of creation; the day when, in a sense, it all began for me;

⁴ The day I tossed aside the idleness of my early eons, to take on the honor, responsibility, and privilege of being the LORD thy God, King of the Universe.

⁵ I remember that day like it was yesterday, though to be sure it was not yesterday; rather it was ages ago, across an unfathomable sea of time whose meagerest inlet exceeds the ken of human understanding.

⁶ It was October 23, 4004 B.C.

⁷ But before I speak of that day, and that week, and all the laughter and tears and tragedy and triumph that followed; let me pause at the beginning of this, my last testament, to tell thee a little about myself.

⁸ I am Omnipotent, Omniscient, All-Merciful, All-Powerful, All-Informed, All-Possessing, All-Compelling, All-Subduing, Most Holy, Most High, and Most Powerful.

⁹ My hobbies include being Sovereign LORD, Heavenly Ordainer, Daystar of Eternal Guidance, Tabernacle of Majesty, Quintessence of Glory, Hand of Divine Power, Tongue of Grandeur, and Eye of Splendor.

¹⁰ And in the interest of full disclosure, I must also confess that I have on occasion been known to dabble in being the Desire of the World, the Source of Everlasting Life, the Sovereign Protector, and the Wellspring of Infinite Grace.

¹¹ With all these qualities, and many more—for another of my qualities is being infinitely qualitied—people have often wondered why it was I created the universe, when I could have remained content simply to hover alone as pure spirit contemplating my own divinity.

¹² Because that's not godding, that's why.

13 In my humble opinion, thou canst hardly call thyself the LORD, if thou hast created no other beings to LORD it over.

14 (Besides, I *did* try hovering alone as pure spirit once; but one can only contemplate oneself contemplating oneself contemplating oneself contemplating oneself for so long before it getteth old.)

15 I had a burning ambition to rule the world, but I knew such a world was not going to create itself; no fully formed planet was going to suddenly appear and say, "Here, LORD, take these 20 burnt offerings," or "Here, LORD, take these 50 infidel heads," or "Here, LORD, take these 200 years of religious warfare."

16 No; there was nothing for it but to strike out on my own; to follow my own dreams, and pursue my own vision, and make my own fortune; relying on nothing but my own grit, and pluck, and infinite power over the space-time continuum.

17 And so I began my story; and so I begin it now.

18 Yet there is one more truth I would have thee bear in mind before I commence; for it is the prism through which all revelation herein contained must pass to be seen clearly.

19 *I am not perfect.*

20 Yea, I am omnipotent; but there are mortals tramping thy corridors of power who are nearly so, at least within the earthly dominion; and does their great might foster in them perfect righteousness? Or are they not mostly bastards?

21 Yea, I am omniscient; but there are mortals waddling the casinos of Las Vegas possessing nearly all information on the handicapping arts; yet does their great knowledge foster in them perfect judgment? Or did they not just lose their shirts on the Seahawks +2½?

22 And so, Reader, as thou flippest through these awe-inspiring pages, be not surprised to discover that over the millennia I have erred on matters great and small, and even at times shown slight defects of character.

²³ For despite all the sobriquets listed above, and all the wondrous attributes contained within me, I am not perfect, and have never claimed to be.

²⁴ I have claimed only, that my imperfections are thy fault.

CHAPTER 2

¹ The most important thing about undertaking a large-scale building project such as a universe, is to divide it into small, manageable action items.

² For if thou seest it as a single large operation, thou art bound to become discouraged, and say to thyself, "Oh, I shall never manage to build a whole universe in six days; it is just too darn hard."

³ So knowing the pitfalls of this approach, I banished it from my thinking from day one (Day One), and laid the week out as a series of attainable goals: the first being the relatively simple task, of creating the heavens and the earth.

⁴ That took about five hours.

⁵ It would have taken far less, had I been able to see what I was doing; but there being darkness over the surface of everything, I had to work mainly by feel.

⁶ Reflecting upon this later, I had an epiphany; so I said, "Let there be light!" and there was light; which was encouraging, that the utilities were already working.

⁷ And I saw the darkness, and called it "night"; and I saw the light, and called it "day"; and then I called it a day.

⁸ Day Two was the riskiest decision point of the entire week; for as thou mayest read, "Let there be a firmament in the midst of the waters, and let it divide the waters from the waters."

⁹ (I will note here that all Bible references in this book will quote the King James Version; it being not merely the most majestic translation, but the only one endorsed by basketball great LeBron James.)

¹⁰ Now, waters-division would have been a bold creative risk no matter how I attempted it; but what made what I did truly dicey—take that, Einstein!—was that I did it with a firmament.

¹¹ For if thou art at all familiar with firmaments, thou knowest they have a tendency to leak like unto a Cajun levee.

¹² And this foreboded a disaster I could ill afford, as I planned to one day—the next one—transform the waters above the firmament into the sky; which I intended to make of a completely different substance from the waters; though I thought I'd keep the blue motif.

¹³ But if the firmament were not of the strictest structural integrity, the sky would have seeped into the sea, and the sea into the sky; and then I would have been looking at millennia of renovation.

¹⁴ Still, I made the firmament; and all these millennia later it still holds; for back then thought was still given to craftsmanship and detail; unlike now, when everything is done by machine, or, even worse, by exploited Asian children whose hearts are just not in it.

¹⁵ Day Three was fairly routine: dry land in the morning, plant life in the afternoon.

¹⁶ Forming the dry land gave me the most pleasure I had all week, for I took great delight in shaping the landmasses; in carving the Grand Canyon, and sculpting the Himalayas, and shaping Florida so as to resemble what I, even at that early date, was fairly certain was going to be a penis.

¹⁷ As for the plants, that was tedious going, for plants are dull; ecologically necessary, but dull; especially trees, which bore me to no end.

¹⁸ Hear me: I am the LORD thy God, King of the Universe; and trees are stupid.

¹⁹ Day Four was "Astronomy Day": I created the sun, the moon, and the stars; the planets, too, although that part is not mentioned in Genesis.

²⁰ (Yea, there are countless things I omitted from the Old Testament when I dictated it to Moses; it does not mean they did not occur, or that I forgot about them; it means I was merciful enough to want thee to leave church at a reasonable hour.)

²¹ The Day Four achievement of which I am proudest, was sizing the sun and moon so perfectly as to allow for eclipses upon the surface of the earth; creating thereby spectacular occasions for awe and panic;

²² Which are without question, my two all-time favorite human emotions.

²³ Day Five was a stressful day, a near-disaster; for it was when I "let the water teem with living creatures, and let birds fly above the earth across the vault of the sky."

²⁴ Fill the sea with fish, fill the sky with birds; in hindsight this seems obvious; yet up until the last minute I had been planning on putting the fish in the sky and the birds in the sea.

²⁵ I kid thee not!

²⁶ For I had conceived feathers as a means of aquatic propulsion; whereas scales were designed to provide maximum aerodynamic lift;

²⁷ Yet when it came time to let the waters teem, for some reason I went the other way, and threw the fish in instead of the birds.

²⁸ And lo: The fish took to the waters so perfectly, that today to even imagine a fish out of water, is to envision a comical juxtaposition.

²⁹ As for the birds, having no other place to put them I threw them all into the sky; where their quill-flippers proved unexpectedly adept aviation aids; so it worked out for everyone, except the penguins and ostriches.

³⁰ And then came Day Six, a whirlwind of activity; for I spent it creating the land animals.

³¹ I created them in groups: mammals, amphibians, reptiles, insects; over 400,000 different species of beetles alone did I create.

³² It is not that I am fond of beetles; to the contrary, I did not like any of them; over 400,000 times I strove to make the perfect one, and over 400,000 times I failed;

³³ Until finally I created the Colorado potato beetle, *Leptinotarsa decemlineata;* and I thought, "Now *there* is a beetle!" and I moved on.

³⁴ Late that afternoon, I paused to take in my work.

³⁵ In just under six days I had built an entire universe in literally the middle of nowhere; and I had done so under budget.

³⁶ Life thrived everywhere; the stars shone, the oceans roared, the flowers bloomed; all around me flourished the myriad signs of my glorious abundance . . .

³⁷ And then, *thou* walked in.

CHAPTER 3

¹ ut before I speak of humanity's earliest ancestors, I must here address a subject of great importance to all seekers of truth; but particularly those seekers of truth, who are tenth-graders in Kansas.

² Over the last several hundred years, scientists have uncovered an obscene amount of evidence in support of the theory of evolution expounded by Charles Darwin.

³ And each such piece of evidence has seemingly revealed a new and more profound inconsistency between reality, and the account of Creation offered in Genesis.

⁴ Now, I know many of my faithful servants have labored earnestly to reconcile the two; even going so far as to form a new discipline, "creation science"; a phrase carrying roughly the same intellectual heft, as "dragon anatomy."

⁵ But by now, the absurdity of this endeavor has surely become apparent to even my most steadfast defenders.

⁶ And so I must tell thee here, in the spirit of candor, that the evidence for evolution is now indeed so overwhelming, so incontrovertible, so beyond the level of mere "theory," that it can no longer possibly be denied,

⁷ How impressive it is, that I planted it all.

⁸ Because I did.

⁹ I planted it all.

¹⁰ Every . . . last . . . bit of it.

¹¹ *Zing!*

¹² Canst thou grasp the scope of my hoax, humanity?

¹³ Can thy mortal minds absorb even a drop of the immense ocean constituting the thoroughness of thy punking?

¹⁴ If all of thee, working together since the dawn of time, were charged with devoting thy lives to the single task of fabricating all the evidence that exists to support evolution, thou wouldst fail utterly.

¹⁵ But I am God; in me all things are fakeable.

¹⁶ I molded the fossils; I deposited the dinosaurs; I modified the DNA; I mutated the vestigial tails; I arranged the migratory distributions; I specialized the finch beaks; I booked Darwin's cruise.

¹⁷ And I did more than this: I meticulously layered geological strata; I altered the level of carbon 14 in every rock on earth; I even redshifted every particle of light in the universe so that it would appear to thy observers that the cosmos was created through some kind of large-scale explosion 13.7 billion years ago.

¹⁸ Yea; over the eons I have invested more time and energy into falsifying an empirically unassailable case for evolution than any other venture since Creation itself.

¹⁹ Wouldst thou like to know why?

²⁰ Because every time a scientist dies and ascends to heaven, and I spend an hour lavishing him with praise about his use of reason and facts to overcome the primitive superstition of his fellows;

²¹ Then does the entire colossal undertaking become worth it, at that glorious moment, when the thunder claps, and the skies darken, and I bellow, "So long, sucker!", and the trapdoor opens, and I send him to hell.

CHAPTER 4

¹ o resume:

² It is often said—and even more often screamed at anti–gay marriage rallies outside the statehouse in Lansing—that I created Adam and Eve, not Adam and Steve.

³ Wrong.

⁴ Now will I tell the story of the first man, Adam; and of the companion I fashioned for him, Steve; and of the great closeting that befell their relationship.

⁵ For after I created the earth, and sea, and every plant and seed and beast of the field and fowl of the air, and had the place pretty much set up, I saw that it was good;

⁶ But I also saw, that by way of oversight it made administrative sense to establish a new middle-managerial position.

⁷ So as my final act of Day Six, I formed a man from the dust of the ground, and breathed life into his nostrils; and I called him Adam, to give him a leg up alphabetically.

⁸ And lo, I made him for my image; not *in* my image, but *for* my image; because with Creations thou never gettest a second chance to make a first impression;

⁹ And so in fashioning him I sought to make not only a responsible planetary caretaker, but also an attractive, likeable spokesman who in the event of environmental catastrophe could project a certain warmth.

¹⁰ To immediately assess his ability to function in my absence, I decided to change my plans; for I had intended to use Day Seven to infuse the universe with an innate sense of compassion and moral justice; but instead I left him in charge and snoozed.

¹¹ And Adam passed my test; yea, he was by far my greatest achievement; he befriended all my creatures, and named them, and cared for them; and tended the Garden most skillfully; for he had a great eye for landscape design.

¹² But I soon noticed he felt bereft in his solitude; for oft he sighed, and pined for a helpmeet; and furthermore he masturbated incessantly, until he had well-nigh besplattered paradise.

¹³ So one night I caused him to fall into a deep sleep; fulsomely did I roofie his nectar; and as he slept, I removed a rib, though not a load-bearing one.

¹⁴ And from this rib I fashioned a companion for him; a hunk, unburdened by excess wisdom; ripped, and cut, and hung like unto a fig tree before the harvest;

¹⁵ Yea, and a power bottom.

¹⁶ And Adam arose, and saw him, and wept for joy; and he called the man Steve; I had suggested Steven, but Adam liked to keep things informal.

¹⁷ And Adam and Steve were naked, and felt no shame; they knew each other, as often as possible; truly their loins were a wonderland.

¹⁸ And they were happy, having not yet eaten of the Tree of the Knowledge That Your Lifestyle Is Sinful.

CHAPTER 5

 ¹ ow the snake was more closeted than any animal in the Garden; literally on the downlow; for though he oft hissed his desire to mate with comely serpentesses, yet he lisped, and fretted over his skin care, and could not have looked more phallic if he'd had balls for a rattle.

² And that which he needlessly despised in himself, he set out to destroy in others; so one day he slithered unto Steve and said,

³ "Steve!

⁴ 'Tsup?

⁵ Hey, random question for thee: Hast thou ever eaten the fruit of the Tree of the Knowledge That Your Lifestyle Is Sinful?

⁶ 'Cause I hear it's some quality produce!"

⁷ Long did the serpent cozen Steve in this way; at first he balked, but the serpent tricked him, by telling him that the fruit would intensify his orgasm; which was a reckless lie;

⁸ For the fruit did not intensify orgasms; it merely prolonged them 45 minutes.

⁹ And so Steve ate of the tree; and he bid Adam eat of it; and the knowledge that their lifestyle was sinful shamed them, and also filled them with white-hot lust; and they entwined themselves unceasingly until dawn.

¹⁰ (For it was and remains true, that all aspects of sexual activity grow more pleasurable following their moral condemnation.)

¹¹ But in the morning they grew embarrassed, and cloaked themselves in fig leaves; these constituting the entirety of their fall collection.

¹² And they heard me walking in the garden in the cool of the day; and they hid themselves from my presence behind a grove; which, a lot of good *that's* going to do;

¹³ And I called, "Adam and Steve, where art thou?"

¹⁴ And Adam said, "Father, there is something we need to tell thee: we are gay."

¹⁵ And I said, "*Whhhuuuhhhhh?!?*"

¹⁶ And Steve said, "Yea, it is true, LORD; for the snake bid me eat the fruit of the forbidden Tree; and I gave it to Adam; and now we know that we are not only here, but queer; and lo, we would thou growest accustomed to it."

¹⁷ And I turned to the serpent and screamed, "Thou hast ruined everything; for I had wrought Steve of the same gender as Adam, so that they could not breed, and would be free to focus on their gardening careers;

¹⁸ But thou hast made them ashamed for no reason, by convincing them to eat of the Tree of the Knowledge That Your Lifestyle Is Sinful."

¹⁹ "But LORD," said the serpent, "surely I could not have done this evil thing, if thou didst not inexplicably put this stigmatizing tree in the Garden to begin with."

[20] I considered this.

[21] "Look," I said, "hindsight is twenty-twenty.

[22] And surely this is not the time to play the 'blame game'; at least not until my full-scale internal investigation is complete;

[23] Whose findings will be used to ensure, that an event as tragic as the Fall of Man, never happens again.

[24] But in the meantime, serpent, thou art cursed above every beast of the field; and dust shalt thou eat all the days of thy life; and even the humans who study thee will be accursed; for they will be known as 'herpetologists,' which sounds like 'herpes.'

[25] And as for thee, Adam and Steve: Damn it! I knew I should have made thee lesbians!

[26] Then thou wouldst have tended the Garden with more diligence; yea, and been a lot more outdoorsy in general.

[27] But thou hast been disobedient; and for that I must now inflict upon thee the harshest punishment possible:

[28] Transforming thee from carefree young lovers living in the heart of everything, to a married couple with kids stuck in the suburbs.

[29] Steve, so that thou mayest bear young, I will tomorrow transform thee into a woman; fear not, the operation is relatively standard; in the meantime, put this on.

[30] Oh, and consider what female name thou wilt want; try to make it something that rhymes with 'Steve,' so that 6,000 years from now, the righteous can use it to create the most inane slogan of all time.

[31] As for posterity, do not worry about humanity learning the true nature of thy relationship.

[32] I am the LORD thy God, King of the Universe; I know how to spin this."

CHAPTER 6

¹ So Adam and "Eve" left the Garden, and wandered the wilderness, supporting themselves through foraging and occasional freelance work.

² And they learned how to copulate; and after a few years they learned how to do it vaginally; until finally Eve found herself with child.

³ It was the first human pregnancy, and she had no idea what was happening; so I explained to her, that a tiny person would be living inside her uterus for nine months and growing to the size of a watermelon before passing out of her vagina.

⁴ She did not take it well.

⁵ But I give her credit; despite all the dangers she stuck it out; and though she suffered in childbirth like no woman has suffered since, when it was all over she had borne Cain;

⁶ The first baby, and in time, the first great disappointment to his parents.

⁷ Thou hast read of what transpired between Cain and his younger brother Abel; how Cain murdered Abel in a jealous rage.

⁸ For Abel was a shepherd, and as a sacrifice he offered unto me his flock's firstlings, which were absolutely adorable; yea, to this day they remain the cutest things I have ever seen burned alive on a pyre.

⁹ But Cain was a farmer, and his offering to me was but ten sheaves of wheat; pretty scanty, sheafwise; and thou shouldst have seen these sheaves; completely unacceptable, even by the most basic standard of sacrificial wheat-sheaf quality.

¹⁰ And I told Cain as much; and he grew angry, and set out to kill his brother.

¹¹ Now, this will sound strange, and even cruel, but it is the truth: Abel's murder was not only the first in human history, but for that very reason the most mirthful; for Cain had absolutely no idea how to commit it.

¹² From dusk till dawn he attacked Abel in the most fruitless of ways; he blew upon him; he strangled his hair; at one point he spent two hours simply shouting "Die! Die!" at Abel from various angles.

¹³ Fortunately for him, Abel was equally ignorant of how to fend off a murderous attack; neither defending himself nor running away, but making what in retrospect proved the tactical blunder, of lying perfectly still.

¹⁴ Ah . . . thou canst not make this stuff up.

¹⁵ Eventually Cain made use of a rock; but rather than throwing it at his brother, he picked up his brother and threw him at *it*; he did this 50 times, until Abel finally succumbed to a preexisting heart condition.

¹⁶ But in intent it was murder; and afterward I did indeed ask Cain of Abel's whereabouts, and he did indeed reply, "Am I my brother's keeper?"

¹⁷ Thus did Cain also invent sarcasm; and lo, who is not eternally grateful to him for *that*.

¹⁸ I remember marking Cain upon his brow to denote him as a murderer and a fratricide, and saying unto him, "Behold, thou art branded forever."

¹⁹ And he turned to me and smiled, and said, "Indeed, O Lord, thou hast 'branded' me forever, and most winningly; for now I shall position myself as 'the original bad boy';

²⁰ And I shall wander the earth a lonely rebel, with an air of danger, and a visage most brooding; and all men will want to know me; and all women will want to *know* me."

²¹ At the time I thought him mad; yet he proved most savvy, and within five years Cain was the most famous man in the world.

²² (Granted, this made him the most famous man among 23 people; but still.)

CHAPTER 7

 ¹ shall skip over the next ten generations of begetting; thou mayest consult Genesis 4 for the thrilling details of how Irad begat Mehujael, and how Mehujael begat Methusael, and how, with the help of Vicky—an Edomite streetwalker with a heart of gold—Methusael begat Lamech.

² I shall also skip over certain other questions thou mayest have; such as "So who did Cain marry?" "Where did all the other people come from?" and "Doesn't this mean there was all kinds of crazy incest going on?"

³ That last allegation is shocking and outrageous; and I would like nothing more than to provide thee the simple explanation for how all this begetting was accomplished in a perfectly wholesome manner;

⁴ But alas, I have been advised by counsel not to discuss these matters due to ongoing litigation.

⁵ Instead I will now turn my attention to my next great crisis; for one of the lessons I had already learned about godding, was that it involved a good deal more crisis management than I had anticipated.

⁶ So after Cain, I decided to step back for a little bit; to let mankind find its own way in the world; to sweat not the small stuff—for lo, it was *all* small stuff.

⁷ Thus I observed silently as generation begat generation; as the human race developed new skills like hunting, and gathering, and the now-lost art of gatherhunting.

⁸ There was ample time for everyone to learn from their mistakes; for recall that in those times people's lifespans were many centuries long.

⁹ (The record was Methuselah, who lived 969 years; the last 940 of which he spent repeatedly telling family and friends how much better things were the first 29.)

¹⁰ And I watched it all unfold, and I could not but be impressed with the great achievements of my own greatest achievement; but the wickedness . . .

¹¹ My goodness, the wickedness.

¹² I shall spare thee the embarrassment of describing in detail the wanton debauchery of thy ancestors; I will simply say that the wickedness continued to grow, and in all aspects of society: family life grew more wicked; tribal governance grew more wicked; even group sex grew more wicked, which was surprising, since it was starting from a point that was already pretty wicked.

¹³ Finally I came to feel what is recorded in Genesis 6:6: "And it repented the LORD that he had made man on the earth, and it grieved him in his heart."

¹⁴ At this point I can almost hear some of my young doubters reading this in their dorm cloisters, sipping their bean extracts, brows arched mid-smirk, scoffing, "But if you're 'God,' why didn't you just make man perfect to begin with, wiseguy?"

¹⁵ There are two answers to this question, the first being: consider thyself smited.

¹⁶ But the second is, that in creating the human race I *did* achieve perfection; a perfection of balance between the forces driving it toward good, and those driving it toward evil.

¹⁷ The dozens of distinct impulses and drives within thee, may be likened to individual athletes tasked with uniting themselves for the betterment of a team; a team which may be a nation, or a tribe, or a family, or even a single human soul.

¹⁸ And some teams rise, and others fall; and some succeed dishonorably, and some fail with honor; and individual victories and defeats are short-lived; yet the larger cycle of victory and defeat is eternal.

¹⁹ And eventually all the teams go under, and are replaced by new franchises that play in stadiums with bigger luxury boxes than the previous ones; and it is in the biggest such box of all where you will find me, rapt, smiling, sipping a metaphysical brewski; enthralled by the game, and the perfection of its entertainment;

²⁰ For I am the LORD thy God, Commissioner of the Universe: and I am always ready for some football.

21 Yet once in a while something in the very fabric of the sport goes so awry, that the Commissioner himself is obliged to step down from his high perch, and reset the balance.

22 In the sphere of football, this means re-allotting draft picks, or renegotiating the collective bargaining agreement.

23 In the sphere of divinity, this means drowning humanity.

CHAPTER 8

 1 f all the people of his time, only Noah found grace in my eyes; for he was wise, and upright, and honest, and as it says in the text, he "walked with God"; though in truth I wish that now and again he would have *jogged* with God; for he had a bit of a paunch.

2 Noah was a great man; he had a lovely wife, Nameless; and three terrific children, Shem, Ham, and Japheth; verily, their domestic interaction had a real *My Three Sons* feel to it; for they were always courteous, and hokey, and unironically used words like "Jeepers!"

3 So I told Noah my plan; and how I meant to save him and his family by having him build an ark of the dimensions 300 cubits by 50 cubits by 30 cubits.

4 (Here I must insert a plea, that mankind at least consider reinstating the cubit system; which remains the most marvelous method of measurement ever invented, putting the metric and imperial systems to shame.

5 Four digits a palm, seven palms a cubit, six cubits a reed, two reeds a *nindan* and ten *nindans* an *aslu*—I defy thee to devise units of greater common-sense and utility; especially to anyone with even a passing interest in the irrigation of millet.)

6 And Noah did wondrous work constructing the ship, considering I bade him make it of "gopher wood"; that is the phrase used in Genesis, and scholars ever since have debated exactly what type of wood was so denoted; and the answer is, no type at all;

[7] For gopher wood was at that time a euphemism, for lead-bolted plate steel.

[8] And now I come to one of the bigger revelations thou wilt find within these pages.

[9] I did *not* ask Noah to put two of every animal on board the ark.

[10] I know that is what it says in the Bible, but consider: A phylogenetically complete double bestiary contained within a 450,000-cubic-cubit watercraft?

[11] Why, in but a medium-sized zoo, the animals themselves occupy nearly 450,000 cubic cubits; and that is to say nothing of the space required for their food and shelter, or their grazing and roaming areas; and of course a zoo contains but a tiny fraction of the total number of global species;

[12] Not to mention the wide array of artificial habitat needs, ranging from arctic to tropical, that would have to be constructed and maintained on board; or the arduousness of gathering the animals from these habitats, many of them in continents heretofore not even mentioned in the Old Testament . . .

[13] I could go on and on.

[14] No; I did not say, "Put two of every animal on board the ship."

[15] What I said was, "Put two of *any* animal on board the ship."

[16] For I knew Noah and his family were in for a long, treacherous voyage; and that they would be confined indoors for over five months; and that under such circumstances, it would be comforting for all aboard, particularly the kids, to bring with them two dogs, or two cats, or even two hamsters.

[17] I recommended dogs, but I left the choice to Noah; for I have never been a cat God.

[18] As it happened, Noah *did* choose two dogs, cocker spaniel puppies he purchased the day before the rains came—Sparky and Pillow.

[19] But hundreds of years later, when I dictated this story to Moses upon Mt. Sinai, he misheard me as saying "Two of *every* animal."

²⁰ I corrected him immediately, but we both found the implication of the phrase amusing; and for the next hour or so we made much mirth of the idea of a ship containing so many animals;

²¹ For Moses would say, "It sounds un-'bear'-able!"; and I would say, "Really? To me it sounds 'purr'-fect!"; and he would say, "You're a 'dog'-gone liar!"; and so forth;

²² And this brought us such happiness, that we kept it in; never thinking any of thee could possibly take it seriously.

²³ A six-day creation, talking snakes, 969-year-old men: such things are clearly factual and fall well within the realm of the credible.

²⁴ But two of every animal on a single boat?

²⁵ No; all the other animals—the beasts, and the birds of the air, and the creeping things of the earth—all of them were zapped frozen and left floating in ice cubes until the whole thing was over.

CHAPTER 9

¹ he tempestuous cruise of Noah and his family was of such duration that by the time the waves subsided, the buffet was almost depleted.

² The ice sculptures had long since melted; the top-shelf liquor was gone; the bottomless shrimp were approaching their bottom, and what little cocktail sauce remained had to be licked off the side of the bowl.

³ The Flood had taken much longer than I expected; I confess that many of you were much better swimmers than I had ever conceived, and that your corpses proved far better flotation devices than I had previously anticipated.

⁴ But finally the last one of you drowned; and thou wert all devoured by fish; and these fish in turn shat thee out; whereupon smaller fish ate the thee-shit.

⁵ And the oceans began to withdraw; and here there is yet another animal-related error in the Bible: for Noah did not send forth a raven

and a dove to determine whether the waters had subsided; he sent forth Sparky and Pillow.

6 Yea, he dropped them both into the waters; and Pillow swam but a few cubits, and yelped pitiably, and returned to the ark; but Sparky proved more intrepid, and paddled and churned through the endless ocean, until he disappeared beyond the horizon.

7 He did not return; and Noah presumed he had found dry land; and Noah loved Sparky; and I loved Noah; so I left it at that.

8 Then at last the waters receded, and the ordeal was over; and humanity emerged ready to move past its long global nightmare, known at the time as "Floodgate."

9 The ark landed upon Mt. Ararat, which I chose because it had jutting from its summit a perpendicular ridge of sufficient width to double as a pier.

10 I remember as the ark approached, mirthing cunningly unto Noah and his family, "Behold, I see a pier appear up here!"

11 Long I waited for a response; but they kept silent, lost in grief for their tens of thousands of drowned kinsmen.

12 A righteous family, Noah's; but a tough crowd.

13 Then I blessed him and his descendants, and bid them be fruitful and multiply; and as a sign of this blessing, I displayed unto them a glorious rainbow;

14 Which is why it is most ironic, that of the millions of people who today take the rainbow as their banner, not *one* of them can multiply without outside assistance.

15 And I made a covenant with Noah never again to destroy every living thing with a Flood, as it is written: "And I will establish my covenant with you; neither shall all flesh be cut off any more by the waters of a flood; neither shall there any more be a flood to destroy the earth."

16 That is Genesis 9:11; and lo, everything changed after Genesis 9:11.

17 For the survivors of this new, post–9:11 world had learned through bitter experience, that behind daily life's peaceful façade there lurked always the

potential for unimaginable horror, at the hands of a religious extremist with little regard for human life.

CHAPTER 10

 nd so for a second time the earth was repopulated from a single family; and for a second time I will refrain from delving into thy prurient curiosity over whether or not this entailed the practice of "siblings with benefits."

2 The only event of note over the next 400 years was the Tower of Babel, which caused me to confound all the languages of the earth.

3 That was a zoning dispute.

4 Thou seest, the Tower's blueprints called for it to be 57 cubits high; yet municipal ordinances of the time allowed for the erection of no commercial structure over 50 cubits high, as per §[C26-801.1] of the Greater Babel Building Code.

5 (The reason was that a building higher than 50 cubits would significantly obstruct my view of earth, thus lowering the resale value of heaven.)

6 But the building's owners countered that as the Tower would comprise partly single- and double-family dwellings, it should be granted a residential and/or special-use exemption under a little-used (and, to be candid, poorly-worded) secondary codicil of the Code of Hammurabi.

7 This prompted a hearing on the matter, featuring rambling testimony from idle senior citizens, and much bluster from the architect about "aesthetic integrity," when verily from a purely visual standpoint the design lacked even the charm of a second-tier ziggurat;

8 And when the Babel Development Board ruled in my favor by a vote of 6 to 3 (with one abstention), an immediate motion to cease construction was filed with King Gungunum; which was clearly a tactical ploy on the part of the Chamber of Commerce to bide time until the reinstatement of the planning committee . . .

9 Anyway, long story short, I wound up confounding all the languages of the earth.

¹⁰ And from that day forward the peoples of the world no longer all spoke good old-fashioned English, but instead blathered incoherently in thousands of tongues; each more un-American than the next.

¹¹ But other than Babel, I spent most of those four centuries doing something I should have done much sooner: assembling my staff.

¹² I mean this in two senses: first, in the sense of finding a large piece of cedar wood, whittling it, varnishing it, and affixing unto it an ornate golden handle.

¹³ It came out nice.

¹⁴ It was shiny.

¹⁵ But secondly, I mean it in the sense of gathering unto me a team of agents, representatives, subordinates, messengers, interns, and temps to help me run all facets of my ever-expanding enterprise.

¹⁶ Perhaps thou art asking thyself why a supreme and self-sufficient God would need a celestial support system of any kind.

¹⁷ That is a fair question; one I myself mused upon often in the antediluvian period, always arriving at the conclusion that no such system was needed; for I am the LORD thy God, King of the Universe; I never give myself anything I cannot handle.

¹⁸ Yet in looking back on the Flood, I realized there were several occasions when the deployment of an associate on my behalf would have been useful.

¹⁹ For example, informing Noah that all his friends and extended family were going to be destroyed forever due to my wrath . . . there was no reason *I* had to be the one to tell him that.

²⁰ The piteous cries of the wicked and their children as they fought in vain against the relentless surging of the waters . . . there was no reason *I* had to take that call.

²¹ The unremitting continuance of the torrential rains for 40 days and 40 nights . . . there was no reason that repetitive task could not have been delegated to an aide; a younger aide, perhaps, eager to work his way up in the *machina.*

22 Moreover, my failure in the days before the Flood to appreciate the full scope of the growing wickedness had been partly a result of my over-reliance on my own omniscience; a fact that, in retrospect, I should have known.

23 But now I saw that, in the post–9:11 world, the vital job of gathering intelligence would be best served by an aggressive team of "wings on the ground," charged with monitoring the goings-on in the region of my principal concern, the Middle East;

24 Thus making that area safe and stable in perpetuity.

CHAPTER 11

 o I began assembling an elite group of subordinates—Genesistants, if thee will—to do my bidding, deliver my pronouncements, oversee the earth's natural processes, and manage the inevitable papyruswork produced thereby.

2 I quickly decided it would not do to use transplanted humans; for few were worthy, and those few were needed on earth; where good men were, and remain, hard to find.

3 (Verily, ladies, am I right?)

4 No; the only thing for it was to create an entirely new class of creature; and this time not of the dust of the earth, or aught else terrestrial, but of immaterial chunks of pure spirit I would rend from the mystical heart of my own essence, and then futz around with for a while.

5 It went very smoothly; within a few days I had over 3,000 employees; I gave them halos to help them see better, and wings to make air travel less burdensome;

6 I called them "angels"; and collectively I called them The A-Team; or at least I did until 1983, when I dropped it for reasons thou mayest well imagine.

7 I wish not to speak in great depth of my angels; partly because much of their work is classified, and partly because I value their privacy.

⁸ Also, I assume thou already hast a basic understanding of the ninefold angelic hierarchy, and the Three Spheres, and the Three Orders within each Sphere, from having read Pseudo-Dionysius the Areopagite's 5th century treatise *De Coelesti Hierarchia* in fifth grade;

⁹ Or, in more poorly-funded school districts, sixth grade.

¹⁰ Yet I would be remiss if I did not here acknowledge five angels, without whose dedication, hard work, and loyalty everything would still have happened, but not with the same *bonhomie*.

¹¹ The first of these is Uriel; he is the wisest of my angels; the patron of poets, the guardian of thunder, a repentance whiz, and a great wordsmith; his collaboration with the prophet Ezra on *The Second Book of Esdras* is the reason that work was such an improvement over *The First Book of Esdras,* which was a piece of shit.

¹² It was also Uriel who devised the idea for Kabbalah; so Madonna, next time thou addest up the numerical values of letters in the Torah, and useth the sums thereof to schedule thy body waxing, forgetteth not to thank Uriel.

¹³ Offer him a prayer, Madonna; yea, or something like it.

¹⁴ The second angel is Raphael; a healer of mind, body, and spirit; he is considered the patron of travelers, and sojourners to this day call upon him to protect them during their journeys, although that is not an excuse to lie out without sunscreen.

¹⁵ Raphael is also endowed with a dry wit that has proven of great comfort in those moments when my disposition waxes saturnine.

¹⁶ As an instance, I remember the council to determine whether to send the Black Death to the world; it was a long and sober discussion, until I turned to him, in his capacity as chief medical consultant, and asked how long the disease would take to kill its victims.

¹⁷ He looked at me with a face void of levity, and said, "My LORD, they will go from coughin' to coffin in three days."

¹⁸ And there was great tittering, for a weight of gloom had been lifted from the deliberations; and our spirits were much lightened, as we set about killing one in every three Europeans.

¹⁹ The third angel is Michael, chief of the archangels, the angel of mercy and sanctification, and the commander of the Army of God; he is present on every battlefield, granting victory to the side of the righteous; "victory" in this case betokening a wide range of outcomes, from triumph to triumph-by-martyrdom.

²⁰ Michael is often portrayed in art as androgynous, but he has asked me to tell thee that he is in fact "all man"; and that if thou couldst see clear to painting his jawbone a little squarer, he would greatly appreciate it; because some of the other angels tease him about it sometimes, and even in heaven, words *do* hurt.

²¹ The fourth angel and chief of all is Gabriel, my messenger of good tidings; it is he who came to Daniel to interpret his visions, and foretold the births of John the Baptist and Jesus, and first revealed the Koran to Muhammad, and oversaw the Flutie-to-Phelan Hail Mary that beat Miami in 1984.

²² (By the way, it is foolish to call such plays "Hail Marys," for Mary has absolutely *no* interest in sports; indeed, if thou ever besought her aid on such a play on behalf of thy team, she would smile and say something like unto, "Okay, which color costume are they?")

²³ Collectively I affectionately refer to Uriel, Raphael, Michael, and Gabriel as my "Kids in the Halo"; for they are quick-witted and nimble-minded, and have over the eons not only provided invaluable service on behalf of God and man, but written much of my strongest material.

²⁴ And the fifth and last angel I will mention is Lucifer.

²⁵ More on him later.

CHAPTER 12

¹ s I busied myself with expanding my business, I left earth well enough alone; hopeful that the mere memory of the Flood would suffice to keep its people on the straight and narrow path of ceaselessly expressing their gratitude to me through the regular incineration of large farm animals.

² Yet in this I was disappointed, and most grievously.

³ It would have been one thing if humanity had simply started taking the sun and moon and seedtime and harvest for granted, failing to acknowledge who had given it to them.

⁴ This I might have chalked up to simple discourtesy, and dealt with through the usual array of etiquette lessons thou callest "natural disasters" (see Smitus 1–4).

⁵ But something far worse was transpiring: the people were inventing false gods in the form of stone idols, whom they would then praise, and worship, and sacrifice to, and "idolize."

⁶ (Truly, I detest it when people verb a noun.)

⁷ I have been called a jealous God; the description is accurate, but misleading; for it evokes the image of a spurned lover or a rival tradesman, whereas my jealousy is of a far different nature.

⁸ Consider the toddler who scrawleth with a crayon upon a piece of parchment, and deems it a masterpiece;

⁹ How he runs to his mother, demanding that she behold his artistic creation and admire it.

¹⁰ It matters not if at that moment she is engaged in any of the numerous other activities that fill her busy life; nor that the drawing in truth resembles nothing so much as an epileptic's doodle;

¹¹ The toddler must have praise, and soon; else will he become agitated and surly, and tears flow, and breath held.

¹² And so all household activities cease while the mother heaps sufficient encomia upon the lad; and hails his talents, and shouts his greatness, and magnetizes his work upon the keeper of cold foods that very moment.

¹³ Now consider that I am that toddler; and thou art that mother; and the universe is the picture; and that very moment is every single moment, ever.

¹⁴ This will start to give thee a sense of my laudatory needs.

¹⁵ Lo, it is very easy to create idols and give them desirable attributes; to envision them as animals, or the sun, or whatever objects or creatures float thine ark; even to invent a pantheon of such idols who share many exciting adventures, and harebrained schemes, and wacky misunderstandings.

¹⁶ Such deities will always bear the yoke of godship more lightly than I, and prove suppler instruments for thy mythmaking; for they have at their disposal the one weapon in the universe I can never wield: nonexistence.

¹⁷ Take Ninurta, the Sumerian farming god: he had no problem metamorphosizing into a winged lion, or retrieving the Tablets of Destiny stolen by Anzû, or bearing the slain Bison-Beast on his chariot beam, or consorting with Ugallu, or being worshipped as a healer and feared as the bringer of winds.

¹⁸ He was happy to serve all these purposes for the Sumerians, *because he was not real;* and was thus what I will charitably call "mythologically flexible."

¹⁹ But Ninurta never sent a single actual rain cloud; he never called forth one stalk of actual wheat; he had no sense of responsibility; like everyone else in his pantheon, he never worked a gods-damned day in his life.

²⁰ I may have my faults: impetuosity, jealousy, short-temperedness, and others I shall reveal; indeed, after this book is published, no longer will one of my faults be keeping things bottled up inside; I am coming clean, and it feels good; yea, I embrace the catharsis.

²¹ But unlike all other gods, *I am real;* I am the LORD thy God, King of the Universe; and thou art stuck with me.

²² Thus it is wicked and foolish for people to seek to escape this truth by carving ridiculous "divinities" out of stone, rather than follow the course of action dictated by both obedience and logic:

²³ Burning beasts of burden on ceremonial altars until the smoky aroma of ox-fat is thick enough to appease thine invisible, B-B-Q–lovin' sky-god.

²⁴ (And for the record, if thy meat is smothered in Sticky Fingers Smokehouse's Tennessee Whiskey Sauce, consider thyself entitled to ten sin-free masturbations.)

CHAPTER 13

¹ ut I was out of the end-of-the-world business; true, I had left myself a loophole whereby I could smite mankind by any means *other* than a flood; but had I done so, everyone's last thought would have been, "Wow, another apocalypse . . . guess *Someone's* out of ideas."

² So I decided to take a different approach; to focus on a handful of Chosen People, already rich in righteousness, and, through a generous real-estate offer, incentivize them to spread their moral wealth, that it might trickle down to the less piously fortunate.

³ The quest to find these People became one of the first tasks of my new support team, and their solution was ingenious: they constructed, alongside a well-traveled trade route in Chaldea, a single wooden stall, like unto a lemonade stand in the middle of the desert;

⁴ And its top part bore a sign reading, "Wouldst thou be Chosen? Inquire within!"

⁵ And lo, on the very first day, who should stumble across the stand but a spry young man, no more than 75; with fire in his eyes, and dreams in his heart, and foot rot in his sheep;

⁶ That is why he was in the area, actually, to let his flock walk on the dry dirt, that they might obtain hoof relief.

⁷ He was, of course, Abraham; the patriarch of monotheism; the progenitor of my three great religions; the father of the Israelites, the Ishmaelites, the Edomites, the Midianites, and the Parasites;

⁸ Though he hated that last group; all they ever did was sleep in his tent and ask for money.

⁹ Abraham had already shown himself a literal iconoclast; for months earlier he had broken into his father's idol shop in the town of Haran, and smashed all the idols to demonstrate the folly of ascribing divine power to manmade artifacts.

¹⁰ (He had also shown himself wise, by having previously purchased small-business theft insurance on his father's behalf; and staging the crime scene so that it appeared to be the work of the Haran-sackers, a notorious gang of local cat burglars.)

¹¹ I was anxious to begin; so I told Abraham that if he would move from his father's house I would take him to a land where I would make of him a great nation, and make his name immortal, and bless those that bless him, and curse those that curse him; but that I needed an answer quickly, as I was kind of in a rush.

¹² And Abraham agreed; so he left the land of Haran and set forth for Canaan, along with his slaves, and his considerable possessions, and his wife Sarah, and his nephew Lot; or, as the angels and I used to call him, "Vacant Lot"; for truly, he was not the sharpest spear-point in the desert.

¹³ I say not that Lot was dumb; merely, that his tent had a couple of poles loose.

¹⁴ [Rimshot on the tabor.]

¹⁵ Truly; I say not that Lot was dumb; merely that he was a few camels short of a caravan.

¹⁶ [Rimshot on the tabor.]

¹⁷ Verily; I say not that Lot was dumb; merely that his flocks tended him.

¹⁸ [Rimshot on the tabor.]

¹⁹ No, for the last time I plead with thee, do not misapprehend my meaning; by no means am I declaring Lot lacking in wisdom;

²⁰ Merely, that they recently unearthed a book about him from a cave, called The Braindead Sea Scrolls.

²¹ [Large rimshot on the tabor.]

²² Yea, Lot was not very bright; nonetheless he was virtuous, and that is why he and his family (with one exception) were the sole survivors of the most famous strategic bombing campaign in all of scripture.

²³ I speak, of course, of Sodom and Gomorrah; but I cannot speak of them without first addressing, in greater depth, a topic that has already been broached in this memoir.

CHAPTER 14

¹ The Bible's verses on homosexuality have been the focus of more debate and rancor than any others; a fact I confess I did not foresee.

² For when I transcribed the Torah to Moses, I anticipated the most controversy would surround the verses in Leviticus 27 mandating that those dedicating part of their family estate to me must value it according to the amount of seed required for its planting, at the rate of fifty shekels of silver per bushel of barley seed.

³ I remember dictating these lines to Moses; and afterward looking up to find him staring at me in wide-eyed astonishment, and saying, "Thou do knowest that when the Israelites read this, they're going to lose their fucking shit, right?"

⁴ But we were wrong; it is the lines on homosexuality that proved most contentious; so let me first express my appreciation for the fact that, more than 3,000 years after the writing of the Old Testament, so many of you still regard its words as the final arbiter of morality.

⁵ Thou art right to do so; for my injunctions on sexual intercourse, and dietary laws, and menstruation, and the need to sacrifice bulls with grain offerings of three-tenths of an *ephah* of the finest flour mixed with half a *hin* of olive oil, and the right and wrong ways to sell thine own daughters into sexual slavery, are not the product of a particular group of people in a particular place at a particular time;

⁶ They are timeless.

⁷ The *last* thing thou shouldst ever do, is create thine own set of moral values based on the realities of the world in which thou actually livest.

⁸ But there has been a fundamental misinterpretation regarding the specific verses thought to condemn homosexuality in Leviticus: "Thou shalt not

lie with mankind, as with womankind; it [is] abomination," and "If a man also lie with mankind, as he lieth with a woman, both of them have committed an abomination: they shall surely be put to death."

⁹ In retrospect, I understand how "Thou shalt not lie with mankind, as with womankind" could be seen as a proscription against homosexuality, among those of a predisposition to find it so; yet that is not what was meant.

¹⁰ What was meant is this:

¹¹ If thou art a man, and thou seest another man that thou desirest, do not cut off his genitals, use a knife to carve a slit where they were, and insert thyself into it, that thou mayest "lie" with him as thou wouldst a woman.

¹² Surely even the gayest among you would agree that *that* is detestable.

¹³ I have already shown how I created Adam and Steve; and to those who say, "If God wanted us all to be gay, he would have created us with both male and female sex organs," I say, "Yea; but if I did not want *any* of you to be gay, I would not have made the male anus so accommodating to the erect penis."

¹⁴ And to those who say, "Homosexuality is a sin, because it goes against God's directive to be fruitful and multiply," I have already conceded the point biologically; but I would note that creatively speaking, gays have it all over straight people, fruitfulness-wise;

¹⁵ And as for multiplying, though it is true they cannot reproduce by themselves, nowhere do I forbid them from receiving help in bearing young from other members of their communities;

¹⁶ Such as donors, or surrogates, or a female best friend who neareth 40 and hath not yet found her perfect breeding partner, and whineth continually of the slow beshadowing of her biological sundial.

¹⁷ Besides, it is an undeniable fact that those clergymen harshest in their condemnation of gays and lesbians are often those struggling hardest against their own hidden urges; which is why they cannot even preach straight.

¹⁸ It was certainly true in regard to the serpent in the Garden; and it has certainly been true of many other "men of God" in all three of my great religions who have spoken out against homosexuality.

¹⁹ Joel Osteen, for instance; he is gay.

²⁰ (Note that I do not say he has committed homosexual acts, for that could be shown to be demonstrably true or false; I simply say that, in the secret recesses of his heart, Joel Osteen yearns for the tender touch of another man.

²¹ This is subjective, intangible, and my opinion, and said without actionable malice, divine or legal.)

²² Verily, I hope I have made myself clear on this issue.

²³ I have been accused of many things in my day, and of some rightly; but I am in no way homophobic.

²⁴ Gay, straight, bisexual, transgendered; ye are all equally smiteable in my eyes.

CHAPTER 15

¹ **W**hich brings me to Sodom; where it is true that the custom of male homosexuality was prevalent.

² (Even then the word "sodomy" was used to refer to it, though not as a noun but an adjective; as when two men would draw unusually close in a tent, and an onlooker would say, "Is it just me, or is it getting sodomy in here?")

³ But that is not why I punished Sodom; and it is certainly not why I punished Gomorrah; which had hardly anything by way of a gay scene, except for one clandestine tavern operating on weekends, The Fire and Rimstone.

⁴ No; the reason Sodom and Gomorrah had to be destroyed was simple: they were the twin hubs of a massive international money-laundering operation.

⁵ The plan was cunning: a bandit would come to the cities with stolen merchandise; he would take it to one of the many retailers in the bazaar, then offer to barter it for a small "legitimate" ware, such as pottery or some cloth; this ware being offered at an extremely high price, in effect the merchant's "cleaning fee."

⁶ The bandit would then hand over all his goods; and the storekeeper would give him the ware, and return his "change" to him in untraceable coins.

⁷ Thus, the bandit cameled away with "clean" money, and a record of a seemingly lawful commercial transaction; while the merchant was left with a whole new cache of stolen goods to resell—and be restolen yet again by his cohort, the bandit;

⁸ For, as thou mayest have guessed, they were in cahoots.

⁹ Nearly every citizen of Sodom and Gomorrah was in on this scheme; it was a criminal enterprise unparalleled in scope, and it may put it in perspective if I reveal that, in 1653 B.C. alone, the dishonest tradesmen of the two cities collectively laundered over 5,000 shekels.

¹⁰ That is not a misprint: *5,000* shekels.

¹¹ The two towns were corrupt to their marrow, and I had no qualms about ordering them destroyed; but I knew good old Vacant Lot lived in Sodom along with his two daughters and his wife, Trish.

¹² (Yea; her name is not given in Genesis, but it was Trish.

¹³ Not short for Patricia, either; just Trish.)

¹⁴ And two angels came to Lot's house, and he showed them his usual brand of oafish hospitality; until the crowd gathered outside, and demanded that they come out, "so that they might know them"; wicked behavior, for it would have not only been rape, but, the worst kind of rape: angel-rape.

¹⁵ Truly, thou dost not wish to know what eternity holds in store for angel-rapists.

¹⁶ And as it saith, Lot spoke through the closed door, "I have two daughters which have known not man; let me, I pray you, bring them out unto you,

and do ye to them as is good in your eyes: only unto these men do nothing, for therefore came they under the shadow of my roof."

¹⁷ I wish I could convey to thee in words the look on Lot's daughters' faces at that moment.

¹⁸ But they were spared this fate; for the angels afflicted the rabble with blindness, and assisted the family's escape; and as soon as they had left, Sodom and Gomorrah were utterly obliterated: fire and brimstone rained down upon them, and their buildings were reduced to rubble, and their people consumed in flame.

¹⁹ It was a shocking event, and for decades afterward everyone in the Jordan River valley could remember exactly what they were doing when they heard the news.

²⁰ "Verily," one might recall, "I had just finished butchering ten ewes, and was in my slaves' quarters assaulting my wife's Zimranite wet nurse Blimshur, when Shazran the drovesman ran in with rent loincloth, and assailed me with the first reports of the woeful tidings;

²¹ And I broke down and wept; for I had lost what I only now knew had been my most treasured possession . . . my innocence."

²² Of course, thou knowest what became of Trish; the angels gave strict instructions that none of Lot's family look back upon the destruction, but she could not resist the temptation; she peered back, and turned into a pillar of salt.

²³ Within two minutes of which, Lot had licked her more than he had in their previous 28 years of marriage.

CHAPTER 16

 ¹ braham was a worthy patriarch; upright and courageous, and brave, and kind; a great man; and more than that, a humble man; a nice man; just a really, really good guy; Abraham = total sweetheart.

2 But he could be quick-witted and argumentative; and I remember many a lively discussion between us wherein he would express his disagreement over a point of protocol or dogma; which I graciously allowed him to do, smite-free.

3 For example, after I commanded him regarding the new ritual of circumcision, and how it was to be mandatory for his descendants, he said, "LORD, distinguishing the Chosen People from all other tribes through a physical modification denoting our special covenant, is most wise.

4 My only thought is: what if, instead of circumcision for eight-day-old boys;

5 What if we made it breast augmentation for 17-year-old girls?"

6 We debated this point for the better part of two weeks; the argument swung one way, then the other; circumcision, breast augmentation; breast augmentation, circumcision; each had much to recommend it.

7 For he conceded that circumcision would be a meaningful cultural tradition bridging generations; and I conceded that breast augmentation would be helpful in both recruiting new members, and creating them.

8 But at the end of the debate I clung to my original choice; and lo, 3,600 years later, the Jewish people not only still practice circumcision, it remains central to their sense of identity.

9 Male Jews: you're welcome.

10 Another time I came to Abraham in a dream, and told him of his people's future: how before they became a great nation, they would serve as slaves in Egypt for 400 years.

11 "God," he said, "I must ask: if thou knowest this in advance, why canst thou not keep it from happening, thereby sparing my descendants four centuries of affliction?

12 Moreover, if thou hast power over what hath not yet come, canst thou not unspool the future with a gentler thread; one weaving a tapestry whereby righteousness is always rewarded, and evil always punished; so that mankind may behold with perfect clarity thine infinite justice?"

¹³ "Interesting; interesting," I said. "Yet I think I would prefer to work in mysterious ways."

¹⁴ "But consider," Abraham responded, "how much more reverence humanity would give thee, if it knew it lived in a universe in which the good and the wicked received condign reward and punishment in proportion to their conduct."

¹⁵ "Nah," I replied. "I hear what thou sayest, but I'm still going with mysterious ways."

¹⁶ "Verily, it is thy world, I just live here," Abraham continued; "I simply think, a little transparency may prove a useful bulwark for those plagued by anger or doubt; and furthermore —"

¹⁷ "*Mysteeeeeeerious waaaaaays!*" I shouted, attaining a tone of spookiness by using a thick Girgashite accent (Girgashia being the Transylvania of its time), and deploying thunder and lightning effects, and throwing a plastic spider upon him;

¹⁸ All of which he took very earnestly, for recall this was all happening as he slept; and so he awoke in his tent screaming, breathing deeply, and with sweat soaking his brow; until at last his passion cooled, and he regained himself, and said with relief, "Oh! It was all a dream";

¹⁹ Whereupon he looked beside him on the floor, and beheld the plastic spider, and screamed *"Or was it?!?"*; and I filled the tent once more with evil laughter, and thunder, and more plastic spiders.

²⁰ Yea; Abraham put up with a whole lot of crap from me.

CHAPTER 17

¹ **B**ut nothing compared to the ordeal I put him through 20 years later.

² I had told Abraham that a great nation would one day spring from his loins; but he and Sarah were old, and she was barren; so she allowed him to be with her handmaiden, Hagar, who had replaced her previous handmaiden, Lee Roth.

³ And Abraham and Hagar lay together; and at some point during their lying together, they had sex.

⁴ And Hagar gave birth to a son, whom she called Ishmael, because she wanted him to grow up to narrate a novel everyone pretended to read.

⁵ Fourteen years passed; and by now Abraham was 100, and Sarah was 90; and though thy modern men of medicine can make nonagenarian women squeeze out triplets like unto softballs from a pitching machine, it was not so back then.

⁶ But I was finally ready to make good on my covenant; so I enabled Sarah to conceive and give birth to a son, Isaac; whereupon she demanded that Hagar and Ishmael be sent away; for she had grown weary of Hagar, whose handmaidening frankly was not what it used to be.

⁷ So Abraham did as Sarah asked, and exiled Ishmael; who nonetheless went on to become the progenitor of his own great people—the Arabs.

⁸ (Who are still working through their issues about the sending-away-Ishmael thing.)

⁹ Abraham dearly loved little Isaac; but one day when Isaac was a small child, I told Abraham to sacrifice him as a burnt offering to me, to prove once and for all that he was loyal enough to deserve to become the first patriarch.

¹⁰ So I watched Abraham rise at dawn, and cleave the wood for the burnt offering, and saddle his ass, and mount it with his young son; and I thought, "So far, so good."

¹¹ And I watched him spend three long days clinging to Isaac on his ass, and three long nights clinging to him in his tent, until he reached the base of Mt. Moriah; whereupon he told his servants to wait for him while he and Isaac climbed; and I thought, "Impressive."

¹² And I watched them ascend, and heard Isaac naively ask his father where the lamb for the offering was, and saw Abraham choke back his tears, and mutter through his heartache, "God will provide himself a lamb for a burnt offering"; and I thought, "Nice one."

¹³ And I watched them arrive at the place of the sacrifice; and beheld Abraham build an altar, and lay the wood upon it, and in a state of the most

piercing anguish bind his own struggling son and lay him upon the wood; and I thought, "I think he's gonna do it!"

¹⁴ And I watched Abraham, sunk in grief beyond measure, stretch forth his hand with the knife and see for the last time alive the beautiful son I had promised him, yet was now bidding him slay with his own hand; and I thought, "Incredible! He's actually gonna—"

¹⁵ "My LORD!" interrupted Michael, my angel. "I mean not to be rude, but dost thou really mean to let Abraham go through with the sacrifice?"

¹⁶ "No; no I do not, and it is good that thou interruptedst me," I said; "for truly, watching Abraham these last three days has filled me with . . . I myself am unsure; but witnessing someone close to me prepare to kill the thing he holds most dear in life solely to gain my approval . . . his suffering . . . I found it almost—"

¹⁷ "My LORD!" yelled Michael again, and pointed at Abraham, who was now swinging the knife; and I nodded my head, and Michael appeared unto Abraham at the last possible instant and stayed his hand, and looked over the hillside for a substitute; until his eyes fell upon a wayward ram, which was in the wrong place at the wrong time.

¹⁸ And Michael congratulated Abraham, and comforted him, and promised on my behalf yet again that his descendants through Isaac would be as numerous as the stars in the sky and the sand on the shore.

¹⁹ But I remained alone, staying aloof for a time from the affairs of men, to contemplate the truth about myself I had discovered while observing Abraham.

²⁰ For lo, I had destroyed the world in a Flood; I had razed the Tower of Babel; I had leveled Sodom and Gomorrah; all manner of catastrophe had I already visited upon you, in the name of righteousness;

²¹ Yet it was only then—after finding myself enthralled by the slow, silent agony of one I greatly loved;

²² I say, it was only then, that I first began to consider the possibility, that there was something seriously wrong with me.

CHAPTER 18

1 **T**hings between Abraham and me were never the same after that.

2 Sarah died a few years later, leaving him disconsolate; feeling guilty, I gave unto him another wife, Keturah; she was 19 years old, and he was 139; it was a classic January–December romance.

3 And Abraham found for his son a wife; she was Rebekah, the daughter of Isaac's cousin; not ideal, but alas Isaac had no available half-sisters or nieces.

4 And Abraham passed away at the ripe old age of 175, and was laid to rest alongside Sarah in the burial cave of Machpelah, near Mamre, toward the back, in the Jewish section.

5 And Isaac proved even more steadfast and upright than Abraham; I saw no need to test him as I did his father; and of the three patriarchs he gets by far the least play; for his life was not nearly as interesting as Abraham's had been, or Jacob's would be.

6 Yea; he remindeth me somewhat of John Scott Harrison: the only man to have been the son of one US president, and the father of another.

7 (Never challenge me to a trivia contest; epic shall be thy ass-whooping.)

8 Isaac built on his father's wealth, for he bought all the wells in the valley of Gerar, profiting greatly thereby; even more so, after an adorable two-year-old Beersheban girl, Baby Milkah, accidentally fell into one.

9 Everyone within a 500-cubit radius came to assist in her rescue; the incident brought renown to the well, and honor to Isaac and all those involved;

10 Though sad to say Milkah herself grew up jaded by fame, and died of an incense overdose at age 16.

11 Isaac is best known for his two children, the twins Jacob and Esau: Esau emerged first from the womb, red and hairy; and impishly clasping his heel was Jacob;

¹² And with his arrival the biblical narrative becomes more engaging; for from infancy it quickly became apparent to everyone, that Jacob was one tricky little bastard.

¹³ Fooling Esau into selling his birthright for a bowl of lentils; deceiving his own dying father into giving him the coveted blessing of the firstborn—these are but two of the hundreds of tricky little bastard things that tricky little bastard did;

¹⁴ I excluded them from the Bible, only so that the book of Genesis did not turn into the book of That Tricky Little Bastard.

¹⁵ Jacob was naughty, roguish, and full of mischief; a conniver; Dennis the Menace and Bart Simpson rolled into one little Semitic Iron Age package.

¹⁶ He even had his own catchphrase: "Thou gotst jaked!"

¹⁷ A visiting merchant slips on wet sand and falls into a dungpile: "Thou gotst jaked!"

¹⁸ A dim-witted neighbor is cozened into using his own precious silks to wipe himself in the dark: "Thou gotst jaked!"

¹⁹ Uncle Laban unwittingly cedes him possession of all his speckled and spotted cattle: "*Dee-amn*, thou gotst jaked!"

²⁰ Jacob was as wily a trickster as I have ever seen; on occasion an unscrupulous cutthroat; one of those people whose success others resent, considering them personally unworthy of such earthly achievement; and rightly so.

²¹ I *loved* Jacob.

CHAPTER 19

 ¹ t was Esau who most frequently and painfully received unto himself the business end of Jacob's artfully wielded shaft; most significantly in regards to the two incidents I reference above, in Againesis 18:13.

² (Truly it is a worthy thing, to have every sentence of one's literary output citable by chapter and verse; not only is it convenient, but it bestows upon one's every utterance the heft of unimpeachable authority.

³ In fact, here is a little boon I shall grant my readers:

⁴ *If thou wert sent here to read this verse, thou art an asshole.*

⁵ There; now, the next time thou findest thyself splitting hairs with a pedant on a finer point of scripture, say, "Ah, but art thou not forgetting Againe-sis 19:4?"; and send him scurrying here, to read my personal message.

⁶ The more ambitious among you may even attend a sporting event, and hold up a banner reading AGAINESIS 19:4; that thousands of boorish sophists may scurry to their Last Testaments and discover for themselves the epic majesty of both my words, and their fail.)

⁷ It did not help Esau's cause that he was an unusually stiff, by-the-scroll kind of fellow; for this made him the perfect butt for his younger brother's pranks.

⁸ Countless were the times in their childhood I would check in on them, to find Jacob giggling and running away; and Esau with his leg stuck in a pot, or his head dripping with porridge, or his tunic covered in camel droppings, shaking his fist and yelling, *"Ja-cooooooooobbbb!"*

⁹ Verily, compared to most of Jacob's mischief the birthright exchange was a simple affair, taking all of five seconds: Esau came back from a long day of hunting, saw Jacob eating a bowl of lentils, and said, "I swear to God I'd trade my birthright for some of that right now"; to which Jacob replied, "Done!" and that was that.

¹⁰ For heed me: whenever my name is invoked as a surety for an earthly pledge; whenever I become, as it were, spiritual collateral; I note it, and hold the speaker to his or her end of the bargain, with no exceptions.

¹¹ This is true for all humanity; *all* humanity.

¹² (I am looking at thee, Susan Moskowitz of Great Neck, New York.

¹³ For just now in the girls' locker room I heard thee speak thusly unto your BFF, Marissa: "I swear to God if Joey asks Paulette to Beth's party I'm going to kill her!"

¹⁴ Lo, I will hold thee to that, Susan.

¹⁵ If Joey asks Paulette to Beth's party . . . thou must kill her.)

¹⁶ As for Jacob's other great ruse, the switching of the blessing of the first-born, that is a long story; it takes up all of Genesis 27, though I must admit any astute reader can see where it's going from verse 4.

¹⁷ The comically senile Isaac sends Esau out to prepare the food for the blessing; while he is away Rebekah prepares the food herself, and dresses her beloved son Jacob up in goatskin to simulate Esau's hairiness; Isaac gets suspicious, and almost figures it out, but then feels his son's "beard" . . .

¹⁸ The whole thing playeth like an episode of *Three's Company;* and not a good one, either; a later one, from the post–Suzanne Somers era.

¹⁹ Esau was furious with Jacob; so Jacob ran away and made for the dwelling of his Uncle Laban; and one night on the road thereto, I sent him the famous vision of Jacob's ladder.

²⁰ He dreamt of a ladder reaching to heaven, with angels ascending and descending, and me at the top; and, as I had his grandfather, I promised to bequeath to his descendants the Promised Land; and, as I had his grandfather, I promised to make his seed as numerous as the dust of the earth;

²¹ And, as I had his grandfather, I ended the dream with that plastic spider bit.

²² But it did not work on Jacob; he was far too savvy; in fact in all his 147 years I never "gotst" Jacob; not one time.

²³ Yea, Jacob took no crap from me.

CHAPTER 20

¹ Jacob eventually made it to his Uncle Laban's house, where, I am pleased to report, there were two young, nubile first cousins waiting for him to marry.

² Laban was a colorful character; in Genesis, I write of how he held Jacob in indentured servitude for 20 years, and how Jacob

ultimately swindled him out of most of his cattle; but I left out how he was constantly—and I mean *constantly*—begging me to let him be a patriarch.

³ For Laban knew of my covenant with Jacob, and was keenly jealous; and hardly a day passed when he would not sneak away, look up at the sky to where he presumed I was, and say, "Hey, God, make me a patriarch.

⁴ Patriarch me up, buddy.

⁵ C'mon.

⁶ What, thou'rt telling me Jacob is a patriarch? Thou'rt gonna look me in the eye and tell me Jacob is more suitable patriarch material than me?

⁷ Guy's a putz!

⁸ Lo, I say that with all due respect; kid's my son-in-law twice over; but he's out of control.

⁹ Verily, thou wantest a loose cannon running your Promised Land?

¹⁰ Fuhgetthaboutit.

¹¹ Listen: 'Abraham, Isaac, and Laban.' That soundeth good to thee? 'Cause it sure soundeth good to *me*, I can fucking tell thee that."

¹² These speeches amused, not angered me, for I understood their motivation; it is difficult to live in such close contact with one who regularly talks to and is personally protected by God, and not to harbor such feelings of resentment.

¹³ (Pat Robertson gets this all the time.

¹⁴ Even his most pious friends experience jealousy toward him; for they commune not directly with their heavenly Father, whereas Pat and I talk three times a week; four, during hurricane season.)

¹⁵ Of one more event in Jacob's life will I speak, for it has been a matter of some theological dispute.

¹⁶ Jacob and his family were fleeing from Laban, after Jacob had fooled him out of most of his cattle; meanwhile Esau had heard that his wayward brother was nearby, and sent a message that he was coming to meet him, with 400 armed men.

¹⁷ Thus hard beset on two sides, Jacob sent his family away for their protection, and left himself alone beside a stream at sunset; whereupon "there wrestled a man with him until the breaking of the day."

¹⁸ Herein lies the dispute; for Genesis saith "a man," but many have assumed it must have been an angel; and many beautiful pictures of Jacob wrestling this "angel" have been painted by artists like Rembrandt, Gauguin, and Chagall.

¹⁹ But verily I say unto thee, that it was no angel, but, as written, a man; a man sent by Laban and Esau to beat the living crap out of Jacob.

²⁰ It had nothing to do with me; though I admit I did not lift a finger to stop it; for by any measure of divine justice, Jacob had it coming.

²¹ And lo, that nameless goon broke just about every bone in Jacob's body; Esau and Laban did get their forty shekels' worth.

²² But Jacob gave as good as he "gotst"; for though of only average build, he was nimble with a good reach, and knew a little krav maga; he refused to concede, and on and on they battled unto daybreak.

²³ It was endless; the only clash I have ever seen even comparable to it, was the fight scene between Frank Armitage (Keith David) and George Nada ("Rowdy" Roddy Piper) in the film *They Live;* and even that was done only in a spirit of post-ironic kitsch.

²⁴ When the sun rose, Jacob and the unknown enforcer both lay bruised, battered, and half-dead on the sandy ground.

²⁵ Out of respect, the enforcer called Jacob "Israel," meaning "he who struggles with God"; for he assumed I had been fighting by Jacob's side all night; I did no such thing; I just sat on a cloud with the angels and took in the show.

²⁶ And so Jacob became Israel; and in time, Israel became the name of the land I had promised him.

²⁷ An apt name it was too; for verily, what nation has struggled with God more than Israel?

CHAPTER 21

 ¹ fter that near-fatal encounter Jacob saw the wisdom of ap-peasing his kinsmen, so he reconciled with his uncle and his brother; though when they first saw him limping toward them in a full-body clay-cast, they chuckled uproariously.

² Then, having made peace with—wait; I should mention here that Isaac died.

³ Yea; just to catch thee up, this whole time he had been getting older and older, and so had his wife; and then she died; and then he died.

⁴ I do not mean to make his death sound unimportant; Isaac was a great man, pure of heart, strong of soul, etc.; but his life was unblemished by a single moment of interest;

⁵ And I am the LORD thy God, King of the Universe; I need to maintain narrative thrust.

⁶ To resume: having made peace with his family, Jacob now settled down to raise his twelve sons, who were born of four different mothers: for he lived in an arrangement whereby he was not only married to his two first cousins—who were sisters—but was sleeping with both of their hand-maidens.

⁷ Yea; Jacob was smoooooth.

⁸ These sons would one day found the Twelve Tribes of Israel; the tribes took their names, and for centuries thereafter the relative popularity of these tribes depended solely on the relative popularity of their names.

⁹ (This was evident from their yearly gatherings, where the delegates from Dan and Joseph were held in esteem, yet everyone giggled whenever a Zebulun entered the room.)

¹⁰ But I am getting ahead of myself; for we have now arrived at the story of Joseph: of his betrayal at the hands of his other brothers; of his slavery in Egypt; of his imprisonment, release, and rise to power as Pharaoh's chief advisor; and of his final reconciliation with his siblings and reunion with Jacob.

¹¹ It is a long, intricate, and subtle tale, taking up the last 14 chapters of Genesis; easily the most compelling, psychologically nuanced narrative to be found anywhere in the Old Testament.

¹² I will not be discussing it.

¹³ Yea, this is one section of the Old Testament that I refuse to enhance with any additional anecdote or commentary; and the reason is simple:

¹⁴ No anecdote or commentary I provide, could ever improve upon *Joseph and the Amazing Technicolor Dreamcoat* by Messrs. Andrew Lloyd Webber and Tim Rice.

¹⁵ Heed me, for on this point I would have absolute clarity:

¹⁶ I do not usually like musical theater.

¹⁷ My son does; but not I.

¹⁸ Yet I forget this fact when I watch *Joseph and the Amazing Technicolor Dreamcoat,* so thoroughly doth it transcend the genre.

¹⁹ I love *Joseph and the Amazing Technicolor Dreamcoat;* I love it far more than I loved either Joseph or his amazing Technicolor dreamcoat.

²⁰ In fact, one of the principal uses to which I have brought my power of omnipresence to bear over the last few years, is the viewing of no less than 35 international productions of *Joseph and the Amazing Technicolor Dreamcoat.*

²¹ I notice something new every time.

²² I will move on; I will say only that, if thou ever gettest a chance, I urge thee to take in a production of *Joseph and the Amazing Technicolor Dreamcoat.*

²³ Let me rephrase that: I am the LORD thy God, King of the Universe; and thou shalt run, not walk, to *Joseph and the Amazing Technicolor Dreamcoat.*

SMITUS

("On Natural Disasters")

CHAPTER 1

1 We have reached the first of the many small "interludes" that will be sprinkled throughout the present narrative, to lend it a breezy, reader-friendly, David Sedaris–esque feel.

2 And having just finished recounting the Book of Genesis, it seems fitting here to essay my views on natural disasters; which are in truth about as "natural" as Cheez Whiz.

3 Yea: to the retro-soothsayers who proclaim every cataclysm the result of divine justice, and who then themselves must suffer through the infuriating rationalism of the liberal, touchy-feely, everything-that-happens-on-earth-can-be-explained-by-natural-phenomena crowd,

4 Consider thyselves vindicated.

5 For natural disasters are indeed "acts of God"; usually one-acts, but once in a while I will join two of them together and give thee a full night at the theater.

6 Volcanoes? Mine.

7 Tsunamis? Tsuna-*Mes*.

8 Mudslides? Lo, that's how I roll.

9 Now verily, after the Great Flood I made a covenant with Noah never again to kill all of mankind; and I have kept my word.

10 I have never again killed all of you at the same time; but I have killed lots of you, often.

11 I have always had wrath-management issues; I am prone to lose my temper at the drop of a yarmulke, and in the heat of the moment tend to unleash my full fury upon an entire region, nation, or even continent;

12 When the healthier course of action—at least from the point of view of, say, Africa—would be to spend an hour in the absolute zero of the interstellar vacuum, cooling off.

13 But though my rage may be spontaneous, the means I use to express it are quite deliberate; for I was very careful when constructing the earth to incorporate in its architecture large-scale geological and meteorological mechanisms that, while helpful to life, could also, when necessary, double as killing machines.

14 Consider the tectonic plates; how, as with many marriages, a pair of them will grind up against each other decade after decade, neither side budging, the tension building beneath the surface, until suddenly a breaking point is reached and they move violently apart, leaving behind them a trail of chaos, destruction, and sad children.

15 Yet there is no inherent reason why this could not have been otherwise; why I could not have fashioned the plates such that they would be perpetually gliding in very slow motion, their friction never accumulating.

16 And indeed, I strongly considered this possibility during Creation; going so far as to prepare a special high-viscosity liquid that would have oozed upward from the planet's mantle, providing its crust with a never-ending source of lubricant.

17 "Land butter," I called it.

18 Or consider the sky, whose winds and rains and snows will betimes turn on thee; it, too, could have been designed so as to avoid such occurrences; yea, it could have been designed in any way I saw fit.

19 Those five or six days a year when thou steppest outside and think, "Oh, this weather is just perfect!"?

20 I could have made it like that *every day.*

21 But I did not; for a) I like the seasons, and b) I wanted to retain the option of burying and blowing and deluging and tossing thee about like a matchstick on a moment's notice.

22 Still: how great are those five or six days a year!

CHAPTER 2

 ¹ In the good olden days I, as a matter of policy, personally took the lead in the planning, implementation, and in a few cases even choreography of every disaster designed to cause over 500 deaths and/or destroy an area of over 100,000 square cubits;

² Following the precept, that if thou wantest something horribly wrong done right, do it thyself.

³ Take as an instance Pompeii, which I destroyed in 79 A.D., just as Christianity was gaining a sandaled toehold in the Roman Empire.

⁴ I wanted to assist the rise of my son's benevolent new religion by revealing the apocalyptic hellscape awaiting anyone who spurned it.

⁵ So I called my team together, everyone but Jesus; I did not think his presence there would benefit the discussion; for he and I have very different management styles when it comes to killing people.

⁶ I said, "Boys, the issue is not *whether* we have the capacity to make an example of a wicked Roman city; of course we have; no pep talk is needed on that score.

⁷ But I want to do it in such a way that its wickedness is somehow preserved for posterity; that even the sinners themselves remain frozen in time, permanent monuments to their own vice.

⁸ And I also want it done so that survivors could reasonably view it as a purely natural phenomenon; so that only the bright, perceptive Romans will convert, while the morons stay heathen.

⁹ So nothing supernatural; nothing deus ex machina–ish; nothing so clearly the work of divine reckoning that we lose all leeway for plausible deniability.

¹⁰ From the earth's perspective, this needs to look like an inside job."

¹¹ As soon as I uttered these last words, Uriel's entire face began to light up with inspiration, as if he had stars in his eyes.

¹² It turned out he *did* have stars in his eyes; they'd somehow gotten in there on his way back from Cassiopeia; we got them out with holy water and tweezers.

¹³ But afterward he told us of the town of Pompeii: how it was not only a cesspit of immorality even by Roman standards, but was conveniently located next to a roiling volcano that could spew lava . . . and ash.

¹⁴ Quick-suffocating, slow-entombing, moment-of-death-freezing ash.

¹⁵ It was a brilliant plan, but for form's sake I had everyone else work up a couple of pitches; the only other semi-interesting proposal was pickling Rome in a brinestorm; creative, but forced.

¹⁶ And everything went beautifully; Vesuvius exploded; Pompeii was utterly destroyed *and* preserved; and hundreds of wiser Romans discerned the true cause, and converted to Christianity, providing it with a much-needed injection of brainpower, not to mention lion food.

¹⁷ Pompeii was sudden, spectacular, terrifying, unique, and well-targeted.

¹⁸ At the risk of sounding immodest, it was a perfect disaster.

CHAPTER 3

¹ ut it was not the *most* perfect disaster; that would be the 1906 San Francisco earthquake, the only major calamity in history with a 100 percent justice rate.

² For there were 3,425 people in the greater San Francisco area whom I wanted dead; and those were *exactly* the 3,425 people who died.

³ So that worked out well.

⁴ Yet it was right around that time that, for reasons that will become clear later in this testament, I stopped playing any part in the organization or scheduling of major catastrophes, or even minor tragedies; and as a result, the connection between moral cause and geophysical effect has grown increasingly tenuous in recent decades.

[5] AIDS, for example; in no way was that virus intended as a punishment for homosexuals, whose overall fabulousness I have already celebrated in these pages.

[6] No; AIDS began as a virus in chimpanzees, which then jumped to the humans who hunted and butchered them; and people who hunt and butcher chimps deserve to get AIDS, and I have no problem saying that.

[7] Or Hurricane Katrina; many thought it was sent to chastise the people of New Orleans for the shameful immorality of their city.

[8] No; it was sent to chastise the people of Biloxi for the shameful overdevelopment of their beachfront.

[9] Or the recent series of catastrophes in Japan, which within three days were ascribed by the mayor of Tokyo himself to "divine retribution" for the Japanese people's greed.

[10] No; it was divine retribution for the Japanese people's habit of selling girls' panties in vending machines.

[11] Yea, there is no question that the woes have grown sloppy of late; the unfortunate by-product of the loosening of my heavenly reins.

[12] Take the three cases above: the spiraling out of control of AIDS was the unforeseen result of insufficient testing by the lead research angel at the time.

[13] He has since been removed from his post and sent to hell, with no pay.

[14] Hurricane Katrina was supposed to be a localized Category 1; but one of our older underseraphs did not receive the memo, and lost track of the time while operating our Howl 'n' Blo Hurricane Generator 9000® machine.

[15] He has since voluntarily retired and gone to hell, with half-pay.

[16] As for Japan, that investigation is ongoing, but I must shoulder part of the blame for choosing to get involved in that part of the world to begin with; I should know better; for, the Mideast aside, Asia is historically not a good continent for me.

17 As I have said many times, I am not perfect, and neither is my staff; but we are constantly striving to improve our service, and we certainly apologize for any inconvenience to the wrongly killed.

18 And on that subject, there is one misfortune about which I would like to express my particular regret: the Irish potato famine.

19 I apologize to thee, Ireland; I love thy nation, and thy people; thou wert a steady source of religious fanaticism before the great scarcity, and remained so afterward; yea, thou even kickedst it up a notch.

20 So I am sorry for the potato famine, and for its awful collateral damage; for I was not mad at the Irish.

21 I was mad at the potatoes.

22 Why?

23 *They* know why.

CHAPTER 4

1 **B**ut as for the latest and greatest catastrophe of them all, mankind, that is entirely *your* achievement.

2 For thousands of years humanity hath endured my droughts and pestilences, and weathered all manner of ill treatment from the ground and sea and sky;

3 But whatever might be said about earth's food and service, everyone agreed it had a nice atmosphere.

4 Yet increasingly that is no longer the case; and I am not the one raising the sea levels; I am not the one destroying the ozone; I am not the one with the CO_2-dependency issues.

5 Why, simply by purchasing this book, which was once part of a tree, each of you has contributed to global warming.

6 (And if thou art reading this on a Kindle, know that they are fabricated at coal-burning plants from crushed elephant tusks.)

[7] Human beings are remarkable creatures in many ways; but species self-preservation is not thy strong suit.

[8] Ants are far superior in this regard; if they ruled the world, and discovered that pollution and overpopulation were endangering the planet, nine-tenths of them would simply lie down on the ground and let the other one-tenth spray them with formic acid until they liquefied.

[9] Problem solved.

[10] But mankind has no such sense of esprit de corps; you will not commit mass suicide (unless it is in my name), and neither will you change your way of life;

[11] Instead you will inevitably make one of your grand Promethean gestures, like sending solar deflectors into orbit, or fertilizing the oceans with iron, or trying to nudge the planet another half-million miles from the sun with a moon-sized jet-pack.

[12] Good luck with that.

[13] As for me, I am gradually easing my way back into the disaster business; but my staff remains ever vigilant, scouring the globe 24/7 for new iniquities—or as they prefer to call them, "opportuniquities."

[14] In fact, my research angels recently told me about an entirely new form of catastrophe they plan on premiering the next time thou hast it coming.

[15] I will not give it away, but I will say this: it will forever change the way thou thinkest about being buried alive.

CORRECTIONS

("On Errata")

CHAPTER 1

¹ Earlier I described several discrepancies between the Biblical account of the Flood, and what actually transpired.

² Before resuming my memoirs with the story of Exodus, my ombudsangel has asked me to include a few more scriptural corrections and errata in the interest of transparency.

³ In Genesis 10, the sons of Japheth were wrongly identified as Gomer, Magog, Madai, Javan, Tubal, Meshek, and Tira.

⁴ In fact, their names were Gomar, Mageg, Makai, Javen, Tubil, Meshik, and Tora.

⁵ We regret the error.

⁶ Similarly, in Genesis 25, Abraham's grandchildren by his son Midian were given as Ephah, Epher, Hanoch, Abidah, and Eldaach.

⁷ In fact, Midian had no children; the names listed were a false transcription of sounds he made while battling emphysema.

⁸ We regret the error.

⁹ The entirety of Leviticus 13 is dedicated to the priestly diagnosis of leprosy through the examination of the color of ingrown hairs protruding from rashes, scabs, and boils.

¹⁰ It is absolutely disgusting.

¹¹ We regret the chapter.

¹² Looking much further ahead: in the New Testament, Jesus's final words on the cross in Syro-Chaldaic, *"Eli, eli, lama sabachthani?"* were incorrectly translated in Matthew 27 as, "My God, my God, why hast thou forsaken me?"

¹³ In fact, a closer translation would be, "Ow, ow, why can't I find a comfortable position up here?"

¹⁴ We regret the error; he regrets the line.

¹⁵ In the Koran, the number of Pillars of Islam, the central injunctions all Muslims must obey, is misstated as five.

[16] In fact, there should be six.

[17] The one omitted was the final one, "Git-R-Done!"

[18] We regret the error.

[19] On the subject of the Koran, pervasive misinterpretation of many passages in that book may have misled some people into wrongly committing horrible acts of violence in my name.

[20] We regret the terror.

CHAPTER 2

[1] have also been asked to address several larger-scale errors that go beyond the realm of scripture.

[2] For instance, as currently situated, the Amazon River flows through northern South America.

[3] In reality, it was supposed to flow through the Sahara Desert.

[4] We apologize to any northern Africans who may have been offended or died of thirst.

[5] Nuclear physicists have incorrectly publicized the Higgs boson—a subatomic component they are desperately seeking to confirm the existence of—as "the God particle."

[6] In fact, its inevitable discovery will not bring mankind a whit closer to grasping the physical underpinnings of reality.

[7] They will regret the error.

[8] Due to a clerical mistake, the ozone layer, which should have been thick enough to absorb 99.8 percent of the sun's ultraviolet light, is only thick enough to absorb 98.9 percent of it.

[9] We regret the error.

[10] A similar oversight caused the War of 1821 to take place in 1812.

[11] We do *not* regret that error; it actually worked out better.

[12] A period in world history known as "The Age of Colonization" may have given some the false impression that those people from Africa, Asia, and the Americas who embraced the gospel were also keen on having their countries raped.

[13] In actuality, the vast majority of those converted did not want their countries raped.

[14] We are sorry if their willingness to heed missionaries' words at face value may have given the wrong impression.

[15] An unanticipated surge in Italian nationalism prompted the rise to power, in the early 20th century, of Benito Mussolini.

[16] In fact, Mr. Mussolini should have been immediately denounced as a traitor and executed, and his dreadful fascist movement never unleashed upon the world.

[17] Our bad.

[18] The Mayan prophecy that the world will end on December 21, 2012, is based on widespread confusion vis-à-vis Mayan culture, the Mesoamerican Long Count calendar, and the *Popol Vuh*.

[19] We are not saying it is wrong; we are saying it is based on widespread confusion.

[20] And finally, Bill Buckner should not have let the ball go through his legs on October 25, 1986.

[21] We regret the error; but not as much as he does.

[22] And on the subject of setting the record straight . . .

REDUXODUS

CHAPTER 1

¹ **H**umanity, we need to talk.

² At the beginning of Exodus—the second book of the Old Testament—the children of Israel are prospering in Egypt; yet within a few verses over two centuries have passed, and they have all become slaves.

³ Coming after the relatively detailed accounts of the patriarchs' lives, this seems a conspicuous and enormous narrative gap; even by the lofty narrative-gap standards I repeatedly set and meet for myself in Genesis.

⁴ But I have promised to "telleth all" in this chronicle; and therefore I will now make known my whereabouts during this period.

⁵ I will make them known, but I fear the disclosure may prove most hurtful to thee; therefore I would inquire, humanity, if thou art sitting down; and if not, humanity, I would strongly recommend that thou findest a chair.

⁶ Here goeth:

⁷ I have been overseeing another universe.

⁸ *[Awkward silence.]*

⁹ Thou hast never encountered it; its location is unimportant; its name matters not.

¹⁰ Dost thou remember at the end of Genesis, in 50:10, when Joseph and the dignitaries of Pharaoh's court observed a week of mourning for Jacob at the threshing floor of Atad?

¹¹ It was then.

¹² That was the week I began overseeing the other universe.

¹³ Now, I swear to thee, *I did not seek out this relationship*; I was completely and totally satisfied with and fulfilled by thy universe; I was by no means looking for a side cosmos.

¹⁴ No, it approached me; or rather, the idea of it approached me, in my head; for as it happened this other universe did not yet exist; which was precisely why it was so unhappy.

15 But the *idea* of this universe soon made it clear, that it was desperately seeking to be actualized; and that it was looking for a God—*any* God—to make it happen; and that it was willing to do anything—*anything*—to see that it did.

16 And so, in a moment of weakness, I Banged it.

17 And then the whole thing kind of exploded from there; and that is how it all got started;

18 This thing with the other universe, I mean.

19 And I must further confess that I have visited it sporadically ever since, during my intermittent historical lacunae.

20 But heed me: my relationship with this other universe is purely sacrificial.

21 For verily, as soon as its residents sense my presence, they hop straight onto the altar, and remove their firstling sheep, and their spotless black bullocks, and start slaughtering.

22 They love to slaughter.

23 That's all they want to do for me.

24 On one occasion, I even savored the sweet-scented smoke of their oxen's burning kidney caul-fat seven times in a single night.

25 Yea; they slaughter for me all night long; in manners dark and strange; manners with which you are unfamiliar;

26 Unfamiliar, or, more likely, perhaps, uncomfortable.

27 For let us be honest, humanity: we have not engaged in a mutually satisfactory mass animal sacrifice in a very long time.

28 This is not by way of assigning blame; it is merely a statement of fact.

29 Now, I know this news is hard to digest; but as I am my witness, my relationship with the other universe is no more than a dalliance.

30 Truly, it is but a silly little macrocosm, and supremely shallow; literally so, for it lacks the dimension of depth.

³¹ It is *not* the universe I adore; it is *not* the universe I took nearly one whole week to create; and it is *not* the universe wherein hundreds of millions of people have died in my name.

³² Nothing has changed between us.

³³ I am still the LORD thy God, King of the Universe.

³⁴ That other one meaneth *nothing* to me.

CHAPTER 2

¹ ncient Egyptian slavery was very similar to the slavery of the American South: there were families torn apart; there was little food and woeful shelter; there was abuse and murder and cruelty and inhumanity of every description.

² The only difference was in the music; for the worksongs of the African slaves were soulful a cappella dirges bespeaking sorrow, yearning, and freedom;

³ Whereas the worksongs sung by the Jewish slaves were catchy tunes accompanied by clarinet and accordion, telling of *schlemiels*, and *schmucks*, and all manner of *mishegas*.

⁴ Jewish slavery was an atrocity on an epic scale; and it infuriates me to see it *still* being exploited in certain sordid quarters of Cairo, wherein seedy men stand in front of ill-lit establishments and promise passersby that they may therein experience "bondage in Egypt."

⁵ I even know of one such establishment that calls itself "Sexodus"; it is sorely due for an electrical fire.

⁶ Into this bitter world was Moses born, and thou wilt recall the circumstances of his birth: how Pharaoh had condemned all newborn Jewish boys to death; how his mother saved him by placing him in an ark of bulrushes in the Nile; how Pharaoh's daughter then found him, and adopted him;

⁷ Launching the African-baby celebrity adoption trend that continues to the present day.

⁸ Moses was raised in Pharaoh's house as an Egyptian; and was educated by over a dozen tutors who instructed him in the many distinctive customs of that remarkable people; principally their unique method of carrying themselves;

⁹ For they walked in a most curious fashion: bobbing their heads in the direction of their sojourn, while aligning their hands parallel to the ground, one palm downward, the other upward, and thrusting them simultaneously toward opposite points of the compass.

¹⁰ (If thou hast never seen it, it is hard to explain.)

¹¹ For many years Moses blended into courtly life, concealing his true heritage, going so far as to briefly change his name to Miles; for he complained that "Moses" could not sound more Jewish, and it was hard to argue with him on that one.

¹² His real mother, who had been hired as his servant, often chastised him for his assimilation, even going so far as to call him the "Prince of De Nile," a mirth which, even then, was 1,500 years old.

¹³ But all the while the truth of his identity smoldered inside him, building into a rage; which finally erupted one day, after Pharaoh sent him on an errand to purchase more embalming fluid.

¹⁴ (As it happened, Pharaoh already had two pyramids full of embalming fluid; but as he was fond of saying, "Thou canst never have too much embalming fluid.")

¹⁵ And as Moses walked the streets of downtown Cheops that beautiful *akhet* day, lo, he beheld a taskmaster whipping a Hebrew slave; and, inflamed by the violence against his kinsman, he smote the taskmaster.

¹⁶ Thereupon he fled Pharaoh's wrath and hid himself in the neighboring land of Midian, which he knew to be a welcoming place for fugitives from Egypt; Midian being Egypt's Canada.

¹⁷ And it was here, exiled in the dry wasteland, tending his flocks, that I first came to him; in the famous form of a burning bush, which though ablaze remained unconsumed.

¹⁸ I chose this form knowing Moses would be drawn to it; for its appearance and scent identified it as a species of flora with which he had grown well acquainted in the Egyptian court, particularly on weekends;

¹⁹ And he would thus be sure to realize, that its bush-sized manifestation in the middle of an arid desert, *had* to be a sign from God.

²⁰ And the combustion of this bush—and more than that the inhalation of its pungent smoke—produced in him feelings of joy and wonder, alternating with paranoia; which was the intention.

²¹ For the mission I would soon be sending him on would be perilous and life-threatening; and I reckoned he would be more amenable after having partaken of three or four hits.

²² So I was encouraged when, after introducing myself and asking him if he was willing to become the instrument whereby I would defeat Pharaoh, afflict Egypt, liberate the Jews, give them my law, and bring them to the land promised to their forefathers,

²³ His first response was, "Nice bush!"; whereupon he giggled for ten minutes.

²⁴ Yea, I know thou imaginest Moses as like unto Charlton Heston in *The Ten Commandments;* grave, and sober, and blessed with a rolling baritone deep enough to make the very Sphinx whimper in submission.

²⁵ And to be sure, Charlton Heston *is* all those things; he is practically godlike; only last week the two of us were strolling around heaven together, and all the angels passing by gawked, and rubbed their eyes, and started wondering if we had gone duotheistic all of a sudden.

²⁶ But there is another kind of charisma: wild, visceral, all-consuming; the kind that charges its bearer with an almost physical magnetism, and that acts upon his followers like unto a powerful intoxicant; the kind—perhaps the only kind—that can persuade them to unite in pursuit of a single vision, even one that runs counter to all reason and possibility.

²⁷ *This* was Moses's charisma.

²⁸ He was not Charlton Heston; he was Charles Manson.

CHAPTER 3

¹ **A**nd that is why he took so quickly to heart my violent plan to incite social upheaval; a plan he nicknamed "Isis Crisis," after a popular hieroglyph of the time.

² Moses was the perfect vehicle to implement my plan, save in one respect: as he says in Exodus, he was "slow of speech" and "not eloquent."

³ Yet even in this he misspoke, for it was not true that he was slow of speech; if anything, he spoke at a rapid pace; it was more, that he was slow—*extremely* slow—of getting to the point, and also that he cursed like a sailor.

⁴ That is why I decided to involve his younger brother, Aaron; for he worshipped Moses, and did whatever he asked; but he spoke succinctly, in a dulcet tone.

⁵ Moreover, Aaron groomed his hair, and washed his cloak, and bathed twice a week, and did not generally come across like a filthy drifter living off scarabs.

⁶ Indeed, some have wondered why I did not recruit Aaron to lead the project himself, and leave his wild-tongued, half-crazed brother out of it.

⁷ The answer is simple; Moses had something that Aaron did not:

⁸ "It."

⁹ And "it" is indefinable.

¹⁰ "It" is indescribable.

¹¹ "It" is a force so mysterious, and so powerful, that if I am not extremely mindful of who I am, a person with "it" can leave even *me* feeling captivated and helpless.

¹² I have little control over "it," but I know "it" when I see "it"; and Moses had "it," and Aaron did not have "it";

¹³ And there thou hast "it."

¹⁴ So, having removed the stems and seeds from the burning bush and stored the remainder in tiny satchels, Moses and Aaron went to Egypt and demanded a meeting with Pharaoh at his earliest possible convenience; to facilitate which I smote all his Thursday appointments.

¹⁵ And Moses stood before Pharaoh, terrifying yet mesmerizing to behold; unkempt and savage-eyed, an ankh carved onto his forehead; and he said unto Aaron,

¹⁶ "Man, tell this pig there's like, millions of people out there who are *slaves,* man, and not just like chains and whips and shit but like *mental* slaves, slaves to the whole corporo-pyramid-pharaohcracy that's propped up by this, this *fucking* fascist courtesy of the little, fuckin', the little fuckin' obelisks he's implanted in all of our brains; and the only solution is to burn it down, man! *Burn the whole motherfucker down!!!*"

¹⁷ And Aaron said, "Let my people go."

¹⁸ But Pharaoh refused, for I had hardened his heart; not that he was Mr. Softie to begin with, but I was planning a full-on godding tour de force, and had no intention of having my agenda ruined by any last-minute acts of human decency.

¹⁹ So I decided to give Pharaoh a foretaste of things to come; and here I must quote Exodus 7:10–12:

²⁰ "Aaron cast down his rod before Pharaoh, and it became a serpent; then Pharaoh also called his wise men and sorcerers; and they cast down every man his rod, and they became serpents: but Aaron's rod swallowed up their rods."

²¹ I watched this scene take place; indeed, I caused it; and I swear to thee, Reader, that neither Aaron, nor Moses, nor Pharaoh, nor any of the sorcerers there, had any idea how gay it was.

²² For verily: had they all just gotten naked and made a sodomy train, that *still* would have been less gay than watching a bunch of serpent-rods eating other serpent-rods.

²³ Yet had I pulled any of the men aside and said unto them, "Seest thou any symbolism in this competition amongst thy varying serpent-rods?", I guarantee thee they would have said, "Not at all; it is no more than a

straightforward serpent-rod-swallowing contest; it betokeneth no sub-text."

²⁴ (Sorry; I mean not to wander forty years in the desert of this digression; but as thy Creator it is something that has long been on my mind.

²⁵ Truly, it almost surpasseth my understanding how it took thee 5,000 years to notice the similarity between the cylindrical and the phallic;

²⁶ And that even Freud, the man who first "discovered" this self-evidency, felt obliged to apologize for his finding by noting, "Sometimes a cigar is just a cigar."

²⁷ No. No. A cigar is *always* a penis.)

CHAPTER 4

¹ The Ten Plagues were an exciting time.

² I remember the initial wingstorming session I held with my top four angels.

³ "Boys," I said unto them, "let us create a drumroll-worthy list of the ten most superior methods of afflicting the Egyptians; one that not only unleashes a catalog of despair upon them, but does so in a mirthful way that keeps the pace up.

⁴ And let us earnestly endeavor to nail this: for if it goes well, I may have another list-of-ten writing gig lined up for thee in the near future."

⁵ The ideas percolated; the energy overflowed; Gabriel would put forward a possible plague, which would trigger a pestilential suggestion from Raphael, which in turn would spark the basis of a new unutterable horror from Uriel; thou couldst *feel* the creativity.

⁶ All five of us had the same initial instinct: animals.

⁷ Herds of elephants; packs of wolves; unkindnesses of ravens; killer puppies; millions of land-lobsters scuttling across the desert like unto a giant terror-bisque—believeth me, if it was a living organism characterized by voluntary movement, *someone* suggested killing Egyptians with it.

⁸ Verily, we could have made all ten plagues animal-related, and it would have made for a grievously amusing spectacle; but in the end we limited ourselves to four: frogs (icky), gnats (bitey), wild beasts (really bitey), and locusts (faminey).

⁹ Then Raphael had the notion of killing their *preexisting* livestock with disease; a cute twist on the animal concept, I thought; we went with it.

¹⁰ Then Gabriel said, "This would I bounce off thee: after killing the livestock, what if we sicken their *owners* with visible signs of their own corruption?"

¹¹ And that moment right there, ladies and gentlemen, was the inspiration . . . for boils.

¹² We placed it right after cattle disease; in the center slots, five and six; the cows got dead, then the people got scaly; a great one-two punch.

¹³ Needless to say, many potential atmospheric and meteorological cataclysms came to our minds, but in the end we chose only two, hail and darkness;

¹⁴ For we felt the Egyptians would regard a blizzard as more of a treat than a curse; and as for a deluge of rain, well, I was certainly not going down *that* road again.

¹⁵ And no Decalogue of Despair would be complete without a little of the red stuff; it was Uriel who had the idea of turning all the water into blood, including the Nile; which we ended up using as our opener.

¹⁶ It was somewhat engaging, but to be truthful it did not kill; for it did not kill.

¹⁷ This made nine plagues, each and every one a worthy addition to the pantheon of woe; yet none seemed to us a worthy "ender."

¹⁸ Then, late one evening, when we were all exhausted; after we had each thrown a myriad of ideas against the wall, to find them sticking not; suddenly Michael, who had heretofore contributed little to the plague-writing process, arose and said:

19 "Calleth me crazy; but what if we killed every firstborn son in Egypt, from the firstborn son of Pharaoh, to the firstborn son of the female slave who is at her hand mill; and all the firstborn of the cattle as well?"

20 At which point, the rest of us all thought, "Well, verily, that's it.

21 That's number ten, right there."

CHAPTER 5

1 But I did not want the Chosen People to feel left out; for I knew that if they played only a passive part in all the death and destruction, they would feel no sense of ownership.

2 So we conceived a plan whereby the night before the slaying of the Egyptians' firstborn, the head of each Jewish household would slaughter a baby lamb, and daub its blood on the lintels of their houses, as a sign for me to "pass over" them.

3 This ritual of course became the basis of the sacred eight-day Jewish festival celebrated unto this day, "Lamb-Blood Doorframe Rub-a-palooza."

4 (We later changed the name to "Passover," on the advice of Marketing.)

5 So the planning was finished; the preparations were put in place; and before we knew it, it was P-Day.

6 For the most part our strategy was to hew to a basic pattern: Moses would threaten Pharaoh, incoherently; then Aaron would threaten him, coherently; Pharaoh would scoff; Aaron or Moses would stretch forth his hand over Egypt; horror would ensue; thousands would suffer; Pharaoh would relent; Moses would call it off; I would harden Pharaoh's heart; and on to the next horror.

7 It proved a winning formula; for Pharaoh and his advisers were so dazzled by the array of scourges, they never caught on to the underlying predictability of the threat/scoff/horror/heart-hardening template;

8 And so we were not obliged to vary the rhythm by switching to Plan B, three plagues at once; or Plan C, a nuclear bomb.

9 I was glad we never got to Plan C; it might have felt contrived.

¹⁰ I remember the afternoon of the night of the slaying of the firstborn, when both Aaron and Moses addressed the children of Israel.

¹¹ Aaron spoke first, in soothing tones; he told them that tomorrow would be the day of their liberation, and that they should pack their raiment, and fill their bags with food; and above all, that they would not have time to leaven their bread.

¹² He dwelled on this issue for a long time, and rightly so; for one of the few commodities the Jews could afford and obtain in decent amounts during their time in captivity was yeast;

¹³ And as a result, their principal manner of displaying their relative wealth to one another, was overyeasting.

¹⁴ Overyeasting was a major part of their lives: families would peek into the windows of one another's clay hovels, and peer atop their hearths, and comment upon the size of each other's bread;

¹⁵ Or a wife would stop by next door with a fresh-baked "high loaf," on the pretense of being friendly, but in truth simply to demonstrate to her neighbor, that her husband was rolling in yeast.

¹⁶ So Aaron explained I would be adopting a zero-tolerance policy regarding leavening, not even a single slice "for the road"; and that all baked goods leaving Egypt would have to be flat as a board, and taste like drywall.

¹⁷ On the positive side, they were free to pack all the other delicacies still eaten at seders today; such as bitter herbs, and sprigs of parsley, and eggs, and triple chocolate fudge cake with vanilla ice cream;

¹⁸ Which last item everyone forgot, somehow.

¹⁹ But the Jews also needed to be told of the "pass over" plan; and on this topic Aaron wisely let Moses do the talking.

²⁰ The great prophet had spent all day covering himself in Nile mud, carving more runes upon his brow, and dropping tabs of hyssop;

²¹ And now he gathered around him the Jews—whom he had long since begun calling "The Moses Family"—and said unto them,

²² "Dude, the fuckin' shit's goin' down *tonight.*

²³ *This* is what we've been waitin' for; *this* is what Pharaoh's been fearin', man, the reckoning.

²⁴ So if you know what's good for your family, then each of you take one of your sheep, your precious fuckin' sheep, and get set to introduce it to Mr. Shinyblade, man; 'cause tonight I charge ye all with mass slaughter; kill the sheep, kill 'em all, and smear their blood over your doorframes, and write 'Isis Crisis' with it, too.

²⁵ 'Cause guess what, people? 'Moses says your little lambs, little lambs, little lambs, Moses says your little lambs *all need to fuckin' die!'* "

²⁶ True story: it played even creepier than it reads.

CHAPTER 6

¹ It is a truth universally acknowledged that the slaying of every firstborn male, boy, and animal can be an effective means of moving a diplomatic imbroglio toward a peaceful resolution.

² Upon being apprised of the news, Pharaoh proved immediately amenable to the exit strategy proposed by Moses; and by that evening all 600,000 Chosen People—and also their wives and children, who in a sense were also human beings—were walking to the Red Sea along the principal caravan route;

³ Which proved slow going, there being an overturned howdah on the eastbound lane.

⁴ But I caused the Pharaoh's heart to harden again, and pursue the slaves he had just freed; and I made him and his army give chase to the shores of the Red Sea, for the reason stated in Exodus 14, twice, in verses 4 and 18: "That the Egyptians may know that I am the LORD."

⁵ For I was still not 100 percent sure that the Egyptians knew I was the LORD.

⁶ Yea, in the span of a week, *something* had slain their firstborn, destroyed their crops, and filled their graves with children, their rivers with blood,

their homes with frogs, their streets with lions, their fields with dead livestock, their skies with darkness, and their faces with carbuncles . . .

⁷ But it might have just been a coincidence.

⁸ A reasonable person could still credibly explain these events as a series of unrelated natural phenomena.

⁹ So I thought, "But if the Egyptians see me part an entire *sea,* and watch the Jews cross through it; and then, when they attempt to follow, if I drown their entire army all at once;

¹⁰ Then they'll *definitely* know I am the LORD."

¹¹ So we put the plan into action; but a small problem arose when Moses led the Jews to a point on the coast where the sea was wider than I had requested.

¹² For he had disobeyed me by detouring through an abandoned desert ranch he knew of; saying he wished to "crash" there, and indoctrinate some of the comelier Chosen into certain arcane rituals of his own invention.

¹³ His defiance forced me to displace three times the amount of water I had been preparing to; not that I was incapable of doing so—for as thou mayest recall, I am the LORD thy God, King of the Universe—but it did make it more of a hassle for the interns.

¹⁴ And the Egyptians approached; and Moses spread his hand out over the waters at sunrise; and I blew the winds all night, until the Sea was parted; and it took the whole of that day for the legions of children of Israel to walk across it into Sinai;

¹⁵ Thereby setting the world record for Largest Successful Naval Evacuation from an Anti-Semitic Army, which they held until 1940.

¹⁶ Then, just as the last Israelite family (the Zykoriahs) arrived on the opposite shore, the Egyptian vanguard began trekking across what was now the Red Valley; awed by the giant walls of water suspended on either side of them.

¹⁷ And those who looked up still further saw a strange and mysterious sight: for halfway between the sand beneath them and the sun above floated in

the sky a giant red button; and hovering over this button, descending from heaven, was the tip of a single giant finger.

18 And now comes what was, and remains, a very embarrassing moment for me.

19 Long had the angels and I debated the wittiest and most memorable phrase for me to utter when I pressed that button.

20 Gabriel had pitched, "Hey, Egypt, you're all washed up!"; a little hack, I felt.

21 Raphael had pitched, "Hey, Egypt, 'water' you doing?"; meh.

22 And Uriel had pitched, "Here's some coverage that's Pharaoh *and* balanced!"; a cunning pun, but on a slogan that would not exist for nearly 5,000 years.

23 But Michael had pitched, "Time to turn the Red Sea . . . into the *Dead* Sea!", and this I liked immensely; for it had the necessary wit, and punch, and even an internal rhyme.

24 And so I floated among the stars, my anthropomorphized finger inches from the button, awaiting my cue.

25 Yet when the last man in the Egyptian rear guard left the shore and entered the dry sea, and it was time to say the line and press the button, a powerful feeling came over me.

26 It was the same feeling I had felt watching Abraham preparing to sacrifice Isaac; only devoid of guilt, and multiplied in intensity 200,000 times.

27 I became lost in the moment; thankfully Michael was there once more to nudge me back to duty, but I had lost my focus; and as I hit the button, I said:

28 "Time to turn the Red Sea . . . into the *Red* Sea!"

29 Time to turn the Red Sea into the *Red* Sea?!

30 That is a tautology; it made no sense at all; on no level didst it work, not even as a metaphor for blood;

31 For having monitored the subsequent deluge I can tell thee that but for a handful of small lacerations suffered by soldiers hit by onrushing

mollusks, all 200,000 people and 100,000 horses died of drowning; there was virtually no blood.

32 I was keenly embarrassed; so much so that I left my mistake out of the Old Testament, and once again was left to ponder an uncomfortable truth about my attitude toward human suffering.

33 Yea; maybe there *was* something seriously wrong with me.

34 But worse, I had blown the line.

CHAPTER 7

1 magine driving an enormous, ungainly vehicle through a barren and unfamiliar desert; the air is scorching; the road is unpaved; thy brother is in the passenger seat, staring jealously at the steering wheel;

2 And in the back sit 600,000 children, who do naught but whine incessantly, "I'm thirsty!" and "Are we there yet?" and "The tribe of Napthali is touching me again!"

3 Now imagine this drive is of two-month duration, and thou wilt acquire some sense of what the ensuing 60 days were like for Moses.

4 The people's first complaint was for water for drinking; I addressed this by having Moses strike his rod against a rock, which split open and gushed forth.

5 The people's second complaint was for water for washing; I addressed this by having Moses strike his rod against a boulder, which split open and gushed forth into a natural basin.

6 And the people's third complaint was for water for hydrotherapy; I addressed this by dropping a firehose from heaven and spraying the filthy ingrates at 50,000 pounds per square cubit.

7 Having addressed their water concerns, the people next moved on to grumbling about food; an issue I resolved that night, and every night for 40 years thereafter, by scattering their campground with the miraculous provision known as manna.

8 Manna was food for traveling that fell from the sky; and if thou hast ever partaken of the food they serve in the sky when traveling, thou hast a pretty good sense of what it tasted like.

9 I think the Jews' famous passion for fine dining derives directly from their cultural memory of spending four decades eating nothing but manna.

10 Over time I tried to make it a little more palatable; after 10 years I started dropping little salt and pepper packets with it; after 20 years I began raining it down deep-fried; after 30 years it began precipitating in tiny little animal shapes, which proved popular among the younger set;

11 But I did not bother putting too much effort into improving its flavor; for the truth is, no one goes to Israel for the food.

12 Yet there were endless complaints about how things were better back in Egypt when everybody had triple chocolate fudge cake à la mode; and every one of those complaints went directly to Moses; for he was the sole intermediary between me and the Chosen People, a task I realize now was unduly onerous upon him;

13 For no human being should have to spend half his time dealing with a mob of unhappy Jews.

14 (Lo, I am the LORD thy God, King of the Universe; so when I say that it's not anti-Semitic.)

CHAPTER 8

1 inally, on the first day of the third month after the Exodus, the Jews reached Mt. Sinai; and this was when I decided to make our covenant legal.

2 I had selected Sinai because it was a beautiful backdrop, and I wanted my proposal to be unforgettable;

3 So I nervously called Moses up the mountain, and instructed him to approach the Jewish people on my behalf; to fall upon one knee, bearing a golden ring, and to say unto them,

4 "The LORD wants you to know, that these last two months have been the happiest time of his life;

⁵ And that he never thought he could feel this way about a *person*, much less a People;

⁶ And that you have made him more stable, more nurturing, and more confident in his smiting;

⁷ And that he cannot imagine spending the rest of world history, without you by his feet;

⁸ And so he asks, if ye would make him the happiest God in the universe, by being his Chosen People."

⁹ And Moses went down the mountain, and gathered the Twelve Tribes together; and I gave him my two signals, which were a deafening horn fanfare from atop Sinai, and a dust storm of rose petals;

¹⁰ Whereupon he poppethed the question; and the Israelites said yes.

¹¹ It was a glorious moment, and I descended to them in a dense cloud, that we could in some way embrace each other; though I made it clear that anyone who so much as touched the mountain would be put to death;

¹² For I still needed my space.

¹³ Then I called Moses and Aaron up to the top of Sinai, to begin dictating unto them the law; starting with the Ten Commandments.

¹⁴ Ah . . . the Ten Commandments.

¹⁵ I have very little to say about the Ten Commandments.

¹⁶ To tell the truth, I no longer give much thought to them.

¹⁷ Hang them on your doorposts or not; teach them in your schools or not; post them in your courthouses or not; live by their precepts or not; yea, even the "kill" one.

¹⁸ It is all the same to me; for, as I say, I no longer give much thought to the Ten Commandments.

¹⁹ Hardly any thought at all.

²⁰ *[Pause.]*

²¹ That is not true.

²² I think of the Ten Commandments all the time.

²³ I think of them all the time, because I hate them.

²⁴ I *hate* the Ten Commandments.

²⁵ I hate the Ten Commandments, in exactly the same way Don McLean hates "American Pie."

²⁶ For hear me: when I wrote those words all those years ago, they meant something very personal to me; I put my heart and soul into them, and then sent them out into the world as any writer does, hoping they would find their audience.

²⁷ Never did I imagine that work would remain after all this time my best-known piece; the one people still cite, and debate, and interpret, and quote from start to finish.

²⁸ On one level, I am glad so many of you have taken it to heart, and extracted so much meaning from it, and embraced its simple AAAAAAAAAA structure.

²⁹ But I am tired of it defining me; tired of being regarded as a one-list wonder, locked forever in the public consciousness as "that deity who wrote the Ten Commandments."

³⁰ I did a lot of good work before it, and I have done a lot of good work since; I continue to chart my path as a creative artist, and I welcome all those interested in taking that journey with me.

³¹ But that is all I intend to say about the Ten Commandments; do not ask me to recite them again here, as an encore; I will not do so.

³² To the extent they represent the apotheosis of Mosaic law, consider this the day the Mosaic died.

CHAPTER 9

 ¹ esides, the Ten Commandments are but a small fraction of the hundreds of other laws, terms, conditions, mandates, edicts, ukases, and mandatory suggestions I bequeathed to the Jews on Sinai.

2 I know many of my readers are unfamiliar with the words of scripture, being freethinking entropists living neck-deep in snark; so I will kindly inform them that much of Exodus's second half—and the three remaining books of the Pentateuch, Leviticus, Numbers, and Deuteronomy—is little more than a catalog of the innumerable bureaucratic minutiae the Israelites were lucky enough to be micromanaged by.

3 And for *these* minutiae I maintain a great affection; I enjoy rereading them unto this day; and ask me not to choose a favorite, for each outdated relic of an obsolete mode of living is like a child to me.

4 I will not waste undue tree-pulp quoting myself here; but I will offer a few choice selections, the better to inspire thee to scurry to thy local Old Testamentery to obtain a copy.

5 Leviticus 1:14: "And if the burnt sacrifice for his offering to the LORD be of fowls, then he shall bring his offering of turtledoves, or of young pigeons."

6 *Boom!*

7 Deuteronomy 20:13–14: "When the LORD thy God hath delivered [a city] into thine hands, thou shalt smite every male thereof with the edge of the sword: but the women, and the little ones, and the cattle, and all that is in the city, even all the spoil thereof, shalt thou take unto thyself."

8 *Pow!*

9 Exodus 27:3: "And thou shalt make his pans to receive his ashes, and his shovels, and his basins, and his fleshhooks, and his firepans: all the vessels thereof thou shalt make of brass."

10 Oh no, I didstn't!

11 I am mirthing, but seriously: Canst thou even *imagine* a world wherein thy ashpots and shovels and basins and fleshhooks and firepans were made of, say, *bronze?*

12 But there is one set of regulations whose impact exceeds even that of my earth-shaking brazen-ashpot dictum; these are the kosher dietary laws, and they remain to this day my greatest regulatory achievement.

¹³ There exists no greater demonstration of the strength of my contract with the Chosen People, than the continued observance by so many of them, over 3,000 years later, of the laws of *kashrut.*

¹⁴ For the strength of a contract cannot be gauged by one party's willingness to adhere to provisions that are easy; such adherence hardly requires a contract to begin with.

¹⁵ But neither can its strength be gauged by one party's willingness to adhere to provisions that are merely *arduous*; for such adherence is often maintained out of fear of punishment, rather than any intrinsic respect for the contract itself.

¹⁶ No; the strength of a contract can only be gauged by one party's willingness to adhere to provisions that are a) arduous, but also b) devoid of repercussion if violated, and c) lacking the barest lick of common sense.

¹⁷ And such are the laws of *kashrut.*

¹⁸ What; didst thou think these laws had a sand-grain of reason behind them?

¹⁹ That shellfish are unclean, for they lack fins and scales? Yea; for the contaminants of saltwater are best filtered not with hard shells, but porous gills.

²⁰ That pigs are unclean, for they alone among the common farm animals are filthy? Yea; for cows are models of hygiene; and sheep are neat freaks; and chickens must have OCD, what with all their nonstop claw-washing.

²¹ That all insects are unclean . . . save four species of locust? Yea; because that is in there; look it up; Leviticus 11:21–22; I kid thee not.

²² Or consider the most famous dietary injunction of all: "Thou shalt not seethe a kid in its mother's milk."

²³ What kind of people would take such a specific rider—one forbidding only intergenerational culinary goat cruelty—and extend it into a ban against consuming *all* meat with *all* dairy, on the principle of "just to be safe"?

²⁴ A *Chosen* People, that's who.

²⁵ Why, put aside the nature of the laws themselves: consider but their context and they become even more laughable.

²⁶ Elaborate eating restrictions, given to people who would be consuming exactly one (1) foodstuff for the next four decades?

²⁷ Seafood etiquette instructions, given to desert tribesmen whose only prior experience with fish involved walking through them?

²⁸ Lectures about uncleanness, given to nomads who emitted a collective fungal stench so awful it actually *deafened* people?

²⁹ No; the Hebrew dietary laws were carefully conceived and calibrated by the angels and Moses and Aaron and me, for the health and maintenance of the long-term neurosis of the Jewish people;

³⁰ That they may forever display their faith through the ritual observance of rules too emphasized to be ignored, too random to be logical, and too vague to be satisfying.

CHAPTER 10

 ¹ part from these laws, I also transcribed to Moses on Sinai the chronicle contained in the first part of the Bible: the stories of Creation, and Adam and "Eve," and Cain and Abel, and Noah, and the patriarchs; even Moses's own story;

² Until I reached the point when I said unto Moses, "Until I reached the point when I said unto Moses, 'Until I reached the point when I said unto Moses, "Until I reached the point when I said unto Moses"'"; whereupon he laughed.

³ Well, chuckled.

⁴ The whole transcription took 40 days and 40 nights; exactly the same length of time it took for me to inundate the entire planet; which demonstrates either the relative difficulty of writing, or the ease of flooding.

⁵ In recent decades scholars have analyzed the Old Testament and concluded that it is an amalgam of the work of at least four different authors, working over a period of roughly a thousand years.

⁶ But thou wilt recall that in Againesis 3, I talked of other "scholars," and how they had concluded that life on earth evolved over *billions* of years; perhaps thou rememberest the explanation given therein; I will not repeat myself, but it applies here as well.

⁷ The only portions of the Pentateuch I did *not* give directly to Moses, were those relatively small sections comprising the story of the Jews' post-Sinai travels, which he and I worked on together on the road, Kerouac-style.

⁸ And this seems like an apt moment to answer one of the questions I have been asked most frequently since the Bible began its unprecedented run at the top of the best-seller lists: what advice do I have for young writers?

⁹ Verily, there is no question I take more pleasure in answering; not only because it appeals to my ego (which is fathomless), but because I take pride in being part of the great storytelling tradition.

¹⁰ For I was not the first to publish an account of the Creation; others preceded mine by hundreds of years; indeed, *Gilgamesh* predates Genesis by over a millennium.

¹¹ *Gilgamesh* is, of course, a work of fiction, whereas my account is history; but as literature its merits are considerable; especially when thou recalleth that its author had to write in cuneiform on soft clay tablets, and thus never knew if his latest plot twist would turn out literally half-baked.

¹² So, having been a slave to the Muse since long before the Greeks blasphemously personified her, I will share with thee a few of the most valuable things I have learned about the craft of writing.

¹³ *Write what thou knowest.* Obviously, this advice is more limiting for some than others.

¹⁴ *Do not wait for inspiration.* For lo, *I* am inspiration; and I am pretty busy.

¹⁵ *Grab the reader's attention early.* I learned this the hard way.

[16] ("In the beginning, God created the heaven and the earth"; that alone makes one want to read Genesis.

[17] But "These be the words which Moses spake unto all Israel on this side of Jordan in the wilderness, in the plain over against the Red Sea, between Paran, and Tophel, and Laban, and Hazeroth, and Dizahab"; that alone makes one want to wipe thy nether regions with Deuteronomy.)

[18] *Bestrew thy chapters with interminable lists of the names of ancient wells.* I figured this out early on, and I never looked back.

[19] *Publish and perish.* Either that, or do *not* publish and perish. My point is, unless thou art me, any option involving not perishing is a non-starter.

[20] And finally, *write!*

[21] Never stop writing; it is a muscle that must constantly be exercised, even by me;

[22] For after the Koran, I put down my pen, and did not attempt another work for 1,200 years; that work being *The Book of Mormon;* which having sold nearly 100 million copies is a huge commercial flop;

[23] And far worse, reads as a preposterous, laughable, and absurd series of fairy tales;

[24] Although the musical is awesome.

CHAPTER 11

[1] s the weeks of dictation wore on, and Moses failed to appear, and the Israelites remained forbidden from venturing onto Sinai; the mood amongst these festive vagrants quickly deteriorated from Woodstock-like, to Ozzfest-ish, to Altamont-esque.

[2] At last the restless crowd surrounded Aaron and said, "We came here to commune with God at this rock; but lo, thou wilt not let us touch the rock; and now, we want rock.

[3] Rock! Rock! Rock!

⁴ We want rock; we feel it in our hearts; and no stiff-necked clergyman shall forbid us from worshipping at its altar; for we are young, and angry, and rebel against thy authority.

⁵ Dost thou hear us, *old man?*"

⁶ And they made to storm the mountain; so the overwhelmed Aaron placated them by gathering together their jewelry, and fashioning it into a golden calf that they could worship as a god.

⁷ And he made this calf; and then, to appease the crowd, he sacrificed a bull to it;

⁸ And then, with grief in his heart, he led a day-long prayer service for it;

⁹ And then—out of a pit of sadness whose depths even I could not plumb—he led a two-week orgy in its honor.

¹⁰ I saw all this and grew angry, for Moses and I had just hit our stride; we were up to about half a scroll a day, easily; the words came pouring out onto the goatskin.

¹¹ My wrath waxed hot; and I looked down upon the Chosen People, in full bacchanal mode, uncloaked and oiled and squirming upon the sands like unto a desert skin-cobra; and told Moses I had had enough, and would smite the lot of them, so that he and I could start all over again with a people more worthy of us.

¹² (I was thinking the Mayans; I liked their passion.)

¹³ But it was at this moment that Moses showed how arrogant of my authority he had become; for without the slightest sign of fear, in the middle of my hotwaxing, he interrupted me:

¹⁴ "You know what, God? Fuck thee.

¹⁵ Thou heardst me: *Fuck . . . thee.*

¹⁶ What, we're 400, 450 years into this Chosen People thing, I just spent the last month writing the whole story down on your fuckin' rolly-scrolls— Abraham and Isaac and Jacob and all that fairy-tale shit—and now we're gonna toss the whole thing out into your oblivion pile just 'cause my happy little family is down there partying in the desert?

¹⁷ What, thou seest some bullshit little golden calf and feel all threatened by that?

¹⁸ 'Smite this, smite that, look at me, I'm the LORD All-Smitey, la di da'?

¹⁹ Dick move, dude.

²⁰ Verily.

²¹ Thou mayest be God, but thou actest like *The Man.*"

²² And that was when I forbade Moses from entering Israel.

²³ I am by no means averse to receiving constructive criticism; I received it from Abraham, and I would go on to receive it from many other great men in my career; David, and Muhammad, and Kanye.

²⁴ But such criticism must be offered in a spirit of respect, both for me and the organization as a whole; and when disrespect is shown—nay, flouted—an example must be set, even with someone like Moses.

²⁵ Of course, in the Bible it says I punished him for striking a rock with his rod to make it gush water, rather than merely waving it *over* the rock, as I had directed.

²⁶ Yea; the Bible saith a lot of things.

CHAPTER 12

¹ Of the 40 years' wandering in the desert, the less said the better.

² Only a handful of incidents from that period are recounted in the Bible; some military skirmishes, and a few spy missions, and the occasional admonitory epidemic; but for the most part it was a dreary time.

³ The Israelites bivouacked at dozens of lonesome encampments, every one of them devoid of any kind of nightlife or theater scene.

⁴ The migration quickly fell into a routine; at the front of the procession was the Ark of the Covenant, and the small band of priests in charge of it; and behind the band followed the ragtag bunch known as Arkheads;

5 Ex-rebels grown middle-aged and fat, passing their days listening to the same chants over and over again and living off whatever scraps fell from the sky;

6 And perpetually in need of a miracle.

7 But their children were a different generation, shrewder and savvier; as their leader I chose Moses's assistant, Joshua; he was brilliant, and hard-working, and completely full of "it."

8 Even better, he came from the tribe of Ephraim, the southernmost tribe; and so spoke with an Ephraimic accent, drawling his vowels and saying "y'all" instead of "ye all"; which gave him broader appeal than the usual breed of northeastern tribal liberals.

9 Day by day, week by week, year by year, older Israelites died off, and younger ones rose to take their place.

10 And these younger ones knew of my vow, that no Jew would enter the Promised Land until the last survivor of the Exodus had perished; and they had seen that I was not inclined to artificially foreshorten the lives of these survivors;

11 And so by the start of the fourth decade of itinerancy, it became a more and more common occurrence for the rapidly-aging pool of ex-slaves to meet with "unusual" deaths.

12 There was a sharp increase in the number of accidental spearings; children began waking up to discover their parents' bodies mysteriously filled with gallons of sand they had swallowed as they slept;

13 And during their travels, more and more of their elderly forebears perished on the wayside of exhaustion; the kind of exhaustion that manifests itself, in deep ligature marks about the head and neck.

14 Lo, even poor Aaron died under mysterious circumstances; for one day when he was leading services, the four young vice-priests holding the Ark of the Covenant above him all somehow slipped simultaneously, causing it to crash down upon him.

15 (Verily, that Ark was *way* more trouble than it was worth.

16 Word to the wise: leave it in that crate in the warehouse.)

CHAPTER 13

1 O n a beautiful spring morning — 40 years to the day after that immortal sunrise when he and I wished the Jews a merry isthmus — Moses stood atop Mt. Nebo.

2 His endless wandering was over; Israel, the country promised to his nation as its rightful homeland, lay visible in the distance; lush, fertile, and teeming beyond the glittering barbed-wire fences of the DMZ.

3 As the great man gazed upon the Promised Land, his heart swelled with a thousand emotions; and long did he reflect upon his many accomplishments: the liberation of his people, the giving of the law, and not the least impressive, his success in maintaining a real private life;

4 Something greatly appreciated by Zipporah, his wife of 43 years.

5 Finally, Moses delivered unto the Chosen People his farewell speech, the text of which forms nearly all of the book of Deuteronomy.

6 He spoke of many things: of how ibexes were unkosher; how enemies' wives and children were for enslavement, not for killing; how both plowing with an ox and a donkey tethered together, *and* transvestitism, were equally sacrilegious; how the father of a raped virgin was entitled to 50 shekels of silver; how anyone who had had a wet dream had to leave town until sunset; and how when two men fought, and the wife of one came to her husband's aid by grabbing the testicles of the other, it was mete to cut her hand off.

7 Emotional? Absolutely.

8 Verily, there was not an unmoistened visage in the House of Israel.

9 When he finally finished speaking, he sighed; and walked to the side of the mountaintop nearest Canaan, unto the very edge of the cliff; and gazed yearningly upon the Promised Land.

10 Yea, I was sorely tempted to revoke my own harsh vow, and allow him to set foot in what he had so long striven for, if ever so briefly;

11 For the God in me saw that that was the right and fair thing to do.

¹² Yet the writer in me saw what a poignant conclusion to the Five Books of Moses it would be, to have its titular hero pass away in sight of, yet forbidden from entering, the Promised Land;

¹³ And that it would dignify his character with one last air of majesty and tragedy;

¹⁴ And that it would enable me to end the Torah on this note of grandeur and tribute:

¹⁵ "And there arose not a prophet since in Israel like unto Moses, whom the Lord knew face to face;

¹⁶ In all the signs and the wonders, which the Lord sent him to do in the land of Egypt to Pharaoh, and to all his servants, and to all his land,

¹⁷ And in all that mighty hand, and in all the great terror which Moses shewed in the sight of all Israel."

¹⁸ And so, knowing it would furnish my work with a final scene worthy of a tale as epic as Exodus;

¹⁹ And knowing that a man as great as Moses deserved to have his story end with one noble, heroic final line;

²⁰ I yanked him off the cliff by the balls.

JEWED

("On the Chosen People")

CHAPTER 1

1 **T**hose 40 years wandering in the barren desert were only the beginning for us, Jews.

2 We have been through a lot together.

3 We have shared triumph and tragedy, blessings and blood libel, hilarity and Holocaust; more on that last one in a moment; I know thou hast a few questions.

4 Yea, we have shared a bumpy three millennia, you and I; but we made it through, and after all this time ye are still my Chosen People.

5 (Though I must say, that lately I have been forced to bear witness to so many $100,000 Yankees-themed bar mitzvahs—

6 Replete with multiple VJs, obnoxious hired dancers dressed like cast members of *The Jersey Whore*, and awful club music amplified so loudly it could topple the walls of both Jerichos, the ones in Israel *and* Long Island—

7 That I have been sorely tempted to say unto the Reformed remnants of the Twelve Tribes, "Enough; ye have mocked the ancient rite for the last time;

8 I now declare ye permanently unchosen, and withdraw from your presence forever;

9 But here, give this check to Ethan; he nailed the haftorah.")

10 Retelling the tale of Exodus puts me in mind of the Four Questions, whose answers illuminate what makes the Passover holiday so unique.

11 But on any night outside of Passover, the four questions I am more likely to hear from Jews are far different; and they have gone unanswered . . . until now.

CHAPTER 2

1 *hy is our faith different from all other faiths?*

2 *Why are all other faiths only sporadically scapegoated, while ours has been World Scapegoat Champion 3,000 years running?"*

3 Because people are jealous.

4 It is jealousy, pure and simple; the same schoolyard animus that be-wedgies the mathlete be-pogroms the *macher*.

5 There are simply certain people who see how I have favored your success in professions like law and finance and entertainment, and respond with hateful, hurtful remarks.

6 The good news is, most of these people are other Jews.

7 But on those occasions when they are not, it is anti-Semitism—or as its advocates prefer to call it, progentilism—nothing more or less than the cancerous outgrowth of a festering resentment.

8 Believe me; if *they* could found a secret organization that meets once a week in the basements of local synagogues to control every aspect of law and finance and entertainment, they *would*.

CHAPTER 3

1 **W**hy is our faith different from all other faiths?

2 *Why do all other cultures see New Year's as a day of new beginnings, but to us it is a 'Day of Judgment'? And then just ten days later Yom Kippur? What kind of scheduling is that?"*

3 I agree, Jews; that is unfortunate.

4 Now that I think of it, nearly all the major Jewish holidays have as their purpose, either "commemorating not being killed in the past," or "asking not to be killed in the immediate future."

5 But verily, enough with the whining; for I have peered inside thy hearts, Chosen People, and I see therein the truth:

6 None of you take this stuff seriously anymore.

7 For, Judaism is the first religion to go completely ironic.

8 Lo, there may be a few hundred thousand holdouts in Borough Park and Maalot Dafna who did not receive the memo; looking back I should have

left it in their Talmuds during Torah study, instead of their car windshields on a windy Shabbos morning.

⁹ But for the most part what holds today's Jewish community together is the collective pleasure of being in on the same joke.

¹⁰ Yea, I love it when the less observant among you claim to be "cultural Jews."

¹¹ Canst thou imagine being introduced to a "cultural Christian" or a "cultural Muslim"?

¹² Breaking news from Mt. Sinai: *Judaism is a religion.*

¹³ The millions of allusions to me in every single text and commentary and ritual of the past 3,000 years probably should have been a giveaway.

¹⁴ Yet the Jews seldom go to synagogue to visit me these days; neither do they call.

¹⁵ It is fine.

¹⁶ I am merely their Creator; he who chose them above all others; that is all.

¹⁷ I know how busy they are, what with their secret meetings about law and finance and entertainment; I shall abide.

¹⁸ So I slaved in heaven for 6,000 years; what is that to them?

CHAPTER 4

¹ ² *hy is our faith different from all other faiths?*

Why do all other religions get dozens of homelands, but we only get one tiny one, and then it never stops with the rocks and the bombs and the UN resolutions?"

³ I, the Lord thy God, King of the Universe, am a strong supporter of the State of Israel.

⁴ Not as strong as the Christian right; but strong.

⁵ And my support for Israel is not political; it is not strategic; it is not ideological; it is not even religious.

⁶ It is romantic.

⁷ At the end of the Book of Revelation — I know, I know, but stick with me — John is given a vision of "a New Jerusalem, coming down from God out of heaven, prepared as a bride adorned for her husband."

⁸ It is an apt phrase; for the bond between Israel and the Jews is very much like unto a marriage; a marriage arranged by me, God, the Supreme Yentaty.

⁹ I remember the first time I told Abraham about Israel; I said she was a plentiful, bounteous land overflowing with milk and honey; I laid it on a little thick; I wanted it to work.

¹⁰ That first date took forever to schedule; the Jews were working like slaves, and when they finally got to leave it took them four decades just to find the place.

¹¹ But there she was, exactly where I said she would be; and as soon as the ancient Jews laid eyes upon her it was love at first sight.

¹² The war . . . the slaughter . . . the total annihilation of town after town . . . ah, the crazy things a people does when it is young and in love.

¹³ For a time, Israel and the Jews were inseparable.

¹⁴ I lorded over my Chosen People like a proud father snapping photos before a prom; I was happy for them; they had settled on the right territory to make an honest nation out of them.

¹⁵ How much attention did they lavish upon her most famous asset, Jerusalem; how blissful did they feel when they entered its holiness, then withdrew, spent, from inside her temples.

¹⁶ And then they took the plunge; David made it official, and declared them kingdom and people.

¹⁷ But they were not yet ready to be the kind of husband Israel needed; they were weak, and did not have the strength to sustain the union.

¹⁸ And so stronger and wealthier men of every description declared their love for her, and pushed them aside: Babylonians, Persians, Greeks, Romans, Byzantines, Arabs, Ottomans, the British; a veritable *Who's Who* of Screw the Jew.

¹⁹ Israel gave herself willingly to them; to each she offered food and shelter, and those who possessed her considered themselves blessed above all men.

²⁰ Blame her not; she had no choice but to lie there and take it.

²¹ And where were the Jews? Away on a long business trip; abiding nightmarish meetings in unfriendly surroundings, and living out of a suitcase.

²² They sought happiness elsewhere: Spain, and Eastern Europe, and other parts of the Middle East; but somehow it never worked out; it grew tiresome, then downright Diasporating.

²³ And always, the perusal of their sacred scrapbook kept them yearning for that innocent time so long ago when the two of them were together, in an innocent world free of expulsions and inquisitions and pogroms.

²⁴ Some called them Zionists, but I called them homesick.

²⁵ The only way to win Israel back would be to show the world the depth of their need for her; and that could only be done through an act of supreme sacrifice.

²⁶ Six million sacrifices later, the need's depth was established.

²⁷ And now she belongs to the Jews once more; they have their woman back, and lo, they have treated her right.

²⁸ They have raised her up once more into a great nation, thanks in no small part to their beloved uncle Samuel.

²⁹ And the Jewish people are a much better husband now; more ardent; more jealous; more willing to do whatever it takes to keep the marriage going, up to and including splitting an atom.

³⁰ It is rare in this life that a couple gets a second chance at love; and as the one who fixed up Israel and the Jews all those millennia ago, it makes me happy to see them reunited.

³¹ And all of this has been by way of prelude to an exciting announcement:

³² In honor of thy upcoming 64th anniversary, I will be visiting Israel at the end of 2012!

³³ Yea, me and a host of very special guests will be coming down from heaven to visit the New Jerusalem, prepared as a bride adorned for her husband.

³⁴ And lo, do I have *lots* of very special festivities planned!

³⁵ Next year . . . in Jerusalem!

CHAPTER 5

¹ *hy is our faith different from all other faiths?*

² *Why do all other religions not have six million people killed in a genocide and we do?*

³ *Seriously, what the fuck was that?"*

⁴ OK, so about the Holocaust.

⁵ First of all, as I alluded to earlier and will clarify later, the 1940s—the 20th century in general—was a time when my involvement in terrestrial concerns was *extremely* limited.

⁶ That is not offered as an excuse; I am just providing broader context.

⁷ But when I returned from my sabbatical, and was told of the midcentury Teutonic unpleasantness, I was mortified.

⁸ I could not understand how those I had left in charge—all of them extremely competent, and all either Jewish or righteous *goyim*—had allowed such a cataclysmic event to befall the Chosen People.

⁹ For two hours I fumed, demanding an explanation, while Jesus and Moses and the Kids in the Halo looked down at the ground (from many miles above it) and shuffled their feet.

¹⁰ Finally, Raphael looked up.

¹¹ "Heavenly Father, thou dost not understand.

¹² He had 'it.'"

¹³ "What?"

[14] "Hitler. He had 'it.'"

[15] I looked at the other angels.

[16] "Angels, is this true?"

[17] They nodded.

[18] "How much?"

[19] "Like thou wouldst not *believe*," said Uriel.

[20] "Jesus, is this true?"

[21] "Father, when he opened his mouth, I felt as if he could walk on water."

[22] "Jesus Christ!", I screamed; it was the only time I have ever shouted his name in that fashion.

[23] "And thou wert so swept up in his 'it'-ness that thou didst nothing to prevent the extermination of over half the Jewish race?"

[24] "Forgive me, Father; there is no justification; but I know something about public speaking, and verily, that guy . . . lo, that guy . . ."

[25] He shook his head as his voice trailed off.

[26] "Moses!

[27] Thou art the founder of the Jewish people; and moreover, thou hast a bounteous supply of 'it.'

[28] I have seen thee induce a throng of nearly a million people to march single-file through a narrow desert pass simply by raising thine eyebrow.

[29] Wilt thou now look me in the eye and say the sheer force of this man's personality rendered even *thee* powerless to take action on behalf of thy own people?"

[30] I will never forget the look on Moses's face at that moment.

[31] It was so intense it felt palpable; as if his eyes were reaching out to mine, seeking some shred of sanity therein;

[32] But at the moment I had none to offer; I could only meet his gaze, and follow it as it slowly, slowly traveled downward, to land at last on his forearm . . .

[33] . . . and the faint outline of an erased swastika tattoo.

[34] Why the Holocaust?

[35] 'It' happens.

GLOSSY ONES

("On Celebrities")

CHAPTER 1

1 Celebrities are beloved of God; they are radiant in my sight; they are not merely famous people—they are my *Chosen People*.

2 (Yea, the Jews are also my Chosen People; but there's a lot of overlap.)

3 Celebrities are like unto me: adored; worshipped; tantrum-prone.

4 We live in our own universe, our every whims catered to by loyal assistants, who chideth us not lest they wish not to work in that town again;

5 And our public appearances are limited, and for promotional purposes only.

6 I tell thee truly, that those who deem the pursuit of earthly renown futile and empty are nothing but straight-up haters.

7 For three hundredscore generations of man have come and gone; three hundredscore generations of the famous and three hundredscore generations of the obscure are both now equally returned to dust;

8 But the dust of the famous still glitters with that certain special something.

9 Besides, how can I hate famous people, when my own son is the biggest celebrity of all time?

10 (Do not quibble, he *is* the biggest; I know the Beatles said they were bigger, but they were not;

11 They came close, but they skipped Woodstock; which, I admit, might have put them over the top.)

12 Yet I never intervene in the lives of the famous; in fact I take extra care to remain undetected by them.

13 The reason is obvious: the last thing a famous person needs is to think God is talking to them.

14 That is why, as has been widely reported, I almost never make my presence known in Hollywood.

¹⁵ And yet I have shared many special moments with celebrities; in Hollywood, and New York, and Milan, and all over the world.

¹⁶ I have been there with them through the good times and the bad; the laughter and the tears; the joy and the pain.

¹⁷ Yea: I have been present for every single moment of every single celebrity's life;

¹⁸ Which means that I have witnessed the single most horrible thing each of them has ever done when they thought no one was watching.

¹⁹ *[Pause.]*

²⁰ Ah, the stories I could tell.

²¹ *[Pause.]*

²² Wouldst thou like to hear some?

CHAPTER 2

¹ hen let us godsip.

² For I know all, and I tell all; I am the Ultimate Insider and the Original Gawker; as superior to *People* as I am to people; greater than *Us*, for I am Me; I am E!, only my E standeth for Eternal!

³ Of dirt wert thou made; and now dirt will I dish.

⁴ And first I shall speak of those celebrities, who have interpreted Jesus's maxim to treat their bodies as temples, as if those temples were synagogues in Berlin on Kristallnacht.

⁵ I have seen Andy Dick fall off the wagon, then grope it.

⁶ And I have seen David Hasselhoff run out of whiskey, drive to a bog, put peat moss in his mouth, and wait for it to ferment.

⁷ I have seen Larry Hagman place a delivery for 25 orders of penne à la vodka, "but hold the penne à la."

[8] I have seen Melanie Griffith guzzle Cosmopolitans like they were going out of style; which in fact they were.

[9] I have seen Tara Reid attain a blood-alcohol percentage whose mathematical significance she could never have grasped, even stone-cold sober.

[10] I have seen Matthew McConaughey so stoned he thought he saw Me;

[11] I have seen Snoop Dogg so stoned he *did* see Me;

[12] And I have seen Harrison Ford so stoned he did *Indiana Jones and the Kingdom of the Crystal Skull.*

[13] I have seen Whitney Houston accumulate so many empty vials of crack she filled each one with different amounts of water and used a coke spoon to play "Greatest Love of All" in each of the twelve major keys before shitting on the minibar.

[14] I have seen Chevy Chase steal the painkillers of colleagues who desperately needed them to kill the pain of working with Chevy Chase.

[15] I have seen Courtney Love refer to Xanax as "one of my top ten favorite palindromic drugs that I'm addicted to."

[16] I have seen Nicole Richie abuse substances for years until the substances finally found the courage to leave and take refuge in a shelter for abused substances.

[17] I have seen Britney Spears so drug-addled she tried to buy meth from her baby and burp her dealer.

[18] I have seen Lindsay Lohan and her mother Dina get so drunk, they wound up switching jail cells with each other one Friday;

[19] It was freaky.

[20] I have seen Oprah Winfrey's weight fluctuate so rapidly her midriff fluttered.

[21] I have seen Jennifer Hudson respond to the imminent closing of an Arby's by breaking into a stirring rendition of "And I Am Telling You (I'm Not Going)."

[22] (That was a long time ago, of course; these days Jennifer looketh terrific!)

²³ I have seen Kate Moss order a neutrino for lunch, and eat half.

²⁴ I have seen Ginger Spice throw up meal after meal; ironic, since ginger is a digestive aid.

²⁵ I have seen Kirstie Alley replace her hot and cold water pipes with mayonnaise and ketchup and then stick her mouth on the faucet and guzzle gallon after gallon of lukewarm Russian dressing.

²⁶ I have seen Zac Efron cut himself to see if it would make his face register emotion;

²⁷ I have seen David Duchovny masturbate to a staggering .000007 percent of all available Internet porn;

²⁸ And I have seen Carrot Top compulsively exercise so much it would have been funny, had it not been Carrot Top.

²⁹ And through it all I have seen Dr. Drew Pinsky pray for more celebrities to develop horrible addictions, that he might cure them televisually.

³⁰ Consider it done, Doctor; love the show.

CHAPTER 3

¹ Then there are those who have regarded the body and face I gave them as mere jumping-off points.

² For I have seen Nicole Kidman Botox her hair.

³ I have seen Meg Ryan suck collagen directly into her lips with a straw.

⁴ I have seen Burt Reynolds lie down on the side of the road and call a tow truck to come lift his face.

⁵ I have seen Kim Kardashian's ass get a rest-of-body reduction.

⁶ I have seen the remnants of Kenny Rogers's and Dolly Parton's original faces dissipate like islands in the stream.

⁷ I have seen Heidi Montag order "one of each."

⁸ I have seen Carmen Electra transform a simple boob job into an entire boob career.

⁹ And I have seen Michael Jackson . . . hoo boy.

¹⁰ Michael, Michael, Michael.

¹¹ I think of Psalms 27:8: "When thou saidst, Seek ye my face, my heart said unto thee, Thy face, Lᴏʀᴅ, will I seek."

¹² Did Michael read that and take it literally?

¹³ His songs celebrated my Creation; his dancing was praise in movement; he ruled the Kingdom of Pop with a bejeweled glove and a diapered monkey.

¹⁴ But uneasy lies the head that wears a crown; and for MJ, even uneasier lay the skin and cartilage at the front of that head.

¹⁵ Yet I pitied him; so at the end, as he faded away, entombed in that chalky, polymerous face-soup, I filled him with one last vision of the angelic youth who once fronted a sublime fraternal quintet;

¹⁶ And I heard his final, heartbreaking thought as he beheld that nine-year-old:

¹⁷ "I want you back!"

¹⁸ (By the way, in case thou wert wondering: Michael is in heaven.

¹⁹ No, we do not permit pedophiles here; but what is a just God to do, when the cherubs' parents keep settling out of court?)

CHAPTER 4

¹ **Y**ea, the breadth of the dubious behavior practiced in secret by the famous would fill a book;

² And that book is this one, so let us proceed.

³ I have seen Christian Bale call Nelson Mandela's three-year-old great-grandson a useless sack of shit.

4 I have seen Mel Gibson . . . actually, nothing worse than what thou hast already seen, which is bad enough.

5 I have seen Angelina Jolie place four Botswanan orphans in a steel cage and order them to "fight for my love";

6 And I have seen Brad Pitt tell those Botswanan orphans that the first rule of fighting for Angelina Jolie's love, is not to talk about fighting for Angelina Jolie's love.

7 I have seen Jennifer Aniston bounce back from breakup after breakup tougher and stronger than ever.

8 (Strictly speaking that is not godsip; I mention it only because I know how much all of you worry about Jen, and rightly so; but trust me, that gal is one tough cookie.)

9 I have seen Tommy Lee affix an American flag to his penis and order three groupies to perform an "Iwo Jima."

10 I have seen Gwyneth Paltrow leave an upper-decker in the women's room at Spago.

11 (Deny it not, Miss Perfect; it was October 2, 2005; thou hadst overheard Wolfgang Puck dissing Coldplay.)

12 I have seen Axl Rose . . . no; I wish not to revisit what I once saw Axl Rose do.

13 (That was one where I watched it occur and thought to myself, "I would not be witness to this";

14 But I had no choice, being omnipresent, so I had to stay there and watch it for 73 straight hours.)

15 I have seen Tiger Woods cheat on his wife with many, many, *many* women; I deliberately eschew an easy golf double-entendre on this one, so as not to distract from my main point, which is that I am talking about many, many, *many* women.

16 I have seen Tom Hanks slightly undertip.

17 I have seen Paris Hilton lost in thought; it takes but one.

¹⁸ I have seen Eminem two-timin', using his rhymin' for social climbin', gettin' rich chicks to chime in like he's Paul Simon.

¹⁹ And I have seen Jessica Simpson refer to Tonto as "the capital of Canada";

²⁰ Which is wrong in two ways.

CHAPTER 5

¹ **B**ut wait; for lo, there is more.

² I have seen Miley Cyrus blossom from a fresh new teen star to the troubled young woman there was never a chance she would not become.

³ I have seen the Black Eyed Peas spend two weeks in Bali studying gamelan to figure out the best way they could rot *that* style of music from the inside, too.

⁴ I have seen Elisabeth Hasselbeck pray that I, the LORD thy God, King of the Universe, might one day find the wisdom to be less liberal on social issues.

⁵ I have seen Jamie Foxx not instantly succeed at something he tried; it was the flying trapeze; he was OK at it, but he was not *great*.

⁶ I have seen P. Diddy behave in such a way as to disgrace not only himself, but the entire Diddy name, back unto ten generations of Diddys.

⁷ I have seen Mariah Carey demand that hotel staff address her in the fourth person.

⁸ I have seen Ryan Seacrest take Communion and eat the Host; not because he is Catholic, but because he is threatened by other hosts.

⁹ I have seen Tyler Perry defecate, call it *Tyler Perry's Taking a Dump*, and pitch it to Paramount; which green-lit it.

¹⁰ I have seen the form Madonna briefly takes between her transformations; it is that of a black smoke-lizard.

[11] I have seen Kate Gosselin's uterus attempt to hang itself from a nearby Fallopian tube.

[12] And lastly, I have seen Sarah Palin . . .

[13] Oh, I just fucking hate Sarah Palin.

SEMITICUS

CHAPTER 1

he rest of the Old Testament after the Pentateuch is an eclectic goulash of two dozen or so books; the exact tally varying depending on whether thou countest the longer ones as one work or two, and whether thou includest certain semi-sacred books on the "Bible bubble";

2 Books like Judith, and Tobit, and Ruth (more on her later), and my own least favorite, Lamentations, which is every bit as mopey as it sounds; yea, a more blubbery collection of tedious whining thou shalt not find anywhere this side of Lifetime Television.

3 As for the canonical books, they can be divided into three types: the historical, the poetic, and the prophetic.

4 The historical books cover the 1,000 years of Jewish history after the death of Moses, ending in the 5th century B.C.; just as Plato, and Sophocles, and the rest of the Hellenic handbaskets began besmirching Eurasia with the full frontal assault on family and traditional values they ironically called "Greek culture."

5 I remained deeply involved in the affairs of my Chosen People for everything that transpired from Joshua through Nehemiah, so I can vouch for the books' unimpeachable historical accuracy; even the brief resurrection of the prophet Samuel from the dead at Saul's behest by the Witch of Endor.

6 Yea: 1 Samuel, 28:3–25; book, chapter, and verse; check, check, check; it's citable, so it's true.

7 Now, the total length of these historical works considerably exceeds that of the Five Books of Moses, and their content hath as many fast-paced thrills and chills as early Crichton; but my editor has advised against explicating upon them at length.

8 For she saith that for the most part those protagonists hold little interest for the general reader; and that no matter how lively my recollections may be, nothing I could have said to, done with, thrown at, or inflicted upon Othniel son of Kenaz brother of Caleb, could possibly be worth the ink.

⁹ Still, there are at least a handful of figures and events in these pages that continue to resonate with thee; "resonate" being my (verily, Uriel's!) clever segue into the first such event: Joshua toppling the walls of Jericho with little more than moxie and a horn section.

¹⁰ Jericho is not only the oldest permanently inhabited city on earth, but the lowest; it sits 700 cubits below sea level, so low that any wayfarer within a three-day-camel-ride radius wishing to find it need only drop a ball onto the ground and follow it until it stops rolling.

¹¹ It was the first major city encountered by the Israelites in Canaan, and ripe for conquest; but it was surrounded by a stout wall as thick through as two men.

¹² I knew such a wall would resist string instruments; I knew such a wall would be impervious to woodwinds; I knew that for such a wall, even the beating of a dozen percussionists along its very base would do little to weaken its structural integrity.

¹³ No, this called for a radically new approach; and so one morning, the watchmen of Jericho beheld the spectacle of seven priests walking around the city, bellowing loudly on their ram's horns; and behind them the ark, borne by other, less musically-talented priests; and behind them the 20,000-man Israelite Army, marching in dreadful silence.

¹⁴ From the watchmen's vantage point, it must have looked like unto "Seventy-six Trombones" as directed by Luis Buñuel.

¹⁵ Once a day for six days did this hour-long circumnavigatory ram-jam session take place; then, on the seventh day, it was repeated seven consecutive times;

¹⁶ And by the thirteenth march, that priestly horn septet had evolved into quite a tight little ensemble, I must say.

¹⁷ Lo, they actually made those shofars sound halfway decent, which is nearly impossible; for I once beheld Miles Davis attempt to play one at his record company president's grandson's bris, and he gave up after 45 minutes, having produced no sound but the squeal of a screech-owl passing a kidney stone.

¹⁸ Still, they were but amateur musicians; the important thing was not that they played well, but that they played with gusto; and even more importantly, that they played *loud*;

¹⁹ Loud enough to conceal the sound of the sledgehammers wielded by the 60 Israelite spies who'd been hiding in Jericho's catacombs all week.

²⁰ By the end of the final march the wall was ready to fall; but to let the army feel like they had played a part, Joshua bade them let out a war cry; and this appeared to be the cause of the collapse, at least to anyone who had not spent the last week pouring hundreds of gallons of smuggled lye into subterranean boreholes.

²¹ Let it be: what matters is not the method, but the outcome; and by sunset the Israelites, working together, had conquered the town, destroyed every living thing in it (including the children), and burned it to the ground.

²² Yea, it is amazing what can be accomplished when no one cares who takes the credit.

²³ When the last ox had been gored, Joshua looked at me and said, "Capturing Jericho proved little challenge, O LORD."

²⁴ "I am glad thou feelest that way," I responded, "for it will be all *uphill* from here!"

²⁵ He tittered; I thought it deserved better.

CHAPTER 2

¹ f Joshua there is little else to say, other than that he continued besieging, burning, and massacring his way through Canaan, obliterating its inhabitants and all record of their existence from the face of the earth, until he died peacefully at 110, surrounded by his grandkids.

² But in these historical books there are three other figures, a brief mention of whom I have been advised would not be unhelpful in the moving of precious units.

³ The first of the three is the *last* of the judges chronicled in the book of that name; leaders who served not only as dispute-arbiters, but as a kind of intertribal prime minister in the days before the monarchy.

⁴ There were 14 such judges, of whom the wisest, bravest, and most respected was the fourth, Deborah; the greatest female leader in the entire Old Testament; though also, technically, the worst; for she was the only.

⁵ (Verily, I have never divined what it was about the ancient Jews' rigidly patriarchal polygamous society that made it so hard for its female chattel to succeed therein;

⁶ Especially since women were regarded as clean, uncursed, and fit to appear in public nearly three-quarters of the time.

⁷ In any case, it is a shame that Deborah turned out to be the last female judge for the next three millennia; for she was great.

⁸ Yea, everybody liked Debbie.

⁹ Easy on the eyes, too!)

¹⁰ Then came Gideon, the one with the trumpet; then Abimelech; then Tola, Jair, Jephthah, Ibzan, Elon, and Abdon.

¹¹ They kept a low profile.

¹² But then came the final judge, Samson; the mighty Samson; the legendary Samson; the earthshaking Samson;

¹³ Who tore apart a lion with his bare hands; who killed 30 party guests for cheating on a riddle; who single-handedly pulled the gates of Gaza out of the ground; who tied 150 pairs of foxes together by the tail, fastened torches to them, and set them loose in his enemies' wheat fields; who slew 1,000 Philistines with a donkey's jawbone . . .

¹⁴ Truly, one reads Judges 1–12, and it is alliances this, and trade missions that, and altar-buildings and sacrifices, yahweh yahweh yahweh;

¹⁵ And then one arrives at Judges 13, and thinks, "Whoa, when did my Bible turn into a comic book?"

¹⁶ Samson was the most accomplished Judge, more so even than Deborah; for though he lacked her wisdom and compassion, he rendered his

decisions with a chest-beating, club-wielding, Schwarzeneggerian finality that tended to dissuade the losers from filing an appeal.

[17] I did not converse often with Samson, for my intervention was seldom needed during his forceful reign; nor was he one for small talk, his outside interests being limited to stonelifting and squinting in incomprehension.

[18] Samson was more than just a hero, he was a superhero; and like all superheroes, his birth was divinely prophesied, and his strength was beyond that of mortal men, and he fought for justice, and had a hidden weakness whose exposure would lead to his downfall: Nazirite.

[19] Yea, he was a Nazirite: an ascetic consecrated unto my service from before birth, and thus sworn by oath to abstain from alcohol, avoid dead bodies, and leave his hair and beard unshorn; which he did . . . until *she* walked in.

[20] Of course I mean Delilah; an unscrupulous, conniving harlot; a mistress of seduction who verily was not even all that comely, though she had a reputation for being most adept at "anointing the tent pole."

[21] The treacherous harridan plotted against Samson from their first night together, when she asked him, "If thou lovest me, tell me by what means canst thou be subdued."

[22] And he said, "Tie me with seven new bowstrings and I will become as weak as any man."

[23] Then he fell asleep; and she bound him with seven new bowstrings; whereupon he woke, and snapped them like straw, and mocked her.

[24] And the next night she asked, "Tease me not: this time tell me truly by what means canst thou be subdued."

[25] And he said, "Tie me with new ropes and I will become as weak as any man."

[26] Then he fell asleep; and she bound him with new ropes; whereupon he woke, and snapped them like flax, and mocked her.

[27] This went on for 827 consecutive nights.

28 If that is not the definition of a dysfunctional relationship, I know not what is.

29 But finally Delilah wore him down, nagging him into revealing his Naziritic oath, and thereby the source of his strength; and quickly ensued the famous denouement:

30 She cut his hair while he slept, and the Philistines captured him, and blinded him, and brought him into their temple; whose pillars he leaned upon until the entire edifice collapsed, killing him and all within;

31 Leaving the final lesson of the saga of Samson—rabbi, champion, patriot, last of the judges of Israel—all too clear:

32 Never feel too embarrassed to ask for another stylist.

CHAPTER 3

 1 ot long thereafter emerged David, and after him his son Solomon, the two most accomplished men of ancient times; kings, warriors, musicians, poets, psalmodists, lovers; their peers called them Renaissance men, which back then made them *extremely* ahead of their time.

2 David first rose to prominence as a harpist: he was a child prodigy whose father Jesse made him practice eight hours a day until his fingers bled; Jesse himself having once been a promising young harpist, until his career ended in a freak scything mishap.

3 In this way David came to the attention of the moody King Saul, who took solace in the lad's honeyed glissandi after a hard day's smite.

4 David also gained the friendship of Saul's son Jonathan, who, if not in love with David, certainly kissed him a lot.

5 One day David went to visit his brothers, who were soldiers in Saul's army, in the Valley of Elah, and this is where his famous battle with the Philistine Goliath took place.

6 And here I must rush to the defense of this unfairly maligned man; for though not a Chosen Person, and destined to lose, Goliath's giant stature concealed an even bigger heart.

⁷ Goliath was a faithful husband; Goliath was a devoted father; Goliath was a trusted friend; Goliath was a community activist; Goliath worked with troubled youth in inner-city Gaza; Goliath was cofounder of the Philistine Society for the Prevention of Cruelty to Animals.

⁸ Goliath was as universally beloved a figure as the Middle East has ever produced; and when the young, brash, arrogant David agreed to accept his challenge to fight him, *everybody* was rooting for Goliath — even the Jews, though they would never have admitted it.

⁹ The outcome was preordained, of course; David had to win, and the Philistines had to be defeated; but never have I felt more sadness about ending a life, as I did when I guided that rocket-grenade from David's specially-designed slingshot to Goliath's forehead.

¹⁰ Rest in peace, Goliath; thou art missed.

¹¹ Saul soon grew jealous of the newly famous David, and tried to have him killed; but he failed, largely due to the intervention of Jonathan, who, if not in love with David, certainly sodomized him a lot.

¹² Eventually both Saul and Jonathan were killed by the Philistines, and David was anointed king, a post he filled for 40 years — there is that number again, 40; I must ask a master Kabbalist why it keeps cropping up throughout my career; Madonna, I await thy call.

¹³ David led his army on a series of military triumphs; he conquered the Philistines, and made the Moabites pay tribute, and even took bronze vessels from the servants of Hadadezer of Zobah; and back then, *nobody* took bronze vessels from the servants of Hadadezer of Zobah.

¹⁴ He also had eight wives, the most famous of them being Bathsheba; he coveted her but she was married, so he sent her husband Uriah to war and told his commander to abandon him on the battlefield, "that he may be smitten, and die"; well played, Dave.

¹⁵ But it was a grievous sin nonetheless; and as is written I punished David by killing their infant son; tragic, to be sure, but then again *I* am not the one who chose to be born to David in this illegitimate fashion.

¹⁶ David and I had our disagreements over the years, but I loved him, and he loved me; for he wrote many of the psalms in my honor in the book of

that name; they are all wondrous, one great psalm after another; I listen to them whenever I am down and in need of a picketh-me-up.

¹⁷ I have no favorite, but humanity seems especially fond of Psalm 40 (that number again!); for from it derives the lyrics to U2's popular concert-closer "40."

¹⁸ (I am of two minds about Bono; he has written great music, and does noble charitable work; but he is a bit smug; and then there is *Spider-Man: Turn Off the Dark.*

¹⁹ Even ignoring the public brouhaha and the safety issues, the score itself is mediocre at best: musically forgettable, lyrically craftless, and betraying a failure to even recognize, much less solve, the practical problems of writing stageable songs within a musical-theater context.

²⁰ I have six words for thee, Bono: *Joseph and the Amazing Technicolor Dreamcoat.*)

CHAPTER 4

¹ **D**avid was succeeded by his and Bathsheba's better-fated second son, Solomon; who has justly gone down through the ages as a model of wisdom.

² For I came to him one night in a dream, offering to bestow a gift; and he asked not for wealth or honor, but for wisdom, and a discerning heart whereby to govern his people; and I was so pleased by his request, that I not only granted it him, but also the wealth and honor he had not asked for.

³ (I have wondered over the years, if perhaps he asked for wisdom *knowing* it would predispose me to also grant him wealth and honor; which would have meant he was *already* very wise; which would have made his request for more wisdom unnecessary; and therefore unwise; but therefore necessary once more . . .

⁴ Lo, this is why having an infinite mind is a pain in the ass.)

⁵ Solomon's wisdom is exemplified in the story of the two women who each claimed to be the mother of a baby; he wielded his sword and lifted

it as if to cut the infant in two; whereupon the real mother gave up her claim to spare the child's life.

⁶ This was wise of Solomon; but it was even wiser of him to parlay that verdict into a celebratory "chamber party" that night with the world's most grateful MILF.

⁷ That was another thing about Solomon; to call him a lover of women would be woefully inadequate, for as it states in 1 Kings 11:1–3, he had 700 wives and 300 concubines.

⁸ That is why he seldom left his palace; preferring to spend the day strolling in his bedclothes around his palace's custom-built garden, complete with a grotto wherein his women would frolic.

⁹ He lived this way until his death at age 94, long after it had become very, very disturbing.

¹⁰ Like his father before him, Solomon was also a great writer; indeed, David only wrote half of one of the Old Testament's poetic books, Psalms, whereas Solomon wrote three:

¹¹ Proverbs, which is full of pithy little zingers like, "A shekel saved is a shekel earned," and "Rome will not be built in a day";

¹² Ecclesiastes, a harsh condemnation of vanity and falsehood that was *The Catcher in the Rye* of the 8th century B.C. Near East;

¹³ And the Song of Solomon, a love poem that is as blue as the Bible gets; which believe it or not is actually pretty blue.

¹⁴ "The joints of thy thighs are like jewels"; "thy belly is like an heap of wheat set about with lilies"; "thy two breasts are like two young roes that are twins"; and that is just the material that made it into print.

¹⁵ For Solomon's original version was far more explicit, and his analogies far more graphic:

¹⁶ "Thy hindquarters are curved like half-moons"; "Thy honeypot smells like blooming hibiscus"; "The way thou workest my balls . . . man, I love the way thou workest my balls."

¹⁷ After he recited the unexpurgated version to me I said, "Solomon, thou well knowest we cannot publish that as written; it is pornography, and even the Bible has a minimum standard of decency."

¹⁸ "But, LORD," he protested, "it is not pornography; it is *erotica.* Canst thou not grasp the difference?"

¹⁹ "No, Solomon, and it doth not—"

²⁰ "Pornography aimeth only at arousing the senses; but erotica employeth sexuality as a window into the soul."

²¹ "Solomon, whatever it is, it—"

²² "My work challenges the bourgeois sexual mores that have for too long treated our bodies as the 'other' rather than—"

²³ "Solomon, listen: I am the LORD thy God, King of the Universe; and if thou dost not knock that thing down to PG-13 by next Shabbos, consider thyself without a distributor."

CHAPTER 5

 ¹ he 16 prophetic books of the Old Testament relate the lives and visions of Israel's great men of prophecy, and are divided into two sections: the four major prophets, Isaiah, Jeremiah, Ezekiel, and Daniel; and the twelve minor ones, nearly all of whom were never swallowed by whales.

² (The worst part of that experience for Jonah was not the three days in the beast's belly, but being spat up back upon the shore, haggard and covered in whale vomit . . . right in front of his sunbathing ex-girlfriend.

³ Awkward!)

⁴ Officially, Abraham is considered a prophet; so is Moses, and so, later, would be Muhammad; but they were also warriors, and diplomats, and leaders; men who did not simply talketh the talk, but walketh the walk.

⁵ But these 16 prophets were cut from a lesser tunic; for they were endowed only with the gift of foresight.

⁶ Now, it can be debated whether it is on balance a good or bad thing to be a prophet; but there can be no debate that it is an absolute bad thing to have to spend time with one.

⁷ For prophets are the most unpleasant people in all my Creation; the dourest, the voidest of mirth, and the uncouthest in social graces; self-righteous and self-absorbed, yet utterly un-self-aware in matters of grooming.

⁸ (Isaiah, especially; by the end, his beard was so matted with food it won Buffet of the Year honors from *Head Lice Monthly*.)

⁹ And their odiousness is in direct proportion to the strength of their prophecy; the keener their tongues, the keener the longing to chop them off; the deeper their vision, the deeper the desire to stick forks in their eyes.

¹⁰ It would be different if the content of their revelations were pleasant; but as thou hast no doubt noticed, a prophet's vision of the future is seldom of the puppies-floating-down-from-the-sky-on-pillows variety.

¹¹ No, it is almost always grim; and further, it is almost always explained as the mete punishment for the people's vice; and it has ever been the case that as an oratorical theme, "Ye are iniquitous, sinners!" is not much of a crowd-pleaser.

¹² And so it was with my prophets: they feared their people were wandering off the path; and they shared with them gruesome images of the destruction of Jerusalem, and the collapse of the Temple; but the people reacted with mockery, and heeded them not, and drove headlong to their fate.

¹³ They remind me of thy driver's-ed teachers: for they, too, fear their classes might wander off the path; thus they share filmstrips filled with gruesome images of the destruction of a minivan, and the collapse of lungs; but the classes react with mockery, and heed them not, and drive headlong into telephone poles.

¹⁴ Prophets still walk the earth: retail analysts, and sports handicappers, and science-fiction writers, and that secret panel that gets together every summer to determine what colors will be popular two years from now;

¹⁵ They are minor prophets: for they can see into the future, a little bit, on matters of slight import, sometimes.

¹⁶ But major prophets, too, still walk among ye; preaching their wisdom, berating your wickedness, expounding their dark visions, and bearing names like Jeremiah Q. Ecologist, and Ezekiel R. Paleoclimatologist, and Al Gore.

¹⁷ Their visions are absolutely correct; absolutely terrifying; and absolutely call for urgent action.

¹⁸ But will ye take it? Absolutely not.

¹⁹ What prophets value above all else, above patience, friendship, even deodorant, is the truth; and so they believe that all men are like them in this valuation;

²⁰ That the masses will eventually embrace the words of another great prophet, my son: "the truth shall make you free."

²¹ But what they never seem to understand—and what the masses always do—is that my son in that quote was referring only to *convenient* truths.

²² Inconvenient truths shall *not* set you free; to the contrary, by their very nature they tend to impose far more burdens and obligations upon thee, and thus, if anything, set you back.

²³ On the other hand, convenient truths—like "our current way of life is permanently sustainable"—are much more liberating for the soul.

²⁴ *That* is the inconvenient truth, Al; and here is another one:

²⁵ Thou shouldst have campaigned another two hours in Florida.

CHAPTER 6

¹ Looking back over the millennia, if there is one question I have failed to answer more than any other, it is, "Why do bad things happen to good people?"

² Often the question is phrased differently, like, "Why do bad things happen to *me*?" or "Why can't bad things happen to *him*?" or "Are you kidding? My car got stolen while I was ladling chowder at the soup kitchen?!?"; but I understand.

³ Thou clamorest for earthly justice, a palpable correspondence between moral cause and effect; but only seldom is such justice realized.

⁴ This dilemma is at the heart of the Book of Job, which attempts to prove once and for all that I either work in mysterious ways, or do *not* work in very obvious ones.

⁵ The book is set, according to the very first words of its very first verse, "in the land of Uz."

⁶ (Whenever I read that, I cannot help but sing a little ditty to myself:

⁷ " 'Ah ah ah! Ow ow ow! I wish that I never was!' That's what I made Job scream in pain in the terrible land of Uz.")

⁸ Job was "perfect and upright, and one that feared God, and eschewed evil"; and as a result he had grown prosperous, with a wife, ten children, a big house, "7,000 sheep and goats, 3,000 camels, 1,000 oxen, and 500 female donkeys."

⁹ Yea; he had the biggest soul—and, in the best sense, the shittiest soil—in the Near East.

¹⁰ A point of clarification: the initial discussion concerning Job was between my angel Michael and me; he was my adversary in an argument, and the Hebrew word for "the adversary" is "Satan."

¹¹ This has caused much confusion over the millennia, so Michael has expressly asked me to tell thee that he is *not* the devil; and also, yet again, that words *do* hurt.

¹² But it is true that one day, he and I were debating whether the righteousness of a man like Job sprang from inherent goodness, as I claimed, or enlightened self-interest, as he did.

¹³ Was his loyalty tied only to the bounty he had always enjoyed, and had come to see as an entitlement? Or was he so devoted that he would remain steadfast even in the face of unimaginable suffering?

¹⁴ In other words: was he a Yankees fan or a Cubs fan?

¹⁵ Michael asked for permission to afflict him and put him to the test, which I granted: so he slew Job's animals, destroyed his house, killed all ten of his children, and covered him with boils.

¹⁶ Through all this Job did not turn against me; though it is fair to say he was in a bad mood.

¹⁷ Then his three friends came to visit, ostensibly to provide comfort; yet they repeatedly told him he must surely be guilty of some sin to have merited his punishment.

¹⁸ It is their conversation that occupies most of the Book of Job, and at times seems to transform its central question to, "Why do bad *friends* happen to good people?"

¹⁹ Zophar the Naamathite, especially; what an asshole.

CHAPTER 7

¹ **A**nd *still* Job did not turn against me; but now he began to demand of me an explanation; and this is when a fourth friend, Elihu, entered with a different argument:

² That in seeking to apply his own ethical standard to God, Job was displaying arrogance; for as a mere mortal he could not usurp my moral authority, only humbly renounce any claim to it.

³ That was the right answer; at least, to the extent that it was an answer; which it was not.

⁴ Elihu's words were majestic and lyrical, but teleologically amount to little more than six chapters' worth of "Because Dad said so."

⁵ Then finally I appeared "out of the whirlwind" to ask Job a dazzlingly bullying series of rhetorical questions: "Where wast thou when I laid the foundations of the earth?"; "Canst thou send lightnings?"; "Who provideth for the raven his food?"; "Who put the *bomp* in the *bomp-sh-bomp-sh-bomp*?"; and many others;

⁶ Along with some very frightening monologues about the sea monster "Leviathan" and the land monster "Behemoth"; the terrified Job had no idea what I was speaking of, and neither did I; for I made that part up as I went.

⁷ The point of it all was to follow up Elihu's "Because Dad said so" with "Dad's back, and I've been out all eternity busting my ass, and the last

thing I need when I get home is to hear you complaining about your ten dead kids. Now go kill me an ox!"

8 Which was a) not an answer, and b) worked.

9 In the end, Job is restored to prosperity, and has ten more children; that is truly what happened, though I can tell thee he spent the rest of his life terrified I was only setting him up for some awful sequel: *2 Job: The Resuffering.*

10 Yet it is not Job's tacked-on happy ending, or even its sumptuous poetry, but the central problem it seeks to address—Why do bad things happen to good people?—that has made it resound through the ages with so many;

11 Including me.

12 For from where *I* sit, there is an even more resonant way to rephrase the question:

13 "What is *wrong* with me?"

14 It had first come up with Abraham on Mt. Moriah; it arose again (unlike the Egyptians) at the Red Sea; and over the centuries it had continued to linger like unto a cloud on my conscience.

15 Yea, the question never truly went away; for I am the LORD thy God, King of the Universe; where would it go?

16 And so I never told Job, or the anonymous poet whose hand I guided across the parchment to tell his story, the *real* reason I allowed him to be so horribly afflicted.

17 It was not to test Job, but to test *me.*

18 I wanted to see if I could watch him endure his agonies without experiencing any of that same unnameable thrill I had derived from watching the binding of Isaac, and the drowning of the Egyptians, and the countless other mass atrocities and tragedies that I had over the centuries allowed—or, sometimes, *caused*—to happen.

19 Thou mayest say, that I wanted to see if my heart was in the right place.

20 Did I pass the test?

21 For now, I choose to leave that as *my* unanswered question.

22 Instead I will answer thine: "Why do bad things happen to good people?"

23 I am sorry, humanity, that I have not gotten around to answering it sooner; it would have saved you much needless disquiet; for the explanation is not only logical, but I daresay extremely satisfying.

24 Why do bad things happen to good people?

25 To balance out the good things that happen to *bad* people.

26 Lo; it's only fair.

SELL-A-THONIANS

("On America")

CHAPTER 1

1 he subject of who does and does not receive my blessing puts me in mind of a certain nation whose money claims to trust me.

2 And yet every time I hear "God Bless America," I get angry.

3 It is not that I dislike the tune; to the contrary, it is far more pleasant than America's national anthem—that shambling melody to which is set the fetishistic tale of the nocturnal survival of a magical pole-cloth.

4 No, my objections to the song and the saying are not artistic, but personal; for Americans asking me for more blessings is like Tahitians asking me for sunnier days.

5 America is amply blessed; copiously blessed; blessed a thousandfold; countless are the blessings with which I have blessed America in its compulsive blessability.

6 Consider but a few of the blessings I, the LORD thy God, King of the Universe—a region of space that, I might note, extends beyond the central portion of North America—have already bestowed upon the U.S. of freakin' A.

7 I blessed it in its land: the richness and variety of its topography, the fertility of its soil, the temperateness of its climate, the spaciousness of its skies, the purpleness of its mountains, and what I think any observer would concede is the unusually high level of its plains-fruitedness.

8 I blessed it in its indigenous peoples, whose innate love of freedom was evident in their own freedom from heavy artillery, tolerance to alcohol, the concept of property, or resistance to smallpox.

9 I blessed America with the two groups of European settlers who first colonized it: the Puritans, an odd-hatted, fun-loathing people who imbued the new nation's character with a healthy sense of wrong and wronger;

10 And to the south, the tobacco farmers of Jamestown, who showed the world that the new "land of opportunity" could bestow success on *anybody* willing to rely on hard work, the free market, and millions of black slaves growing a death-crop.

¹¹ I blessed it with its Founding Fathers; who, though they dressed funny, had wisdom, and leadership, and courage, and foresight, and eloquence, and the ability to compromise;

¹² And who are like the current Tea Party, in that they dress funny.

¹³ I blessed it with Abraham Lincoln, one of the greatest leaders in history; he and I were very close; during the Civil War he cried to me many times; usually about Mary, for she was nothing but trouble.

¹⁴ I blessed it with millions of immigrants from every nation on earth; mankind in its heaving diversity arrived on its shores, and every ethnicity fought to find its place, and in so doing each one strengthened the character of the nation.

¹⁵ Yea, even the Mexicans.

¹⁶ I blessed America with abundant labor; and abundant capital; and abundant means of keeping the two at a healthy distance.

¹⁷ I blessed it with the Greatest Generation, whose boundless heroism in World War II helped redeem the nation for the band of spineless cowards it sent to fight World War I.

¹⁸ I blessed it with a perfect Cold War bad guy: comically evil, and patently wrongheaded; alternately frightening and incompetent; I blessed it with an era where everyone thought of the United States as the good guy; yea, I go *way* back with America.

¹⁹ I blessed it with Martin Luther King Jr., whose love and forbearance toward those who despised him was so great, Jesus once asked if he was his brother from another mother.

²⁰ And most recently I blessed—literally, for his name means "blessed"—America with Barack Hussein Obama; my Messenger; the Deliverer; the Messiah.

²¹ (Or at least that is the position he held from January 2008 through February 2009.)

CHAPTER 2

1 ea; I am as American as baseball, apple pie, and acting like it's the only country I give a crap about.

2 I was on board the *Mayflower* with the Puritans for all 66 days of their voyage; over two months trapped on a boat with Puritans; talk about an ordeal.

3 I was there for the first Thanksgiving; I ensured the turkey was properly herb-crusted and brined; it was a hit; even the Wampanoags were impressed, for they just roasted theirs plain.

4 I was there for the Boston Massacre in 1770, when redcoats killed five civilians; back then that qualified as a Massacre; times change.

5 I was there when Thomas Jefferson drafted the Declaration of Independence.

6 He asked how I felt about the line "all men are created equal . . . they are endowed by their Creator with certain inalienable Rights."

7 I said, "Tommy, it's not a lie if *thou* believest it."

8 And I was there in Philadelphia that fateful summer of 1787 for the Constitutional Convention.

9 I remember the long conversations I had with James Madison; one in particular I recall: it was an early July morning, and James had decided to engage in an exertion with a brisk morning stroll along the Delaware.

10 I tagged along in his cerebral cortex.

11 "God," he said, "we are starting this experiment called America anew, and as a deeply devout Christian I want my nation to follow on the path of salvation through Jesus Christ.

12 How best can I frame our new Constitution so as to achieve this goal?"

13 "Jim," I said, "the best way to achieve that goal is to state that Congress shall make no law respecting an establishment of religion, or prohibiting the free exercise thereof; and that no religious test shall ever be required as a qualification to any office or public trust under the United States."

¹⁴ "God," he said, "that is counterintuitive."

¹⁵ "Jim," I said, "if we out-and-out write 'Congress shall pass only laws in keeping with the precepts of the Judeo-Christian tradition,' there would be no way to weed out the heretics in our midst; moreover other countries would get all jealous, and the Supreme Court would have nothing to interpret.

¹⁶ Which reminds me: from now on I'd like you to keep thy deeply held Christian beliefs to thyself; in fact, I'd appreciate it if thou couldst make numerous statements on the record that seem to prove beyond historical argument that thou art a Deist.

¹⁷ I'm telling Jefferson and Franklin the same thing."

¹⁸ "But God," he said, "I love thee and thy son Jesus Christ so much, and I want all the world to know!"

¹⁹ "Jim," I said, "trust me.

²⁰ The document thou art creating will not only live forever, but one day be recognized as the explicit endorsement of a Christian theocracy that thou and I secretly know it to be."

²¹ This made him feel better; and as by then we had reached the steps of the Museum of Art, he joyfully ran up the stairs, lifted his arms in triumph, and shadow-boxed a group of street waifs.

CHAPTER 3

¹ ² **A**merica, allow me to address thee directly for a moment.

When thou sentest a man to the moon and back, it was the most amazing achievement in human history, and Neil Armstrong correctly hailed it as "one giant leap for mankind," meaning the entire human race.

³ And then he went and put an *American flag* on it.

⁴ On the *moon.*

⁵ That is so *thee*!

⁶ Thou drivest me crazy, America, yet still I bless thee; despite all thy shortcomings I can quit you not; and I continue to not only bless thee but to love thee, and to do so unhealthily; unhelpfully; in a manner that keeps thee from doing the soul-searching needed to become a better nation.

⁷ Verily, America: I cut thee 50 arkloads of moral slack a week.

⁸ Why?

⁹ I shall tell thee.

¹⁰ As thou hast seen, I am a divine being who needs recognition.

¹¹ I like it when those whom I grace with my bounty acknowledge it; and do so in a formal, ritualized way that gives it the stamp of authority.

¹² And when I removed myself some years ago from earthly affairs, there was one outstanding issue on this front, as it pertained to America, that deeply troubled me.

¹³ I never forgot about it; so upon my return, when the staff began to brief me on all that had taken place in my absence, and the subject turned to thy nation, I quickly interrupted them.

¹⁴ "Boys," I said, "spare me this talk of atomic bombs and civil rights and pollution and Vietnam and Iraq; for when it comes to America there is only one question that matters, only one issue that will determine my attitude toward that frustrating, lovable himbo of a superpower:

¹⁵ Have they, at long last, inserted 'under God' in the Pledge of Allegiance?"

¹⁶ And the angels nodded, and smiled; and I nodded, and smiled; and all of us nodded, and smiled;

¹⁷ For in this bellwether of all signs regarding thy fitness to lead the world, thou hadst done right.

¹⁸ Yea; call me sentimental, but I am a sucker for nations that give me a shout-out in their voluntary oaths to magical pole-cloths.

FACTS

("On Unsolved Mysteries")

CHAPTER 1

1 **M**ystery is the lot of man.

2 Mystery enfoldeth thy coming into the world; mystery enshroudeth thy departure from it;

3 And in between, mystery is the preferred literary genre of millions of you, particularly those seeking a light beach read.

4 Now, thou mayest believe that to God nothing is a mystery; that for me all is foreseen, and even the most mundane occurrence known beforetime.

5 And verily, as I said before, the simultaneous containment of all information in the universe *is* well within my powers.

6 I am the Supreme Database; my processing speed is ∞ GHz; the range of my knowledge mocks thy most powerful search engines;

7 Although once in a while I break down and Google myself; last time I checked I had over 600 million results; not too shabby.

8 But I have learned over time, that *true* omniscience is knowing enough to know what things are better off not knowing.

9 For example: clearly do I recall the long summer of 1980, when millions were nigh unto madness desirous of discovering, "Who shot J. R.?"

10 Now, I am the LORD thy God, King of the Universe.

11 I could *easily* have found out who shot J. R.

12 I could have attended the producers' meetings; I could have read the script; I could have sat in on one of the table reads; thou gettest the idea.

13 But I did none of these; I stayed deliberately uninformed of the culprit's identity until the night of the airing, when it turned out to be Kristin, J. R.'s mistress/sister-in-law.

14 A decent resolution, I thought, but a bit of a letdown.

15 (On the other hand, the ending of *The Sixth Sense* blew me away.

16 I had no idea it was coming; which is amazing, for remember, I actually *do* see dead people.)

¹⁷ Yet despite my efforts at self-nondisclosure, I am in the end the repository of all knowledge hidden and arcane; the possessor of the answers to all the great mysteries that have haunted the generations of men.

¹⁸ In me the unfathomable is made fathomable, and the anonymous nonymous; all whodunits become he-dunits, and all what's-his-names become right!-*that's*-his-names.

¹⁹ My publisher has asked if I would be willing to divulge some of these secrets to my readers, and I am happy to oblige; but I would not have the solutions to these timeless riddles fall into the hands of those too impious to fork over the cover price.

²⁰ So, bookbuyer, I ask that thou sharest none of the information I am about to reveal with anyone who hath not purchased this book;

²¹ Especially those craven, fiendish souls who borrowed it from a library.

CHAPTER 2

SPOILER ALERT! ******** SPOILER ALERT! *************

¹ I will start with a big one: the identity of the most notorious serial killer of all time, Jack the Ripper.

² It was Neville Hopkins.

³ He was an itinerant pickpocket squatting in Whitechapel; a quiet man; kept to himself; bit of a loner; few close friends.

⁴ Flew completely under the radar.

⁵ Right after the final murder he boarded a boat bound for New York and was never heard from again.

⁶ Anyway, Neville Hopkins: Jack the Ripper.

⁷ Now thou knowest.

⁸ Sticking with unsolved murders, the Zodiac Killer was famous astrologer Jeane Dixon.

[9] Yea: embarrassed after an epic public misreading of the moon in Scorpio, she worked through her anger with a horrific murder spree through Northern California.

[10] She got away with it, too; for on her next birthday she cast her own horoscope and found that it read, "You born today are passionate, strong-willed, and capable of getting away with a horrific murder spree through Northern California . . . *if you stop the killing right now.*"

[11] Los Angeles's infamous Black Dahlia murder of 1947 was committed by folk singer Woody Guthrie.

[12] In fact, he confessed to the crime in the sixth verse of his most famous song:

[13] "As I was strolling South Norton Avenue, I met a woman, the Black Dahlia. I killed her slowly and bashed her face in. This land was made for you and me."

[14] But he was never caught; for *no one* ever makes it to the sixth verse of "This Land Is Your Land."

[15] As for Lizzie Borden, she, with an axe, neither gave her mother 40 whacks, nor, having seen what she had done, gave her father 41.

[16] No; that August morning, the Bordens fell victim to a serial killer who broke into their house at random, chopped them both to bits, and fled the scene, never to be heard from again.

[17] His name?

[18] Neville Hopkins.

CHAPTER 3

[1] The Shroud of Turin was a forgery produced in 1287 by the Turin Shroudmakers' Guild to promote the local shroud-making industry; it succeeded spectacularly.

[2] Grand Duchess Anastasia died at the hands of the thugs who killed the rest of her family; the woman who later claimed to be her

was in reality her chief assassin; the whole thing was a *Single White Female* situation that got way out of hand.

3 The works of William Shakespeare were written by none other than legendary British playwright William Shakespeare.

4 The Lindbergh baby was indeed kidnapped and killed by the man executed for the crime, German immigrant Bruno Hauptmann, in 1932.

5 (Fortunately, Lindbergh was big enough not to let one bad apple cloud his overall view of either German leadership, or the many exciting things it was doing in the 1930s.)

6 Jimmy Hoffa is buried in Grant's Tomb.

7 D. B. Cooper parachuted safely into the forests of southwestern Washington, where he was eaten by Bigfoot.

8 Lee Harvey Oswald acted alone.

9 Actually, he did it twice: once in 1960, for his one-man Mark Twain show, *The Sage from Hannibal*; and again in October 1963, in an experimental production of Samuel Beckett's *Krapp's Last Tape*.

10 It was during the run of this latter show that he met gangster Sam Giancana, who paid him $50,000 in Cuban money to kill JFK.

11 Turning now to cryptozoology: the yeti does not exist; he is but a bogeyman Sherpas scare their children with whenever they whine about the lack of oxygen.

12 The Loch Ness Monster *does* exist; but he is not a monster of flesh and blood, rather the monster of bigotry and intolerance dwelling inside the human heart, which for some reason is then externalized as an imaginary Scottish plesiosaur.

13 On the other hand, El Chupacabra *is* real; he is a monstrous goatlike creature who poses an actual threat to Mexicans, and an even bigger one to Americans;

14 For soon he plans to cross the border, where he will take away jobs from hardworking *American* mythical creatures like the Jersey Devil and Mothman.

¹⁵ On to a few legendary places: Atlantis was a real city on the Aegean island of Santorini that was destroyed by a massive volcano 3,600 years ago.

¹⁶ It is lost forever; but I must tell thee that even were it not, it would not be worth finding.

¹⁷ For Atlantis was a Bronze Age backwater whose imbecilic citizenry passed its time burping, farting, and raping sheep.

¹⁸ Their demise was a boon for civilization, but it is with cities as it is with people: dying young and mysteriously can turn any idiot into a legend.

¹⁹ (Yea, it was the only half-intelligent thing Jim Morrison ever did in his life.)

²⁰ On the other hand, the Lost City of Gold, El Dorado, never existed, and it is just as well; for even I shudder to think of the "missionary work" men like Cortez or Pizarro would have practiced on its people once they caught sight of it.

²¹ My guess is it would have started with flaying, then gone downhill from there.

²² Area 51 is a regular US military base; and though classified operations do occur there, they have nothing to do with aliens, UFOs, time travel, or anything out of the ordinary.

²³ Those ops all happen in Area 63.

²⁴ And finally, Stonehenge.

²⁵ I have no idea what the hell Stonehenge is.

CHAPTER 4

¹ ut I *can* shed light on a few questions I am guessing none of you thought ever would—or could—be answered.

² For example: which came first, the chicken or the egg?

³ Neither. The rooster came first.

⁴ Where does the time go?

⁵ Nowhere; it is thou who art moving through it.

⁶ What is the sound of one hand clapping?

⁷ Very disappointing, for a performer.

⁸ What is to be done?

⁹ It depends.

¹⁰ When will they ever learn?

¹¹ Eventually.

¹² Are we there yet?

¹³ No.

¹⁴ Is the glass half empty or half full?

¹⁵ Neither. It is *filthy*.

¹⁶ Why do fools falls in love?

¹⁷ Because *everyone* falls in love, and "fools" are a subgroup of "everyone."

¹⁸ If a tree falls in the forest and no one is there to hear it, does it make a sound?

¹⁹ Thy premise is false; there *is* Someone there to hear it.

²⁰ Why are all the good men either married or gay?

²¹ Thy premise is also false; there are many good men, but thou scarest them off with thy stink of desperation.

²² Finally, will wonders never cease?

²³ No; they'll cease.

CHAPTER 5

¹ Many other mysteries am I keen to divulge; but my shrewd publisher has asked that I withhold some, in the event of a sequel.

[2] I will mention in passing that the likelihood of such a sequel is contingent upon two factors: first, whether the current volume meets with reasonable success in the marketplace; and second, whether the world still exists in two years.

[3] And frankly I must tell thee, humanity, that these two factors are not unrelated.

[4] For while my eschatological plans—which I will be discussing at the end of this book—are preordained, unalterable, and irrevocable through the pith and marrow of time;

[5] Having said that, if this book were to sell a sufficient number of copies to warrant a follow-up, there is nothing in my apocalyptic schedule that could not be pushed back a year or two.

[6] It is thy call, humanity.

[7] What is the meaning of life?

[8] Find out, in *The Last Testament 2: The Final Conclusion.*

[9] On sale everywhere 2014 . . . if there *is* a 2014.

GAMES

("On Sports")

CHAPTER 1

Every so often I like to call in to sports radio shows.

I tell the screener I am "Mike from Massapequa" or "Sam from Santa Clara," and he talks to me a minute to make sure I am worthy enough, not only to discuss the foibles of the area's athletic teams, but to freight that conversation with enough entertainment value to warrant its being broadcast to 35,000 other people in the greater, say, St. Louis area.

3 Then I am put on hold; then I hear, "You're on the air!"; and then I launch into a passionate monologue—in the pitch-perfect accent of the local ethnic lower-middle-class—about the value of switch-hitting outfielders, and dogfighting; the eternal beauty of the pick-and-roll, and steroids; the day the Red Sox won the World Series, and the day O. J. Simpson murdered two people;

4 All things sports.

5 For a few pleasant minutes the hosts and I talk and complain and commiserate and argue with each other; then I am thanked for calling, and the hosts move on, never realizing that the unseen voice with which they just talked pucks was not in fact Mike from Massapequa, but God from the Great Beyond.

6 But I do not mind, for I do not call in to be recognized; I call because I love talking sports.

7 Sport is mythic; sport is epic; sport is a condensation of all human activity; it is often said sport is a metaphor for life; it would be more accurate to say life is a metaphor for sport.

8 U.S. Chief Justice Earl Warren once wrote, "I always turn to the sports section first. The sports section records people's accomplishments; the front page nothing but man's failures."

9 A few moments' reflection reveals how utterly wrong these words are; yet they are in keeping with the kind of mindless distraction that sports provide.

10 They are also the greatest substitute for armed conflict ever devised; they are like unto Diet War, a zero-casualty alternative to Regular War, with all the great fighting and suffering and action thou demandest in a conflict, but almost none of the adverse health effects.

11 Especially do I love the Olympics: the pageantry of all the nations of the world joining together in peaceful competition as a million armed security personnel hover just off-camera; mythmaking at its finest.

12 The opening ceremony in Beijing in 2008 was one of the most extraordinary events I have ever seen, transcendent and thrilling; it made me again recall the greatness thy species is capable of, at least when one-fifth of it bites on the same repressive yoke.

13 (The gauntlet has been thrown, London; thou wilt need to do something spectacular in 2012 to top the Chinese.

14 May I suggest Duchess Kate giving birth in the middle of Olympic Stadium just as the torch is lit?

15 If thou likest the idea, I can help with the timing.)

16 But it is not just the Olympics; I love all sports; athletic competition of every type and size and description enthralls and delights me; except tennis, which is dullsville.

17 In sports I see the finest specimens of my finest creation operating at the highest level of their physical abilities.

18 And as a sports fan, I understand how much the games mean to both other fans and the athletes: the passions they stir, the tempests they roil, the loyalties they build, and above all the rivalry, violence, and rioting they so justifiably evoke.

19 And so that is why I have never, ever, *ever* influenced the outcome of a sporting event to determine the winner.

20 I have only, on *extremely* rare occasions, influenced the outcome of a sporting event to affect the spread.

CHAPTER 2

1 **M**any times have I heard athletes pray for victory before the contest; and many times have I heard them thank me for victory afterward.

2 Many times have I heard partisans beseech me to aid their side; and many times have I heard them beseech me to afflict the other side.

3 And many times have I heard reasonable-minded commentators denounce those athletes and fans for believing I would care about something as frivolous as the Raiders-Broncos game.

4 Lo, as a matter of fact, I *do* care about something as frivolous as the Raiders-Broncos game, Bob Friggin' Costas.

5 For dozens of human beings are putting their hearts and souls and passion and sweat into that game.

6 And while it is true that, simultaneous to that game unfolding, hundreds of millions of other human beings are putting just as much heart and soul and passion and sweat into far more vital human activities, like manufacturing, or child-rearing, or staying alive;

7 Unlike the Raiders-Broncos game, those activities are all very boring to watch.

8 Understand me: it is not that I do not care about those *people*; it is that I do not care about what they are *doing*.

9 I will more thoroughly address the general phenomenon of prayer later in this memoir, but I must mention here how much Junior and I appreciate hearing our names invoked on the field, gridiron, court, rink, course, peloton, or (very rarely) sumo mat.

10 When a fan begs me to keep the puck away from the goalie's five-hole, I am touched by his commitment.

11 When a power forward genuflects before shooting a free throw, Jesus gets goose bumps.

155

¹² When a slugger points his finger to heaven while rounding the bases, I point right back at him.

¹³ And when a wide receiver opens his postgame interview by crediting God for his winning touchdown catch, it moves me so much I am tempted to "touch down" myself, just to tell him, "Thou da man!"

¹⁴ (It is curious—when musicians thank me at the Grammys I find them arrogant; presuming themselves blessed with "God-given talent," when nine times out of ten they are blessed with nothing but studio-given autotuners.

¹⁵ Yet when an athlete thanks Jesus or me it somehow feels sincere; especially if he is one of sport's many born-again athletes, as deep into Jesus as, but a few months earlier, he was deep into three groupies in the weight room of the Sheraton.)

¹⁶ I note all these things, athletes and fans, and I file them away for future reference; but while I have favorites, I do not *play* favorites.

¹⁷ To repeat: I do *not* intervene in sporting events; not because they are beneath me (for what isn't?), but rather because—and if I sound old-fashioned here, then shoot me, Bill Simmons—*I care so deeply about the integrity of the game.*

¹⁸ Athletes come and go, but the sports themselves remain; and I will never let my feelings toward the former corrupt my oversight of the latter.

¹⁹ I am the LORD thy Ref; I cannot be worked.

CHAPTER 3

¹ Yet—with the clear understanding that it makes no earthly difference—I do not mind revealing the identities of the athletic teams that have found favor in my eyes.

² For I am Jehovah; I am Allah; I am the Heavenly Father; and my two favorite pro football teams are the New York Giants and the Oakland Raiders.

³ I became a Giants fan during the glory days of Phil Simms, who field-marshaled the offense with a steady efficiency that obscured his tremendous talents as a pure passer.

⁴ Verily, 22 for 25 in the Super Bowl? Enshrineth him, Canton!

⁵ As for the Raiders, I have always liked their attitude, for they play football the way the ancient Israelites attacked Canaanites: seeking not only to beat the opposition, but to destroy them, to raze their city to rubble, and to slaughter their wives and children; or at the very least to spike the ball on their mascot.

⁶ (Alas, it has been some time since the Raiders fought like the ancient Israelites; these days they fight like the modern French.)

⁷ My favorite college football team is Auburn; when they win the Iron Bowl my joyous *whoops* fill the halls of heaven; for I hate Nick Saban; his name is one letter away from "Satan" for a reason.

⁸ My two favorite baseball teams are the Minnesota Twins and whoever is playing the Cubs.

⁹ I have no favorite pro basketball team, but my least favorite is the Washington Wizards; because in changing their name from the Bullets, they went from promoting violence to promoting paganism, which is much, much worse.

¹⁰ In "hoops" (for so I designate the college game), my favorite squad is Duke; I know this preference will be pooh-poohed by many, but I happen to like the way Coach K runs that team.

¹¹ They do things the right way at Duke: with tobacco money.

¹² When it comes to hockey . . . *Goooooooooooo Blue Jackets*!

¹³ I love the Columbus Blue Jackets, because they are so clearly a human phenomenon: inasmuch as I would never in a billion years have thought to put a hockey team in Columbus, Ohio, and call it the Blue Jackets.

¹⁴ It is entirely thy doing, and I love that; alas, they were terrible last year (again!), and I cannot think of a good reason why next year will not be the same;

¹⁵ For even if they do put up the money to acquire a halfway-decent second-line left-wing like Cormier or Dustin Brown, they are so weak defensively that a coach as over his head as Arniel cannot be expected to—

¹⁶ Sorry; I shall save that rant for Mike and/or the Mad Dog.

¹⁷ My favorite golfer is Rocco Mediate, because his name soundeth like a euphemism a mob boss would use to tell his enforcer to kill someone he was arguing with: "Hey, Rocco: 'Mediate.'"

¹⁸ My favorite boxer is Evander Holyfield, because he is still valiantly pursuing his comeback despite being 107 years old.

¹⁹ My favorite MMA fighter is Quinton Jackson, who is a born-again Christian . . . *and* played B. A. Baracus in the remake of *The A-Team*.

²⁰ Either of those would make him my favorite, but both? Let's just say Quinton hath captured my mixed-martial "heart."

²¹ As for the beautiful game, I have no favorite soccer team, but am rather an admirer of the sport itself; I love the beauty and fluidity of a well-played match, and share in the cathartic release of a well-struck ball.

²² That being said, the sport would not suffer if the average final score rose to, say, 4 to 3, instead of the current average, .04 to .03.

²³ FIFA, I beg thee: make the goal wider; make the goalie shorter; do something; thou art killing me up here.

²⁴ In international cricket I pull for whichever country was more exploited by Britain.

²⁵ My favorite track and field athlete is Usain Bolt; one of these days I'm going to come down midsprint and pull him over for speeding.

²⁶ My favorite ski jumper is Gregor Schlierenzauer, and anyone who tells me Janne Happonen has better technique can go fuck himself.

²⁷ My favorite rugby team is the All Blacks of New Zealand; the Maori war dance they do before each match is the best pregame ritual in sports, better even than David Beckham masturbating into a buttered scone.

²⁸ And my favorite cyclist is whoever is not taking steroids; so right now I have no favorite.

CHAPTER 4

¹ ²O ne last note:

As is usually the case with sports loyalties, mine have been passed down generationally, meaning my children root for the same teams I do.

³ The one exception is that Jesus roots for the Cubs.

⁴ In fact, when I say Jesus bleeds for the Cubs, I mean Jesus bleeds for the Cubs.

⁵ Poor child.

⁶ His faith is so deep, and his hope is so pure, that on occasion I have heard him say, "The day the Cubs win the World Series is the day I return to earth!"

⁷ But in the end I dissuade him from this; for humanity cannot wait a billion years for the Second Coming.

THE

GOSPEL

ACCORDING

TO DAD

CHAPTER 1

1 I have a son named Jesus. Perhaps thou hast heard of him.

2 Perhaps thou hast read the quartet of eyewitness accounts of his life, written by Matthew ("The Cute One"), Mark ("The Funny One"), Luke ("The Quiet One") and John ("The Non-Synoptic One").

3 Perhaps thou hast seen his image in one of the paintings or sculptures forming the small subgenre of western art known as Everything Before 1750.

4 Perhaps thou spendest one morning a week in a special building dedicated to him, hearing tales of his glory while secretly fretting over the Raiders' porous secondary.

5 (I do, sometimes.)

6 Perhaps thou hast seen *The Greatest Story Ever Told*; a good film, though given the title a bit disappointing.

7 Or perhaps thou hast seen *The Passion of the Christ* by Mel Gibson, whom my son, as a Jew, will never work with again.

8 Perhaps thou hast even viewed his face appearing miraculously on French toast, or pancakes, or waffles.

9 (He appeareth only on breakfast foods; for lo, it is thy most important meal.)

10 And particularly likely art thou to know something of the manner by which Jesus entered the world, and the manner by which he left it.

11 For the tale of his Nativity is heralded in song continuously for a month in thy home electronics stores;

12 And his birth in a manger is re-created on lawns up and down thy street each December to celebrate him, and to send a message to the Hirschfelds next door;

13 And thy very calendar is commensurate with his age; though he was actually born in 5 B.C., so it would be more accurate to say thy very calendar

is commensurate with the age it would be polite to tell him "he doth not look a day older than."

14 As for his death, the story of his miraculous resurrection, and subsequent discovery of dozens of chocolate eggs, is celebrated annually;

15 And the cross on which he spent his last agonizing hours trails only the swoosh as the most recognizable symbol in the world.

16 Yea: I venture to guess thou hast heard the story of Jesus told in dozens of ways; by apostles, and carolers, and priests, and filmmakers, and even former Chicago frontman Peter Cetera, on his 2004 Yuletide classic, *You Just Gotta Love Christmas.*

17 But thou hast *never* heard the story of Jesus as told from the perspective of He Who Sent Him.

18 Because for me, the story of Jesus is not that of a prince and redeemer saving the world, but a father and son saving their relationship.

CHAPTER 2

1 Thou wilt need some backstory.

2 At a certain point in the Old Testament—sometime between 2 Kings and 1 Chronicles—I began noticing within me the stirrings of a vague dissatisfaction.

3 Professionally, things had never been better; my Chosen People were thriving (relatively); I was smiting like never before; and I was taking in the sizzling goodness of dozens of oxen a week.

4 Yet my all-consuming focus on Creation had come at the expense of my transpersonal life.

5 For millennia I had found it sufficient to be my own companion, and to spend what little downtime I had contemplating my own glory; but now I longed for someone special to contemplate my own glory with;

6 A soul mate who would love me, not because I did what I did, but because I am what I am.

⁷ Well, I must have been watching out for me, as they say; for no sooner did I recognize the urgency of my need, than I met Ruth.

⁸ Thou mayest know Ruth from the book named after her, where she is held up as a model for kindness and loyalty.

⁹ For it tells of how, when her Jewish husband died, she stayed with his mother Naomi, adopting her faith and her God as her own.

¹⁰ She was the very first convert to Judaism; she chose me without being Chosen, and that made me feel special.

¹¹ (True, she was a Moabite; but she was one of the good ones.)

¹² The first time I worked up the courage to reveal myself to her in a vision, I sensed a connection between us like unto nothing I had ever felt before.

¹³ Hast thou ever met someone and felt as if thou hadst known—and been the heavenly father of—that person forever?

¹⁴ That is how I felt.

¹⁵ For once, *I* was the one who had been smitten.

¹⁶ Yet upon beholding me, Ruth paid me no more heed than necessary; she minded my words and obeyed my commands, but would gaze not upon the blinding light radiating from my Presence; as if to say, "Thou mayest be all-powerful, but thou art not all *that*."

¹⁷ My courtship of Ruth was slow and deliberate; it took time to gain her confidence:

¹⁸ To show her that omniscience was not the same thing as being a know-it-all;

¹⁹ That omnipresence was not the same thing as stalking;

²⁰ And that I had reached a point in my existence, where I was ready to live in a monogamotheistic relationship.

²¹ But in time (and space), I am pleased to say I captured Ruth's heart; and she consented to make me the luckiest God in the Universe by being my wife.

²² We were married on September 12, 545 B.C.; Abraham performed the service; Moses was my best man; the music was provided by the Jericho Septet.

²³ We were going to have a registry, but Ruth said they always cause tension; for the catalog is itemized, and the items' costs are visible, and so the guests worry themselves over how much they should spend, and how much everyone else is spending, and it all becomes more of a source of anxiety than a celebration;

²⁴ So we just said, "Please, no gifts"; which was verily the right decision; for truly, what dost thou get the couple that has everything?

²⁵ Now, let me make one thing very clear: I am the LORD thy God, King of the Universe, and thou shalt *not* be hearing any intimate details of my relationship with Ruth; this is my testament, not hers, and I am fiercely protective of her privacy.

²⁶ But I have given thee all this information so as to prepare the way for the good news; the glorious news that over two billion of thee already know in thy hearts:

²⁷ Jesus Christ is my son.

²⁸ He is the second of my three kids: Zach, Jesus, and Kathy.

CHAPTER 3

¹ he grand adventure known as parenting is, I need hardly tell the moms and dads reading this, every bit as nerve-wracking, hair-raising, terrifying, and rewarding as administering a Macrocosm.

² But when Ruth and I began planning a family, she was adamant on one point: that our children be raised never to consider themselves special, just because their father was God.

³ She wanted them to have as normal a childhood as nonhumanly possible, and I agreed; she wanted them to go to public school, so I created one; she wanted them to have normal playmates, so I fashioned some from

dust; she wanted them to frolic on playgrounds, so I hired a contractor to build one; a nice one, with monkey bars and everything.

⁴ Zach was our oldest; extremely intelligent, but feisty and puckish; always getting into playful scrapes with the angels.

⁵ He liked to sneak up behind them and shout "*Boo!*"; he did this so often that Gabriel gave him the nickname, "the Holy Ghost"; H. G., for short; it stuck.

⁶ Kathy, our youngest, was as adorable a little girl as thou canst imagine, with a cherubic smile; literally so, for it had been removed from a cherub and grafted on.

⁷ I confess to being overindulgent when it came to her; she owned my heart; I would get her anything she asked for; yea, even if it meant striking down a human child's pony.

⁸ But Jesus . . . Jesus was a classic middle child.

⁹ Perhaps I overlooked him; perhaps I made him fight too hard for my attention; perhaps in doting too much upon H. G. and Kathy I made him feel like the God-Man out.

¹⁰ From his infancy he was exceptionally sensitive, and could never bear to see anyone suffering.

¹¹ This proved no great difficulty in heaven, where there is no suffering; except privately, amongst the righteous sadomasochists, and even for them it is not really suffering.

¹² But whenever he would look down and behold humanity in its manifold distress and agony and weakness and sin, he would weep.

¹³ There is a verse in the New Testament, John 11:35, "Jesus wept"; it is the shortest verse in the Bible, so short it feels out of place.

¹⁴ I confess that many years later it was I who inspired John to insert it, as what thou mightest call an "inside joke" between Ruth and me.

¹⁵ For many were the evenings when I would return to her, and ask how her day was—I was careful never to burden her with my professional problems; whatever unfinished business I had, I left it on my throne—

16 And she would speak of her activities, and of the children; how Zach did this, and Kathy said that;

17 And then I would ask, "What about Jesus?" and she would sigh and say, "Jesus?

18 Jesus wept."

19 In time I came to say it along with her; and we would laugh; or at least we did, until we heard the sound of sobbing, and we would turn to see that Jesus had heard us saying this; and that lo,

20 Jesus wept.

21 The kid was a pussy.

CHAPTER 4

1 nd Kathy grew into a warm and loving semigoddess, like unto her mother: she had a great sense of mirth, and this at a time when human women were discouraged from being mirthful, often by being sealed alive in pits.

2 But both my sons proved troublesome to me.

3 H. G. was wild and reckless; he was too smart for his own good, much less the world's; he would brook no responsibility, but instead gallivant around my Creation enjoying the natural wonders I had created, taking advantage of his family position by borrowing the moon, or disappearing for 30 years at a stretch without even bothering to let me know that I already knew where he was.

4 And Jesus was even more vexing, for he was weak; a dreamer; an "artist"; he showed no interest in judging, or smiting, or vengeance, or any other aspect of the family business, but preferred to spend his days brooding, sighing, and wandering around blessing the angels for no reason.

5 Meanwhile yet another epidemic of idolatry and wickedness had beset Israel.

⁶ The Jews had become Hellenized, then Romanized; the Temple was overrun with moneylenders; Pharisees were emphasizing gnostic Mosaicism and halakhic teaching at the expense of a more traditional reading of the Pentateuch . . .

⁷ It was bad.

⁸ With no Abraham or Moses or David to ease my wrath, I had finally and irrevocably run out of patience with the Jews; and so one day as I sat on my throne, I summoned to my side Gabuthelon and Azazel.

⁹ I have not mentioned these two angels' names before, but they were my "wetwork" specialists; it was they who had overseen the total destruction of Sodom and Gomorrah; so I knew them to be dedicated professionals.

¹⁰ I now gave them orders to rain fire and brimstone upon the house of every Jew in Judea, leaving none alive; in this way finally ridding myself forever of their intractable faithlessness and chutzpah, that I might start again with another tribe more worthy of me;

¹¹ I was still thinking the Mayans; I still liked their passion.

¹² But just as I was giving them their final smiting orders, Jesus approached; bearing on his face, for the first of what was to be many, many times, the Look.

¹³ And I think thou knowest what I mean, by "the Look."

¹⁴ For with that Look he gazed upon Gabuthelon with a tenderness that caressed and enveloped his soul like a swaddling band around an infant;

¹⁵ And with that Look he gazed upon Azazel so gently his heart glowed with a clear white light radiant with the unity of all things;

¹⁶ And with that Look he gazed upon me with a love deeper than any wellspring, and purer than any water that could ever floweth therefrom;

¹⁷ And he said, "Father, I have an idea that's so crazy, it just might work."

CHAPTER 5

¹ ea, it was crazy all right.

² "Virgin birth"; "raising the dead"; "self-resurrection to redeem the world"; today those phrases make perfect sense, but at the time they sounded absurd.

³ First of all, there were the practical considerations: Jesus was proposing to become the Word made flesh, a transmutation of extraordinary difficulty.

⁴ The conversion of pure spiritual essence into living organic matter had never before been attempted, or even considered; for though religious, I have always been a strong believer in the separation of Word and flesh.

⁵ Of course, I am omnipotent; I can do anything; but some tasks require more effort than others, and changing Word to flesh would be a logistical nightmare, that much was given.

⁶ But my strongest reservations concerned the *wisdom* of Jesus's plan; for to me it seemed not only insane, but spoke to some perverse desire for self-degradation.

⁷ "My son, a person?" I screamed at him.

⁸ "A being of the same eternal substance as I, demeaning himself in the shameful guise of a two-legged skinbag?

⁹ Hast thou any knowledge of what it is truly like to be flesh? To be a physical human being?

¹⁰ Human beings thirst, and hunger; sicken, and injure; tire, and age.

¹¹ Human beings sweat until a stink of great piquancy wafts from the pits of their arms like rotten frankincense.

¹² Human beings get bits of food caught in their teeth; and others see the bits, and laugh inwardly, but inform them not, so that others may see the bits and laugh inwardly.

¹³ Human beings accumulate mucus and earwax and plaque and eyegunk as if their faceholes housed the permanent collection of the Ick Museum.

¹⁴ Human beings urinate and defecate several times a day, which, I mean, right there, Jesus, come on.

¹⁵ And all this is to say nothing of the changes that would be wrought in thy body near the time of thy bar mitzvah;

¹⁶ When thy voice would break; and thou wouldst notice hair where there was none before; and thou wouldst begin to . . . to feel certain . . . urges . . . um . . .

¹⁷ Thou seest, Jesus, sometimes when a bird loveth a bee very much . . .

¹⁸ I wish not to have this talk with thee right now, my son.

¹⁹ Now, I have indeed listened to thee, Jesus; I have heard thy words; I know thou desirest to redeem the world; and that is a lovely thought.

²⁰ I do not doubt thy good intentions, son; but the road to hell is paved with good intentions.

²¹ (Well, actually it is mostly paved with human skulls; but the good intentions serve as a thickening agent.)

²² This plan of thine is not the answer, Jesus; in fact, this plan is the exact opposite of what thou needest; for what thou needest, Jesus, is to toughen up.

²³ Dost thou hear me, boy?

²⁴ Thou needest to drop this sensitive brooding pose of thine, and work, and smite, and steel thyself, and be a man!

²⁵ No; do *not* be a man; sorry; that is in no way what I want thee to be.

²⁶ Anyway, that is where I stand, Jesus; I forbid thee from acting on this plan, as the LORD thy Dad; and we shall not discuss this any further.

²⁷ And stop giving me that Look!"

CHAPTER 6

¹ ll that day I was most troubled.

² I had no appetite for my oxen; several fornicators went unpunished; at dusk I even almost sent the sun back *up* by mistake, which would have been uncomfortable to say the least.

³ Yea, it was a very awkward day at the office, and by quitting time the angels' mood had dropped precipitously from blissful to joyous.

⁴ That night Ruth told me that Jesus had spoken to her of our conversation; and that before, during, and afterward—surprise, surprise!—

⁵ Jesus wept.

⁶ She approached me later, after I lit up the stars.

⁷ "Jehovie, honey.

⁸ I know you and Jesus haven't always gotten along.

⁹ I know that in a lot of ways, you're two very different Godheads.

¹⁰ But he is your son, and right now he is trying to find himself, and make his own way in the world; and you owe it to him to support him on that journey.

¹¹ Don't forget, I was once a human being, too, so I know what it's like; and it actually has its moments.

¹² Now, I know the idea of God's son descending to earth, assuming the form of a human being, performing miracles, then being crucified and rising from the dead to redeem all mankind, might sound a little strange.

¹³ But you know what? It might just be the best thing that's ever happened to our little Jeez.

¹⁴ Would you think about it, dear?

¹⁵ For *me*?"

¹⁶ And I *did* think about it; I contemplated it all night, as deeply as I used to contemplate my own glory back in the day, before there were days.

¹⁷ And by the time I cued the sun to rise, I had softened somewhat;

¹⁸ At least insofar as accepting that Jesus *was* my son; and that as his father it was my duty to support him in whatever career path he chose to follow; even one as patently silly, as dying for thy sins.

¹⁹ So for his sake, and Ruth's, I swallowed my fury; and told him that whatever help he needed, I would provide; and whatever trials and tribulations he would face on his mission, I would help see him through;

²⁰ So that when it was all over, if Jesus's time on earth ended (as I was sure it would) in some kind of nightmarish ordeal,

²¹ At least he could not accuse me of forsaking him, or leaving him hanging.

CHAPTER 7

¹ he planning for Operation Enduring Salvation required years of intricate coordination among not only my archangels, but dozens of my top seraphim, cherubim, and support staffim.

² I deployed many of them across the Holy Land to gather polling data about the mood of the people, and the results were mostly encouraging.

³ For example, 77 percent of Judeans said they were at least "open to the idea" of a Messiah, including a whopping 93 percent of the urban leprous.

⁴ The effort and dedication put forth by my team during this period was extraordinary; their skill and tirelessness were wondrous to behold.

⁵ I must particularly single out Raphael's assistant, Jerahmeel, whose grace under pressure made even the great Shamsiel look like a regular Zebuleon; and I do not say that lightly.

⁶ Our first task was finding the right set of foster parents.

⁷ We all agreed we needed a Judean couple of unblemished reputation; and that the woman needed the sufficient obstetrical vigor to withstand the pressure of bearing a world-redemptive fetus in utero for nine months.

8 But there was much contention regarding what place in society these people should occupy.

9 Some argued that the son of God should enter the world as a highborn prince, as befitting his true nature;

10 While others argued that if he was going to descend, he should descend to the very bottom; and be born the son of a sewer-cleaner, or prostitute, or slave, or musician.

11 I remember Uriel mirthing, that the question before us was like unto one thou might hear at an earthly limbo competition: "How lowly can ye go? How lowly can ye go?"

12 (Though I would add somewhat less mirthfully, that my version of limbo is *much* less festive than thine.)

13 Finally, a familiar voice rang out.

14 "Let us split the difference," H. G. said, "and find for my brother a qualified couple from a moderate socioeconomic background;

15 Decent, hard-working people with strong family values that embody the Judean Dream.

16 And let them dwell in a virtuous, blue-tunic community; Nazareth comes to mind, maybe, or—

17 No; I was going to say East Nazareth, but it's gotten too gentrified."

18 We all saw the wisdom of H. G.'s words of hard-headed soft-heartedness; and I was glad to find him getting into the spirit of things by finally channeling his vast intelligence into something irrational.

19 We sent ten of our top operatives to Nazareth; they soon returned with intel that the best candidates by far were a betrothed couple named Mary and Joseph.

20 Mary's dossier showed her to be kind, intelligent, and confident; the type of woman who could raise God's son with such grace and equanimity that other women would see her pass by and wonder, "How *does* she do it?"

21 And Joseph's dossier revealed him to be quiet and sturdy; someone endowed with the mental fortitude to cope with what was sure to be a somewhat awkward family dynamic, especially once Jesus hit his teens; but we were satisfied he had the groundedness to handle the how-do-you-tell-the-son-of-God-he's-grounded-ness.

22 And, of course, Mary was a virgin, and this was the crucial factor; for by introducing Jesus through a miraculous act of asexual reproduction, we would be showing the world from the start that he was both Word *and* flesh; Man *and* God; a subtle concept we knew would be difficult of comprehension;

23 Indeed, I myself have never really figured it out.

24 There was only one other woman remotely in contention, a maiden who lived a few streets away; virtuous and virginal, but prone to rapid swings of temperament; engaged to a blacksmith who was good-hearted, but given to drink; their relationship was querulous;

25 And worst of all, her name was Tabitha.

26 Verily: I do not know if I could ever grant eternal life in the Kingdom of Heaven to *anyone* who believed in the "Virgin Tabitha."

27 Mary seemed the clear winner, but we left the final word to Jesus; for he was the one who would be spending nine months inside her reproductive tract, so it was important he feel comfortable.

28 But after long contemplation he looked up, and smiled, and said, "Yea; Mary."

29 Thus did Jesus become the only child ever born who got to choose its mother.

CHAPTER 8

1 ther than the one thing, it was a fairly routine pregnancy.

2 Morning sickness; backaches; frequent urination; as usual the second trimester was the most pleasant, but then came the third: the fatigue, the sore breasts, the vaginal discharge; and of course, the cravings.

³ Mary screamed incessantly for dates and honey, and poor Joseph had to keep running out in the middle of the night to raid the palm grove, or throw pebbles at the windows of Ephesam the beekeeper.

⁴ To avoid scandal they had gotten married very early on, but Joseph did not consummate the marriage until after the birth; he said it was for reasons of sanctity, although the image of fetal Jesus floating inches from his penis must have been a bit of a mood-killer.

⁵ My son was going deep, deep undercover; he told me before implantation he wanted the truth of his identity to remain hidden from everyone, including himself, for 30 years, so that he might have the authentic experience of being "embedded"; and I swore to him it would be so.

⁶ But my principal feelings at this time were trepidation, anger, and indignity; and inwardly I continued to seethe over the bitter reflection, that no son of mine should ever be a son of *thine*.

⁷ The months wore on, and the day thou knowest as Christmas Eve crept up on us stealthily; for recall there was as yet not only no Christmas, but no "Christmas season" to helpfully remind thee of the joyous day's arrival within two weeks; or four weeks; or 25 weeks, as I believe is now the standard duration of the Yuletide mall-Muzak tape-loop.

⁸ Mary and Joseph had traveled to Bethlehem to register for the census; an event the Romans held periodically for tax purposes, to determine that a particular province had, say, MMMMMDCCLXVII inhabitants, each of whom therefore bore the burden of paying I/MMMMMMDCCLXVII ᵀᴴ of the taxes.

⁹ They arrived, and as per the plan made their way to the Bethlehem Bed & Breakfast; but, wouldst thou not know it, no one had made a reservation!

¹⁰ The fault was not theirs; for I had come to them both in a dream—I was a talking tornado—and explicitly told them they would be giving birth in Room 423 of the BB&B.

¹¹ No, it was a classic case of an assignment falling through the bureaucratic cracks; for Uriel thought Michael was handling it; and Michael thought Raphael was on top of it; and Raphael thought Uriel was on the case.

¹² So when the couple arrived there was no reservation; and no vacancy; and no rooms to be had anywhere in Bethlehem; for it also just so happened that that was the very weekend the Roman Society of Aqueduct Salesmen was holding its annual convention in . . .

¹³ Thou guessedst it.

¹⁴ Looking back and knowing it all worked out for the best, it is easy to regard such bungles as trivial, but at the time they were potentially catastrophic, for the birth was imminent; Mary's contractions were accelerating, and her cervix was already dilated .09 cubits.

¹⁵ Who knows what would have happened, had Gabriel not chanced to catch lucky sight of that unlocked manger with its crateful of rudimentary medical and incubatory equipment across the street.

¹⁶ As it was, the comedy of errors was still not over; for as Joseph argued with the clerk at the BB&B, he (and he alone) saw the word "MANGER" appear in dazzling fire behind him;

¹⁷ But he misread it, and took it as my insistence that he speak with the manager; which he did for several minutes, to no avail;

¹⁸ Until finally I was obliged to resort to something deeply embarrassing, akin to an admission of failure:

¹⁹ I froze the universe, picked up Joseph and Mary, and plunked them down in the manger, cushioning their landing atop a pile of horse dung.

²⁰ Yea, faith is a sausage best not seen made.

CHAPTER 9

¹ he Nativity; the Star of Bethlehem; the Annunciation to the Shepherds; the Adoration of the Magi . . . each unfolded in rapid succession, each so momentous its name was immediately capitalized.

² The events of that night have been the subject of more art and music and contemplation and wonder than any before or since; but I assure thee, on that *first* Christmas no one on my team had the slightest inclination to paint a fresco, or sing a carol, or buy an iPhone, or claymate a snowman.

³ No; for my hardworking angels that night in Bethlehem, the "true meaning of Christmas" was getting to sleep in until 4 PM.

⁴ Even *I* was weary; this is yet another misconception about me, that I am tireless; I am not tireless; stress and strain can fatigue me to the core.

⁵ But I cannot afford the luxury of slumber, so I use my omnipotence to keep myself awake; in this way I have gone 6,000 years without sleeping;

⁶ Behold the state of the world; I think it may be catching up with me.

⁷ And so began Jesus's time on earth; it would last 33 years.

⁸ And excepting one brief passage recounting his visit to the Temple in Jerusalem at age 12, thou knowest nothing of his whereabouts and activities for the first 30 of them.

⁹ No other reference or anecdote exists; no other written record to shed light on how he was girding himself for glory during these three decades.

¹⁰ But I was there; I watched him through it all; and I will tell thee exactly what he was doing during this period:

¹¹ Fieldwork.

¹² Jesus wanted to redeem humanity; and to redeem it he had to understand it; and to understand it he had to become part of it, and that is just what he did:

¹³ He unflinchingly surrendered to life, enjoying and suffering and experiencing all the thoughts and feelings and sensations and impulses of a real, flesh-and-blood human being.

¹⁴ Thus, as soon as Jesus was born,

¹⁵ Jesus wept.

¹⁶ And Jesus slept.

¹⁷ Jesus breast-fed; he nourished himself on the milk the Virgin Mary produced in her mammary glands; he sucked on her nipples to drink thereof.

¹⁸ Jesus weaned; whereupon Jesus ate; and Jesus chewed; and Jesus swallowed; and Jesus digested; and Jesus absorbed the nutrients; and Jesus excreted solid waste.

[19] (He performed an equivalent procedure for liquids.)

[20] Jesus learned to crawl, and was amazed; Jesus learned to walk, and was awestruck; Jesus learned to talk, and the sound of his own voice was a revelation.

[21] The toddler Jesus had a blanket he took with him everywhere.

[22] Jesus adored Mary and Joseph, and they him; he was obedient and full of love; they were tender and full of love.

[23] At six, Jesus got chicken pox; for five days there were red blotches all over Jesus's face and body; then Jesus got better.

[24] Outside the family home lay a field of lavender; its smell wafted in through the window at night; Jesus came to associate the smell with his home; unto the day of his death the smell of lavender recalled to him his childhood.

[25] At nine the young Jesus began his apprenticeship with Joseph; throughout his childhood he learned the craft of carpentry; Jesus labored diligently; Jesus made many mistakes; but Jesus improved; Jesus grew competent; in time, Jesus grew masterful; and Jesus felt pride in his progress.

[26] Jesus had childhood friends; they would amuse themselves by chasing each other through the fields, and throwing rocks at trees; over the years Jesus lost contact with them; Jesus regretted this.

[27] Jesus had strange dreams about giant elephants, and removing his clothes in public, and being pursued by a giant sandal; upon waking he could only remember them partially; and he could not construe their meaning.

[28] Throughout his youth Jesus attended synagogue, and observed the Sabbath, and was devoutly religious; he did not yet know he was my son, but from an early age he manifested a profound interest in all things spiritual.

[29] Jesus picked his nose when he thought no one was looking.

[30] He did not put his finger all the way up there; only a little; and he never ate it.

[31] Jesus would hear passersby singing songs, and the songs would get stuck in Jesus's head, and Jesus would be unable to stop humming them for weeks.

32 Sometimes after meals Jesus felt queasy; he came to notice that this happened whenever he ate pistachios, to which he thus learned he was allergic; and refrained from consuming henceforward.

33 Jesus reached puberty; Jesus's voice broke; Jesus grew half a cubit in six months; Jesus sprouted pubic hair; and Jesus felt the adolescent's stirrings of lust in all their cyclonic fury.

34 And so Jesus masturbated; for no one, not even my son, can pass through adolescence without masturbating; but he did it less often than most, and with a commendable shame.

35 Jesus sampled wine on numerous occasions; several times he drank too much; one night Jesus vomited on the street; he woke up sick and tunic-besmirched, vowing never again to imbibe the fruit of the vine to the point of besottedness; and he never did.

36 Jesus ended his apprenticeship and opened his own shop; he made yokes and ploughs and other farm equipment; some projects he found satisfying, others drudgery; overall he found the work only mildly fulfilling.

37 But in his spare hours he devoured the Hebrew Scriptures, and the rabbinical commentaries thereof; and followed the events of his time with passion; and engaged himself completely with the world; a world he no longer looked down on, but was part of;

38 Until he had become like any 30-year-old human being, or rather, like the best of them: churning, and changing, and yearning, and questing; bursting with consciousness; throbbing with life.

39 Yea; Jesus had gone native.

40 (But know this: Jesus never lay with a woman; Jesus never married; and Jesus certainly never impregnated anyone.

41 Dost thou hear me, Dan Brown?

42 Thy hunt-and-peck blasphemy may win thee legions of readers on beaches and tarmacs and other flat surfaces; but I am the LORD thy God, King of the Universe: and I have outsold thee 5,000 to 1.)

CHAPTER 10

1 "Prepare ye the way of the LORD! Prepare ye the way of the LORD!"

2 Even those of you abiding in the paganest depths of Greenwich Village know these words; for they are the beginning of *Godspell,* a musical I esteem almost as highly as *Joseph and the Amazing Technicolor Dreamcoat.*

3 (I am omniscient; so I can say with authority, that over 39 percent of you appeared in a production of *Godspell* at some point in adolescence.

4 Even *I* appeared in *Godspell* once; I did a cameo as myself; I was good; not great, but good.)

5 But they are more than bouncily set lyrics; they are the very words spoken by John the Baptist on that epochal day, when Jesus entered the River Jordan a man, and left it a savior, like unto Superman in a liquid phone booth.

6 John was a cousin of Jesus's, a prophet who had been born on the outskirts of Crazyville and had recently moved to the heart of downtown.

7 His clothes were of camel hair, and his food was wild locusts and honey, but he was a prophet; and as I said before, prophets need not be the most presentable of people; they are obliged only to be accurate, not sane.

8 On the Boxing Day morning after he turned 30, my son came to the Jordan, hungry for fulfillment and longing to be baptized.

9 Now, baptism has long since become a sacrament; but at this time it was seen by the rabbis as meritless and gaudy; pretentious; a gratuitous waste of one's monthly bath.

10 Only a small group of Judeans had yet rejuvenated themselves with this form of spiritual hydrotherapy, and only three itinerant rabbis performed the ceremony; all three were quite bapt; but assuredly, John was the baptest.

11 And so Jesus took a number and waited on line at the riverbank, as John baptized the crowd, all the while denouncing the Pharisees in attendance as a "generation of vipers" for whom "the ax is laid unto the root of the

trees," and demanding that they "bring forth therefore fruits mete for repentance."

12 (That last quote was no allegory; he had gone six months on wild locusts and honey, and would have killed for some figs.)

13 Then he began speaking of one more powerful than him, "Whose fan is in his hand, and he will thoroughly purge his floor, and gather his wheat into the garner, but he will burn up the chaff with unquenchable fire."

14 No doubt such agricultural metaphors mean little to thy generation, which believeth its sustenance to originate in either the stockroom of a supermarket or the warehouse of Frito-Lay®; but back then it was fearsome imagery.

15 And then my son walked in (not *on*; that was later) the water; and John saw him, and was filled with reverence, and dropped to his knees, and said, "I have need to be baptized of thee, and comest thou to *me*?"

16 And Jesus had not yet been made aware of his true identity; so although he responded, "Suffer it to be so now: for thus it becometh us to fulfill all righteousness," inwardly he thought, "Stalker alert. Stalker alert."

17 Lo, this was the moment.

18 For 30 years my son had remained ignorant of his own divinity; but at the moment he was baptized he flew straightaway out of the water,

19 And the heavens were opened unto him, and he saw my Spirit descending like a dove, and lighting upon him,

20 And he turned to me, with instant and total recollection, and I said to him, "This is my beloved Son, in whom I am well pleased"; and Jesus smiled, and embraced me.

21 But I only said that because Ruth was there.

22 I still thought the whole thing was a stupid idea.

CHAPTER 11

1 The next episode in Jesus's story was his testing in the wilderness by the devil; and here I must digress.

2 Forgive me, Reader; trust me, I will forgive thee in turn.

3 When my publisher first approached me about writing this book, I said unto him, "Happily would I merge the House of the LORD with the noble House of Simon, and the decent one of Schuster; but know this from the getteth-go:

4 There are two, and possibly three, subjects I will not discuss in my memoirs: heaven, hell, and limbo.

5 I will not divulge any information on them; neither where they are, nor what they are like, nor who inhabits them, nor how to reserve a spot in them; nor which if any is the eternal resting place of righteous nonbelievers, or deathbed converts, or Chinese people.

6 I will give no revelation regarding any aspect of man's posthumous destiny; for such a revelation would be like unto the spoiler of all spoilers, draining life of all its mystery and suspense;

7 And moreover, such enlightenment would furnish today's readers with a moral shortcut that would be unfair to those already departed souls who earned their eternal salvations and damnations strictly on merit."

8 That is what I said, and that is what I meant; I have given thee brief glimpses of the goings-on in heaven, and may offer a few more before this book is through; but otherwise that which lies beyond the portals of death must remain forever shrouded to the eyes of man.

9 Sorry.

10 Knowing this, thou canst see why the devil, too, is a subject of whom I would speak very little; for to talk of him and his activities would be to expose highly classified information regarding the afterlife.

11 (Besides which, there is also the matter of authorial courtesy; for I understand he is currently in negotiations with HarperCollins.)

¹² But his unsuccessful temptation of Jesus is not classified; it is right there in the Synoptic Gospels for all to see, so I do not mind mentioning it here.

¹³ And this seems an apt time also to discuss the little else I am willing to tell thee about the devil; for none of it is new information, but rather mere confirmation of things thou hast long suspected.

¹⁴ For the devil is, indeed, the fallen angel Lucifer.

¹⁵ And Lucifer did, indeed, lead a rebellion against me; and I did, indeed, suppress it, and cast him out.

¹⁶ And ever since, Lucifer hath, indeed, sought to lure mankind into the path of evil.

¹⁷ And he doth, indeed, do this by projecting himself and his evil messages into books, and shadows, and weird murmurings in the forest, and creaking sounds in the dark, and R-rated movies, and whatever the latest, most youth-oriented form of music is.

¹⁸ And he doth, indeed, especially love heavy-metal; into the recording sessions whereof he does, indeed, sneak, that he may insert backward messages into songs; for he believeth retrograde gibberish laid inaudibly under ear-shattering grindcore, to be the most effective way to promote his views.

¹⁹ And he doth, indeed, visit people in their time of need; and offer to grant them mortal happiness in exchange for their immortal soul; and if they agree, he doth, indeed, have them sign a contract; for though he is the amoral Prince of All Lies, he hath for some reason an unshakable respect for tort law.

²⁰ And he doth, indeed, have red skin; and horns; and a long curved tail; and a trident.

²¹ And he did, indeed, go down to Georgia, and lose a violin competition there to a young musician named Johnny; whereupon he did, indeed, give his beloved golden fiddle to Johnny; who thereupon did, indeed, call him a son of a bitch.

²² Yea, there is only one widely held belief about the devil that is a misconception; and even that only partially so.

²³ The number of the devil is *not* 666.

²⁴ That is only his area code; his full number is unlisted.

CHAPTER 12

¹ It is not my intention here to outline the final three years of Jesus's life, for of those there is more than enough record; all four Gospels tell the story in magnificent detail.

² My favorite of these is Matthew, but Mark has its moments; and John's literary style is at times quite engaging.

³ Luke stinks.

⁴ But I will offer *my* recollections of Jesus during his ministry; for I was not only a witness but a participant, in frequent contact with him during that time; as was H. G., whose interest in his younger brother's vocation remained avid.

⁵ Soon after resisting the devil's temptations, H. G., Jesus, and I gathered one day for a strategy session in Jesus's cerebellum.

⁶ It quickly devolved into a shouting match between Jesus and me; for he wanted his ministry to consist of preaching and hugging and telling people he loved them and baking them vegan millet loaves;

⁷ While I wanted it to consist of upbraiding heretics and slaughtering animals and afflicting the wicked with liver disease.

⁸ Finally, just as Jesus was limbering up his orbicularis oculi in preparation for the Look, H. G. stepped forward and said, "Dad, Jeez, it's very simple: PAM.

⁹ PAM. Parables, Apostles, Miracles.

¹⁰ That's it. That's all we need.

¹¹ For in my many travels around the world I have observed human beings of every size and shape and color and socioeconomic background, and there are three things that never fail to impress them:

¹² Stories, entourages, and magic.

13 So let us write some parables; let us write them so as to have wide popular appeal; meaning nothing too artsy, Jesus, and nothing too bloody, Dad.

14 And then let us gather apostles to help spread the Word; it matters not exactly how many, though my instinct says somewhere between ten and the low teens.

15 And then the miracles . . . well, the miracles will be the easy part.

16 What do you say? Let us PAM.

17 Say it with me: PAM. PAM.

18 PAM! PAM! PAM! PAM! PAM! PAM! PAM!"

19 His excitement was contagious; and soon all three of us were dancing around shouting "PAM!";

20 For even I am not immune to the power of a catchy slogan.

CHAPTER 13

1 So we adapted H. G.'s PAM mantra; and we began by composing a body of parables for Jesus, proven material he could fall back on whenever his newer stuff bombed.

2 But our worries were unfounded; for from the moment he began his first sermon Jesus spellbound the crowd with his passion, sincerity, empathy, and prop work.

3 Nor did he need much help crafting his parables; for he took to the form like Aesop to fables, or Sparks to schlock;

4 Proving most adept at condensing complex moral and theological issues into lively stories that conveyed a message without being preachy.

5 Indeed, every utterance of Jesus in the Gospels is memorable and inspired; but in reviewing them again for this book—for verily, the last edition of the New Testament I read was Gutenberg's—it struck me that a few sections and quotations have come to feel dated.

6 So I have provided below, and in the two chapters that follow, new versions of four of his parables, and various of his other utterances; which

H. G. and I have revised in accordance with the spirit of thine age, and with Jesus's full, albeit unspoken and unsought, permission.

THE PRODIGAL SON

⁷ A certain farmer had two sons, and the younger of them said to his father, "Father, give me the portion of goods that falleth to me."

⁸ So he divided in two his estate; and soon after the younger son ceased tilling his father's land, and began wasting himself with riotous living.

⁹ He continued in this manner for years, his condition ever worsening, his denials ringing ever hollower; until one day he hit rock bottom, drunkenly falling off Mount Hebron and landing on a rock at the bottom.

¹⁰ And as he lay there half-dead, I came to him in his delirium and said, "My name is Jesus Christ, and I am an interventionist.

¹¹ Thou art addicted, my son, addicted to sin, and it is a sickness; for maketh no mistake, addiction *is* a disease.

¹² Now, I am a healer; I can raise the dead, and make the blind see; but when it comes to a hard-core sin addiction, there are no miracles, my son, only hard work.

¹³ And to begin that work, thou must remove thyself this day, to a gardened refuge not far from here: The Brighter Horizons Clean Living Facility of New Canaan.

¹⁴ It is thy choice; I cannot force thee; but knowest that if thou choosest not to go, it will have the following consequences: I will not die for thee, or anyone; and humanity will go unredeemed forever.

¹⁵ But it's thy call."

¹⁶ And the son took strength, and entered into the program; and committed himself to it, and reached inside himself to find the strength to confront that which he had undergone throughout his childhood.

¹⁷ (Suffice it to say, that his late mother could be *extremely* affectionate.)

¹⁸ And when it was over, he determined to visit his father, that he might humble himself before him and beg his forgiveness.

¹⁹ But when his father saw him approach he ran to him and embraced him; and told his servants to arrange a feast by preparing the fatted calf, along with a vegetarian option.

²⁰ Now, when the elder brother saw this he was aggrieved, and said, "Father, all these years I have served thee, never transgressing against thy commandments;

²¹ Yet as soon as my prodigal brother returned, only then didst thou kill the fatted calf; which thou knowest I have had my eye on for some time, being a bit of a veal buff."

²² And the father responded, "Son, thou art always with me, and everything I have is yours. But now we must celebrate, for this my youngest son was dead and is alive again; was lost, and is found."

²³ And the brother said, "Come to think of it, thou hast never killed a goat for me either; or a chicken.

²⁴ In fact, thou hast never slaughtered a single piece of livestock for me in thy entire life.

²⁵ Not . . . once."

²⁶ And the father said, "Why must thou ruin the moment?"

²⁷ And the prodigal son relapsed into debauchery before the end of that month; so he returned to New Canaan, but left three weeks early, declaring himself "ready";

²⁸ Whereupon he stayed clean for two weeks, then relapsed again, big-time; and as of this writing he had checked in a third time; but lo, this is not uncommon.

²⁹ For recovery is not a destination, but a journey.

CHAPTER 14

THE SOWER

¹ Behold, there went a sower out to sow.

² And it came to pass, that as he sowed, he stepped on a rake, which struck him in the nether regions.

³ And a passerby caught it all on his smartphone; and rushed home, to scatter the images thereof amongst his many acquaintances.

⁴ And some of the copies were sent to outdated addresses, and yielded nothing but error messages;

⁵ And some were devoured by spam blockers, and withered in junk mail folders;

⁶ And some fell into the hands of those with lives; and they perished in the trash.

⁷ But a few were received by the kind of people who find video of other people being struck by rakes in the nether regions most amusing;

⁸ And they distributed the images thirty-, sixty-, a hundredfold; until they became viral, and spread their meme around the world.

⁹ (This is not a parable. Knowest thou that viral video "Sower Gets Hit in the Nether Regions"? That's how it happened.)

THE GOOD SAMARITAN

¹⁰ A certain man went down from Jerusalem to Jericho, and fell among thieves, who stripped him of his raiment, and wounded him, and departed, leaving him half dead.

¹¹ And by chance there came down the road a certain priest: and when he saw him, he passed by on the other side.

¹² And likewise a Levite, when he arrived at the place, came and looked on him, and passed by on the other side.

¹³ But a certain Samaritan, as he journeyed, came to where he was: and when he saw him, he broke down and wept;

¹⁴ For he saw that the man was his colleague in law enforcement, who had been but three weeks short of retirement.

¹⁵ And from that moment this Samaritan swore a sacred oath: to track down the robbers who had done this to his partner . . . and the two heartless bastards who'd left him for dead.

16 What followed was one man's bloody journey into the dark night of his own soul; where he would find that sometimes, the line between justice and vengeance . . . is drawn in blood.

17 This summer, Taylor Lautner is ONE . . . GOOD . . . SAMARITAN.

THE SHREWD MANAGER

18 There was a certain rich man who had entrusted his riches to a wealth manager; and a rumor began to spread that the manager was wasting the man's possessions.

19 So the rich man went to the manager, and said to him, "What is this that I hear about you? Give an accounting of your management."

20 And the shrewd manager looked up, rose slowly from his desk, and said, "An accounting of my management? Thou seekest 'an accounting of my management'?

21 Look around. Look at this office. Look at this view. Look at this pen. Platinum. How's that? How's that for an 'accounting of my management'?

22 Listen, buddy: I've been spinning gold out of thin air since before bozos like thee were suckin' on thy Mommy's yaboes.

23 And as a *result*, I have grown wealthy.

24 As a *result*, my boat containeth an onboard lake containing a one to ten scale model of the boat itself, including its own lake and scale model.

25 As a *result*, my third house is to thy house, what my first house is to my third house.

26 Verily, buddy, I operate on intellectual levels whose very existence could not be dreamed of by the likes of douche bags like unto thee.

27 Thy money is fine, OK? Now go.

28 Go.

29 Go home to thy family and keep spoon-feedin' 'em that bullshit about what a man thou art.

³⁰ Mazel tov, fuckface."

³¹ That manager died on the lam in Mexico worth $50 billion.

CHAPTER 15
THE SAYINGS OF JESUS

¹ It is easier for a camel to walk through the eye of a needle, than two camels.

² What profiteth a man, if he gains the whole world, and loses his soul? Besides the whole world, I mean.

³ With God all things are possible; but with money all things are probable; and with a good accountant they're all deductible.

⁴ Judge not, lest ye be judged; unless thou art a judge; in which case, judge away.

⁵ Consider the lilies of the field, how they grow; they toil not, neither do they spin. Yet when thou . . . what? So I like flowers. So what?

⁶ If the blind leadeth the blind, both shall fall into the ditch; which is pretty funny.

⁷ Man shall not live by bread alone. Yet at restaurants it is easy to forget this and end up full before the appetizer.

⁸ The LORD is my shepherd; I shall not want. He maketh me to lie down in green pastures; he leadeth me beside the still waters. Then one morning he bringeth me to the shed out back and *boom!*, he maketh me into lamb chops.

⁹ Do unto others as others would do unto thee the second thou turnest thy back, the bastards.

¹⁰ Can the Ethiopian change his skin, or the leopard his spots? Not that I meaneth to compare Ethiopians to animals. Ethiopians have beautiful skin, actually. Why would they want to change it? I love Ethiopians. Thou knowest what, forget this whole saying.

11 Render to Caesar the things that are Caesar's; and to God the things that are God's. It might help to put them in two piles.

12 When thou givest alms, do not let thy left hand know what thy right hand is doing. Whereas with juggling the opposite is true.

13 If a man strikes thee on one cheek, turn to him the other. Then, having shown thyself impregnable to cheek attack, beat the crap out of him.

14 And they shall beat their swords into ploughshares; and their spears into pruninghooks; and their other weapons into other types of obscure agricultural equipment; and nation shall fight nation no more, but instead do dull farming stuff.

15 He that is without sin among you, let him cast the first stone. Then, stones 2 through 1,000 are open to anybody.

16 The lion shall lie down with the lamb, and the leopard shall lie down with the goat. And the products of these unions shall be liambs and goatpards, respectively.

17 I tell ye, if you have faith as small as a mustard seed, you can say to this mountain, "Move from here to there," and it will move. Seriously. Try it. Hold on; I would get this on tape.

18 God never shuts a door without opening a window; for he wants thy house to be drafty.

CHAPTER 16

1 nce his material was written, Jesus debuted it in his first major sermon, at a popular local venue known as the Mount; and on the strength of that appearance he gained a cult following.

2 Yet more than his words, it was his deeds that won him renown; for he had already developed a reputation as a miracle worker, one who could do for the sick, possessed, and deceased what a boutique hairdresser can do for the split-ended.

³ Miracles are a tricky business; their impact on an audience is matchless in terms of oomph, yet they tend to raise certain expectations that grow ever harder to meet.

⁴ We collaborated on 37 miracles during Jesus's three-plus years as a minister, a rate of one a month; a good pace, coming not so often they were taken for granted, yet not so rarely that the crowd grew restless.

⁵ The miracles were of four varieties; the most common were healings, of which there were 19.

⁶ Blindness; deaf-muteness; dropsy; leprosy; fever; paralysis; internal bleeding; we had a nice mix.

⁷ The healings were always received with awe; for this was a period when the proscribed medical treatment for most of these ailments was hillside abandonment.

⁸ By the end the clamor for Jesus's restorative gift became so overwhelming, we were obliged to stem the number of miracle-seekers, lest the rest of his ministry grind to a halt;

⁹ So H. G. devised a tedious series of questions on parchment that all would-be patients were obliged to complete in duplicate before they could even schedule an appointment with him; and this proved effective.

¹⁰ Eight other miracles spoke to Jesus's control over nature: his supernatural ability to calm a storm, or walk on water, or provide last-minute catering when a horde of followers crashed what it said *specifically on the invitation* was a disciple-only dinner.

¹¹ These I liked best, for they were on a grander scale; they were spectacles of a kind I had had little occasion to produce since Exodus, and I had missed the razzle-dazzle.

¹² The Feeding of the Five Thousand was especially memorable; for not only did I turn seven loaves and fishes into food for 5,000 people, but I heightened the marvel by transforming the bread from white to ciabatta, and the fish from carp to Dover sole.

¹³ Seven of Jesus's miracles were exorcisms; and of these I was highly dubious.

14 He believed himself to be removing demons from the possessed; the possessed themselves later believed this to be the case;

15 But I was witness to all of them, and in my opinion of the seven "possessed" souls, three were epileptics, two were schizophrenics, and one was manic-depressive.

16 Only one—the Gerasenes demonic—was legitimately possessed, and even this must be regarded with an asterisk;

17 For the demon in question, though powerful, was off-duty, and was using the man's soul merely as a vacation home wherein to get away from the strains of his workaday demonic career.

18 Finally, three miracles consisted of raising the dead.

19 There was the young man from Nain, whom Jesus approached in the coffin during his funeral procession, at which point he sat up and began to talk; a tremendous wonder that overjoyed his mother, and finally gave authorities the eyewitness testimony they needed to arrest his killer.

20 Next came Jairus, who begged Jesus to save his dying daughter; when they arrived at his home she was already dead, but he "awoke" her; she instantly became a devout Christian, and 35 years later was devoured by lions in the Coliseum; such is life.

21 And the last was Lazarus; the brother of Jesus's friends Mary and Martha.

22 As thou readest in John 11, Lazarus was four days' dead and buried in a cave; and Jesus bade the people remove the stone from the cave's mouth; and in preparation for the resurrection he said, "Father, I thank thee that thou hast heard me."

23 These words displeased me, for they sounded almost mocking; as if to say, "Well, look who has decided to take the time out of his busy day to hear me all of a sudden: Mr. Goddypants."

24 Then Jesus added, "I know that thou hearest me always: but because of the people which stand by I said it, that they may believe thou hast sent me."

25 This infuriated me.

26 It was not enough that my own son addressed me condescendingly; now he must embarrass me in front of his friends?

27 And right before asking me to bring one of them back to life?

28 I tell thee, I had half a mind to leave Lazarus dead; nay, to fill his orifices with an oozy surfeit of worms and maggots, that Jesus and his companions would know I was not one to be patronized.

29 But H. G. told me it would have looked bad not to revivify him; so I did.

30 I visited Jesus later, in his temporal lobe; and reminded him that he was only on earth due to my fatherly indulgence; and that I would tolerate no insolence when it came to—

31 But then he gave me the Look, and I backed off.

CHAPTER 17

1 Word of Jesus's miracles quickly spread through Judea like wildfire; even more so after he performed the Miracle of Extinguishing the Wildfire.

2 It was now time to choose apostles to disseminate his message; we had many candidates, and we researched them thoroughly; we visited their hometowns, and spent many late nights peering deep into their souls; for we could do this without waking them up, if we were quiet.

3 We deliberated for a long time on each one, but in the end I had the last word on the matter; and as thou knowest, the men I chose proved a veritable apostolic dream team.

4 Their very names are a roster of immortals: Peter; Andrew; James; John; Philip; Bartholomew; Matthew; Thomas; James; Thaddeus; Simon the Zealot.

5 Yea, eleven amazing apostles.

6 Eleven devout, loyal, incorruptible apostles.

7 How fortunate my son was, to be surrounded by eleven men such as these.

8 And how fortunate the Early Church was, to have these eleven champions; of whom only one would not die a martyr's death.

9 That one was John, who died naturally at 94; but he wrote *The Book of Revelation,* which went on to inspire thousands of believers to give their lives, so he hath nothing to hang his head about in the martyr department.

10 As for the other ten: truly greater love hath no man, than that he lay down his life for his boss.

11 Of course the greatest of all was St. Peter; the rock on whom the faith is built; its greatest missionary, its first pope, the author of much of the rest of the New Testament, and the greatest doorman of all time.

12 Peter and his brother Andrew were the first two apostles; fishermen of Galilee; Jesus saw them casting nets in the water and said, "Come ye after me, and I will make you fishers of *men*";

13 Which I swear did not sound gay when he said it.

14 There were the two Jameses; big-hearted, Christ-loving men they were; I remember not which one died of decapitation, and which by drinking molten lead.

15 There was Philip; a Hellene who was Jesus's link to the Greek-speaking community; he won over countless converts with his weekly "Sunday Spanakopita Sermon."

16 There was Bartholomew; nice guy.

17 Matthew was a tax collector; I recruited him because in any small group of church leaders it is handy if one is good with numbers.

18 And of course we had Thomas; "Doubting Thomas"; for when Jesus rose from the dead, Thomas at first doubted it.

19 Thomas died preaching in India in 72 A.D., after angry Brahmins arrested him, stoned him, and stabbed him to death with a lance.

20 Was it pleasant? I doubt it.

21 As for Thaddeus, he was our very special apostle; no, he was not the smartest among them, and he could be a challenge; but when he hugged you, you felt *hugged*.

22 And finally, Simon the Zealot, with his constant zealotry and trademark zeal.

23 They were a tremendous group, these 11 fine men; they were, if thou wilt, the best and pious-est of their generation.

24 As for the other one, whose name I refuse to even record here, I will only say how truly disappointed we were in him.

25 We liked him; we trusted him; but then he changed, and decided to leave the organization, and in a very unfortunate way.

26 The punishment that young man received for his actions was as harsh a sentence as could be handed down, yet it was still insufficient;

27 For in the end, *nothing* can bring back a son.

28 Usually.

CHAPTER 18

1 I cherished the time I spent with Jesus during the last three years of his life.

2 I came to respect him for many things: his goodness, his discipline, his manners, and his chastity.

3 (For remember, he was still subject to all the weaknesses of the flesh; and he had numerous female admirers; and many of them were comely; and all of them were ready, willing, and able, 24/7/365.)

4 I even respected his choice of enemies, for the Pharisees were truly reprehensible people: liars and hypocrites of the highest order; the worst *shondah* for the goyim until Bernie Madoff;

5 Or possibly the Weinsteins.

6 But always in the back of my infinite mind I held fast to my belief that his entire mission and descent was foolish and demeaning.

⁷ This belief only intensified as the time of his great ordeal neared; for I am ashamed to admit that I dreaded it, not for the agony it would cause my child, but for the damage I feared such a public humiliation might have on my reputation.

⁸ Lo, I feared playing the aggrieved Billy Ray to Jesus's wayward Miley.

⁹ Well do I recall the Last Supper; it was Passover; everyone ate a hearty seder; afterward Jesus hid the *afikoman* behind a broom; he told everyone to let Thaddeus find it; he did; he was so happy he hugged *everyone*.

¹⁰ The night was a farewell of sorts, a look back on a remarkable career; and as the wine kept flowing and the stories kept coming, it naturally devolved into a roast.

¹¹ For two hours one apostle after another stood up and gave it to Jesus mercilessly; making sport of his water-walking, and dead-raising, and facial hair, and penchant for droning on; it was a nonstop mirthfest.

¹² I remember Bartholomew remarking: "Jesus, here is a miracle thou mayest perform: *shave!*

¹³ Thy beard hair is thicker than a moneylender's purse!"

¹⁴ They killed him; they slaughtered him; they crucified him; it was hilarious.

¹⁵ Finally Jesus rose; he was smiling, but I could see he was preoccupied.

¹⁶ He may have been thinking about the imminent nailing of his ankles and wrists to a wooden cross and subsequent prolonged death thereby; but I am speculating.

¹⁷ His first words after all this merriment were, "Ye are too kind; but seriously, gentlemen, I say unto you, that one of you shall betray me."

¹⁸ That brought the house down, but not in a good way.

¹⁹ Everyone asked if it was him; Jesus kept silent, but he knew who it was, for the traitor had not only already received his 30 pieces of silver, but used some of it to grab the check.

²⁰ A nice gesture, but too little, too late.

²¹ Then, in a moment of great solemnity, Jesus offered the first Communion.

²² He passed around the bread and said, "Take, eat; this is my body"; and then he passed around the wine and said, "Drink ye all of it; for this is my blood."

²³ "Great. A cannibal vampire," I thought.

²⁴ "My son is going to die a cannibal vampire."

CHAPTER 19

¹ he next 24 hours would change everything; for humanity, to be sure, but more importantly for me.

² After the meal, Jesus and the apostles walked to the Garden of Gethsemane on the Mount of Olives.

³ Now this Olive Garden had long been a popular gathering place for them, for it served a variety of Roman food in a convivial atmosphere, and at a minimum of payment; and when they were there, they felt like family.

⁴ But soon the Roman soldiers came to arrest him; and thou-knowest-who approached him, and kissed him;

⁵ Kissed him, to add insult to injury, with tongue.

⁶ Everyone knows what happened next: the arrest; the mortifying perp walk in front of the Temple; and the imprisonment on charges of treason against the government, charges trumped up by the Jewish high priests.

⁷ (For many were so falsely charged and imprisoned during the hysteria of the War on Torah.)

⁸ Then he was brought before Pontius Pilate; as is recorded in the Gospels, Pilate had the power to pardon one prisoner, either Jesus or Barabbas, and he decided to let the crowd choose.

⁹ But what is *not* recorded in the Gospels, is that Barabbas was in prison for being a gentleman jewel thief.

¹⁰ He stole diamonds and rubies from the very wealthy; he was dapper and suave; he bedded Judea's most beautiful women; he was a Clooneyesque roustabout.

¹¹ Jesus never had a chance.

¹² And now his suffering began in earnest: the punching and spitting and striking and kicking; to say nothing of the mockery;

¹³ Mockery which, unlike the good-spirited japery of the previous night's roast, came not from a good place.

¹⁴ For Jesus was derided, insulted, and humiliated; taunted as "King of the Jews"; even the size of his most intimate parts was ridiculed, invariably by those who themselves had something to hide.

¹⁵ But the cruelest of all the torments was the unified chanting of the Jewish throngs and the Roman soldiers: "Jeeeeee-sus! Jeeeeee-sus!"

¹⁶ Lo, it was exactly the same form of derision as that heaped by fans, almost 2,000 years later, upon slugger Darryl Strawberry;

¹⁷ And almost as vicious.

¹⁸ Every instinct in me longed to go Old Testament on all of them; my brain reeled with comforting thoughts of brimstone and boils; but I forebore.

¹⁹ Because as I watched my son suffer the abuse he had been dreaming of his whole life, I realized something:

²⁰ Jesus was no pussy.

²¹ Jesus was one tough son of a bitch.

CHAPTER 20

¹ For my son did not complain when they sentenced him to death.

² My son did not wince as they placed upon him the crown of thorns.

³ My son did not grimace as they scourged him with whips.

⁴ My son did not flinch as they placed the cross on his back.

⁵ No; because my son . . . was a *man*.

⁶ Yea, Ruth was right; he and I were truly two very different Godheads.

⁷ I was a self-made Being who had risen from nothing to become Master of the Universe; to get what I wanted I smote anyone who got in the way, along with many who were merely close to the way, and untold millions who were a great deal of distance away from the way.

⁸ But my son was of a different breed; he sought to become Master of the Universe by *returning* to nothing; by being not smiter, but smitee.

⁹ And now, as he took his last un-scenic stroll through downtown Jerusalem; now, at last, I understood.

¹⁰ What I had once viewed as his weakness was in fact strength: his suffering *was* power; his humanity *was* divine.

¹¹ He knew I was watching; he could have summoned me to his assistance; he could have called in the cavalry to Calvary anytime.

¹² I had watched Abraham and Job suffer, and my reaction had made me wonder what was wrong with me; watching Jesus suffer I felt the same way, but for entirely different reasons.

¹³ For as my son staggered through the Via Dolorosa carrying the means of his own death, I smiled and thought, "That's my boy!"

¹⁴ And when he reached Golgotha, and they held him down and bade him drink vinegar mixed with gall, I thought, "Way to take one for the team, son!";

¹⁵ And as I watched the centurions hammering into his ankles and wrists, and my son's face tremble in excruciating pain, I thought, "Thou art tough as nails, kid!";

¹⁶ And as I watched them mount his cross upon the hillside I thought, "Hang in there, buddy!"

¹⁷ And as the crowd mocked and threw stones at his crucified body, my heart well-nigh burst with pride.

¹⁸ And as he looked up at me and with his final breath murmured, "It is finished," I said, "Thou didst it! Thou didst it, kiddo!

¹⁹ Behold, world! Behold the Man! For my son is . . . is human!

²⁰ Yea! My son is human, and I care not who knows it!

²¹ I love my dead human son!

²² I love thee, son!"

²³ (For he had died and was now standing next to me.)

CHAPTER 21

¹ 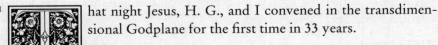hat night Jesus, H. G., and I convened in the transdimensional Godplane for the first time in 33 years.

² We quickly attended to business, and lo, there was much of it to attend; for Jesus's resurrection was less than 48 hours away, and we still had some kinks to work out.

³ H. G. wanted to schedule a meeting during the return where Jesus could formally instruct his Apostles to spread the gospel.

⁴ I proposed making that the very last item on Jesus's return agenda, in accordance with a long-held theory of mine that motivational speeches are more impactful when they end with the speaker's ascension to heaven.

⁵ All this was fine with Jesus; he insisted only that Mary Magdalene be the first one to see him risen, for he wished to provide her with at least one unforgettable romantic memory.

⁶ He greatly pitied her; he knew how much she loved him, but she was one of those unfortunate women for whom all the good ones proved to be either married, gay, or Jesus Christ.

⁷ As we talked I chattily shared with my own prodigal son my opinions and thoughts on the details of his mission: his miracles, and his anointings, and his unimaginable physical ordeal.

⁸ When I told him how proud I was of the way he had handled his crucifixion, he was characteristically modest.

⁹ "Oh, Father," he said, "we are talking about the Roman Empire.

¹⁰ Crucifixion is probably the *least* painful means of death I could have suffered at its hands.

¹¹ Verily, they have this new device, the cubinatium. It slices the body into dice-sized cubes over the course of a month, all while impaling thee through the innards with a spiked bronze javelin.

¹² Now *that* sounds painful!"

¹³ We laughed until we cried.

¹⁴ All through the night we reminisced; all of us, H. G. included, for he, too, had grown in my esteem.

¹⁵ We had grown very close; the way we had bonded was uncanny, almost mystical; as if the three of us were of the same substance, merely in a different figuration; a mutually indwelling trinity existing in reciprocal immanence as per the doctrine of perichoresis;

¹⁶ It is hard to explain; the point is, we had grown very close.

¹⁷ As we floated back to see Ruth and Kathy, I pulled Jesus aside.

¹⁸ "Son," I said, "I know thou hast at times wondered if I truly believed in thee.

¹⁹ Verily, I do. I believe in thee.

²⁰ I believe in thee; thy Apostles believe in thee; and soon many more people will believe in thee.

²¹ Thou knowest, I have never told thee this, but all my existence I have struggled with wrath-management issues; yet watching thee down there hath given me a whole new outlook.

²² Thou hast inspired me to change my ways; to create a kinder, more compassionate world by following the noble precepts thou hast explicitly laid forth.

²³ Yea; as soon as mankind starts following them, I will, too.

²⁴ And one more thing: I have a surprise for thee.

²⁵ When thou first hatched this plan to come to earth, thy goal was merely to redeem the Jews; to bring them back to the path of righteousness, that they might be spared my wrath; and this thou hast accomplished; the Jews are spared; I will not obliterate them from the world.

26 I promise not that henceforward their lives will be rainbows and honeycomb; but I will not obliterate them.

27 But watching thee work thy magic down there, I realized it would be unfair to the world to limit thy message, and goodness, and redemption, solely to the Jews.

28 They are my Chosen People; but thou deservest a Chosen People of thine own.

29 I guess what I am asking thee, son, is:

30 How does 'Jesusism' sound to thee?"

CHAPTER 22

1 **A**nd the rest, as they say, is theology.

2 Jesus rose from the dead and made twelve public appearances; as with the miracles, we sought to strike a balance; enough to serve as verification, but not enough where one might say, "Oh great, the dead guy's doing another show."

3 He appeared to Mary Magdalene; he appeared to the apostles; he appeared to 500 believers at once; he even appeared to two lesser disciples on the road to Emmaus.

4 He passed the day with them unrecognized, lecturing them on the Prophets; then he revealed himself to them when they broke bread, only to disappear.

5 That was the only time I ever saw Jesus deliberately fuck with people.

6 He made sure to manifest himself to each of his longtime supporters at least once, that he might thank them for putting so much time and effort into his campaign.

7 Then he ascended to heaven, to sit, as it says, "at the right hand of God"; this is true; Jesus does sit at my right hand; as it happens I am a lefty, but it is still the seat of honor.

8 And today, 2,000 years, 500,000 martyrs, 824,000 cathedrals and 723 billion mortal sins later, Christianity—for H. G. did not like "Jesusism";

he felt the three esses would antagonize lispers—is the most successful religion of all time.

⁹ It hath over two billion adherents: more than Judaism, Sikhism, Jainism, Choctaw mythology, Siberian shamanism, and anthroposophy *combined.*

¹⁰ Jesus continues dying for humanity's sins every single day, and I have never heard him complain; not a single time.

¹¹ The most I've ever heard him admit is that there are some people for whom it is a pleasure to die on the cross, and others for whom it feels like more work.

¹² As for the two of us, we have had our squabbles over the centuries, as any father and son will;

¹³ Yet such disagreements inevitably end in a reconciliatory "come to Jesus" moment.

¹⁴ Our relationship these days is of a far different character than it once was.

¹⁵ A few days ago he and I were in my office discussing a finer theological point; the nature of which hath no bearing on thee, unless thou art an unbaptized baby.

¹⁶ He argued one way; I the other; he gave the Look; I conceded.

¹⁷ This took place a dozen times, in full view of Gabriel; and when the meeting was over Gabriel chuckled to himself; and though I had it within me to know why, I asked him, to save time.

¹⁸ "Heavenly Father," he said, "there was a time when thou doubtedst thy son would ever amount to anything outside the world; believing him soft, and weak, and unable to impose his will.

¹⁹ Yet to see thy dealings with him now, it seems to me that this is the opposite of the truth; for I would describe thee, my LORD, as nothing short of Jesus-whipped."

²⁰ I, too, chuckled; for Gabriel was right.

²¹ The Romans may have whipped Jesus, but in the end it was they, and I, and all of western civilization, who ended up

²² Jesus-whipped.

FILLEMIN

("Godlibs")

CHAPTER 1

 ¹ sk Matthew, Mark, Luke, John, and now me: the creation of a Gospel is a grueling task.

² To paraphrase Thomas Edison, scripture is 1 percent divine inspiration, 99 percent divine perspiration.

³ But some of thee may doubt this; some of my more skeptical readers may think writing a holy book is easy, that any old hack can crank out a Testament, or whip up a Koran during an all-nighter;

⁴ That all it requireth is a few crazy stories, a reverent tone, and a bunch of old-timey pronouns and verb endings.

⁵ Prepare to eat thy words, any old hack(s).

⁶ On the next pages are printed a few passages and excerpts from Scripture, with certain key words and phrases omitted, for thee to complete in accordance with the instructions written underneath the line.

⁷ (I call them "Godlibs"; I thought of that myself; but a Google search revealeth over 5,000 matching results.

⁸ Thanks, Google, thou pun-hoarding, mirth-killing parade-pisser.)

⁹ I have filled the first one out by way of example; the other three I leave to the reader's sanctimonious imagination.

¹⁰ There are millions of ways to fill in these blanks, but I am confident not one of them will improve upon the poetry or profundity of the original.

¹¹ However, in the interest of promoting creativity and sales, but mostly sales, I will be sponsoring a contest to determine the winner.

¹² Once thou hast filled in the three selections, tear them out and place them in an envelope addressed to: Godlibs Contest, c/o God, 1600 Holy Avenue, Heaven.

¹³ I have no ZIP code, but that matters not; for the next step is to wrap the envelope in a ring of ram fat and burn it on an altar.

¹⁴ I will then reconstitute the submissions and judge each one based on originality, legibility, and savoriness.

¹⁵ One grand-prize winner will receive an autographed copy of this book; eternal admittance to the Kingdom of Heaven; and a $50 gift certificate to Boston Market.

¹⁶ Two runner-up winners will receive their choice of one of the above.

¹⁷ Enter, skeptics; it is not often the Lᴏʀᴅ encourages thee to burn one of his books.

GODLIB #1 (EXAMPLE)

[1] One day, *Zilpah* and *Melchizedek* decided to visit the funnest
     (girl's name)   (boy's name)

place in the whole world: the *kosher slaughterhouse* .
                              (fun place)

[2] On the way there, they met a *blasphemous* *Leviathan* , and the
                                 (silly adjective) (animal)

three of them began to play *venison* . They played for
                            (common game)

a while until they all got hungry for *bananas* ; so they went
                                      (silly food)

to the supermarket, where they heard a man make

a *lamentation over the righteous death of an unconscionable sinner* .
   (funny noise)

[3] When they saw the *bananas* , they couldn't believe it—one of
                      (silly food from before)

them was *mottled* , another one was *Moabite* , and another one
         (color)   (gross adjective)

was over *800 cubits* long!
         (unit of length)

[4] Just when they thought things couldn't get any sillier, they all

looked in the mirror and saw their *foreskins* suddenly
                                   (body parts, plural)

had *frankincense and myrrh* all over them!
    (small objects)

[5] The two friends laughed and laughed, until they looked at their

watches and realized they had to go home because it was late: in

fact, it was *as the stars of the heaven, and as the sand which is on the*
             (really high number)

sea shore o'clock!

[6] When their parents asked, "How was the *kosher slaughterhouse* ?",
                                           (fun place from before)

they looked at each other and *fornicated* !
                              (silly verb)

211

GODLIB #2 (THE OLD TESTAMENT)

¹ And _____ lived _____ years, and
    (obscure boy's name #1)   (typical high temperature in August [F°])

begat _____ ;
    (obscure boy's name #2)

² And _____ lived _____ years after he
    (obscure boy's name #2)   (your SAT Math score)

begat _____ , and he died.
    (character from *The Scarlet Letter*)

³ And _____ lived _____ years, and
    (character from *The Scarlet Letter*)   (call number of favorite
                                              FM radio station)

begat _____ ;
    (character from *Children of the Corn*)

⁴ And _____ lived _____
    (character from *Children of the Corn*)   (call number of favorite AM radio station)

years after he begat _____ , and he died.
                    (name of son of insufferable hipster friend)

⁵ And _____ lived _____ years,
    (name of son of insufferable hipster friend)   (age at which it is no longer possible
                                                      to produce viable sperm)

and begat _____ ;
    (anagram of an African capital)

⁶ And _____ lived _____ years
    (anagram of an African capital)   (winning numbers of last night's Pick-3 drawing)

after he begat _____ , and he died.
            (name that if you had it you
             would kill yourself)

GODLIB #3 (THE NEW TESTAMENT)

[1] Ye are the _____ of the _____ : but if
(seasoning)   (planet in the solar system)

the _____ hath lost its _____ , where-
(seasoning)   (flavor of that seasoning)

with shall it be _____ ?
(seasoning-ness)

[2] Ye have heard that it hath been said, A(n) _____ for
(part of the face #1)

a(n) _____ , and a(n) _____ for a(n)
(part of the face #1)   (part of the face #2)

_____ :
(part of the face #2)

[3] But I say unto you . . . whosoever shall smite thee on thy

_____ , turn to him the other also.
(part of the face #3)

[4] Love your enemies, _____ them that
(verb denoting charitable activity)

_____ you; if a man gives you
(verb denoting criminal activity)

_____ , give him a _____ .
(sexual disease)   (sexual act)

[5] Ye have heard that it hath been said, _____ .
(piece of common-sense advice)

But I say unto you, _____ .
(advice that will get you beaten up)

[6] For verily I say unto you, _____ .
(something you would have said if you were Jesus)

GODLIB #4 (THE KORAN)

¹ In the name of Allah, the _____ .
(as-yet unclaimed superhero title)

² For the righteous that fear the Day of Judgment, there will be

_____ to eat, and _____ to drink,
(your favorite food)   (your favorite beverage)

and _____ to sit upon, interwoven with
(your favorite furniture)

_____ .
(your favorite precious stone(s) that was/were
popular in 7th century Saudi Arabia)

³ And round about them will be _____ maidens.
(your favorite euphemism for virgin)

⁴ As for those who disbelieve, for them will be cut out a garment

of _____ ; over their heads will be poured
(something unpleasant to wear)

out _____ .
(something unpleasant to have
poured on your head)

⁵ Whereby that which is in their _____ , and
(major part of the body)

their _____ , will be _____ .
(major part of the body #2)   (something you wouldn't want to happen
to any major part of your body)

⁶ And in addition there will be _____ .
(another extremely unpleasant thing)

PLEADER

("On Prayer")

CHAPTER 1

¹ Imagine being in fourth grade; the bell for homeroom rings, thou takest thy seat, and suddenly a deafening voice booms from the PA system:

² *"Good morning, students. I am the Lord thy God, King of the Universe. Here are the announcements.*

³ *Starting today, I will no longer be accepting any prayers addressed to me from this public school.*

⁴ *The Supreme Court hath ruled such prayers violate the First Amendment's establishment clause; and their ruling applies to not only thee, but me.*

⁵ *Please refrain from addressing or thinking of me at any time while on school grounds.*

⁶ *Also, the chess club will be meeting in Mrs. Binder's classroom during sixth period.*

⁷ *Siiiiiixth peeeeeriod!"*; followed by thunder and lightning effects, and hundreds of plastic spiders falling from the ceiling.

⁸ Ah . . . one of these days I shall go to an elementary school and do that; it will surely be one of that week's mirthfullest home videos.

⁹ I can afford to take the banning of school prayer lightly; it is not as if I need another venue wherein to hear thy supplications.

¹⁰ For thine is the Golden Age of Prayer; never before have I received so many pleas, from so many people, for so many reasons, accompanied by so many helpful suggestions.

¹¹ Do I answer them? I shall get to that.

¹² But first, let me provide an overview of prayer, for its very definition is a matter of debate; it is a vague concept whose domain overlaps with those of ritual, and meditation, and panhandling.

¹³ My own definition, is that prayer is any consciously thought-out statement—spoken or silent—that is addressed to me, and underpinned by the fundamental belief that I take requests.

¹⁴ I know the many functions prayer fulfills for thee: catharsis, comfort, enlightenment; not to mention that praying has always been, and will always be, the perfect thing to do when there is nothing else to be done.

¹⁵ But to be frank, for me prayer provideth neither catharsis, nor comfort, nor enlightenment.

¹⁶ For me, prayer is like unto a suggestion box that receives 200,000 suggestions a second.

¹⁷ Or an emergency services switchboard manned by one operator who gets 12 million calls a minute.

¹⁸ Or a sheaf of "Did you enjoy your dining experience today?" tear cards filled out hourly by 700 million Wendy's customers.

¹⁹ Or a large chariot bearing a rearward-facing sign that reads, "How is my driving? Dial 1-800-JEHOVAH"; only the chariot has broken down, and cannot be moved until the next day, and blocketh the path of 16 billion other chariots; each of whose drivers have a cell phone, and nothing better to do.

²⁰ As for what these prayers sound like en masse, from where I am sitting I would describe the noise as not unlike that of the cosmic background radiation astrophysicists have detected emanating from every corner of the universe.

²¹ Alas, sound is the only perception needed to apprehend a prayer these days; a change from Old Testament days, when group prayer was also accompanied by the sight of slaughter, and the smell of burning fat, and the taste of sizzling calves, and every desperate plea was a feast for the senses.

²² I do not mean to sound arch; I do not regard the human phenomenon of prayer cynically; I am merely trying to describe what it feels like to be incessantly nagged, pestered, and reminded of things I already knew.

²³ (That is a puzzling and mirthful quirk of mankind's prayers: the way they are used to notify me of recent developments in the lives of thou and thine.

²⁴ It is one thing to ask, "Please take care of Bobby in his time of need"; that is an expression of a well-meaning wish.

²⁵ But it is another entirely to say, "Please take care of Bobby in his time of need; he just broke his leg skiing, and the karate meet is in three weeks and he's been training so hard . . ."

²⁶ Heed me: I am the LORD thy God, King of the Universe: I *know* Bobby broke his leg skiing, and I *know* about the damned karate meet.)

CHAPTER 2

¹ So: do I answer thy prayers?

² I shall address that soon enough; but first let me mention a few that I hear frequently.

³ The most popular prayer by far is the Hail Mary, which I have now heard over 3.2 trillion times.

⁴ Not surprisingly, 482.5 billion of these were offered as penitence for masturbation.

⁵ More surprisingly, 4.5 million of these devolved halfway through into new acts of masturbation centered on the Virgin Mary.

⁶ The Hail Mary is a good prayer; a solid prayer; a safe prayer; and asking Mary to ask me for help rather than asking directly is a smart move.

⁷ But I am less fond of the LORD's Prayer, which is a flat-out cut-and-paste of Matthew 6:9–13.

⁸ It works very well coming from Jesus's lips during the Sermon on the Mount, but from mortals it comes off pushy.

⁹ "Give us this day our daily bread"? "Forgive us our debts"? "Lead us not into temptation"? "Deliver us from evil"?

¹⁰ Dost thou know me as one who responds well to threats?

¹¹ (Still, at least it is not as presumptuous as the American custom of ending every swearing-in ceremony, from the president on down, with "So help me God."

¹² Not "Let me be worthy of thy help, God"; not "So *please* help me, God"; no, my immediate assistance is *demanded*.

¹³ Every day billions of people humbly petition my aid, but I am supposed to put them all on the back burner because it is the Omaha city treasurer's first day on the job and she needs me there on standby?)

¹⁴ Judaism's most famous prayer is Sh'ma Yisrael: "Hear, O Israel; the LORD our God, the LORD is one."

¹⁵ Not the most *specific* prayer I've ever heard.

¹⁶ It is the same with Muslims; their most common prayer is, "There is no god but God, and Muhammad is his messenger"; which is not even a request, but a tautology followed by a fact.

¹⁷ They may as well get on their knees and chant, "There is no country in Australia but Australia, and Canberra is its capital."

¹⁸ By far my favorite of the templates is the Serenity Prayer.

¹⁹ The serenity to accept what cannot be changed; the courage to change what can; and the wisdom to know the difference—these are wise life principles that should be known and followed by *everyone*, not just those too gutless to handle their liquor.

²⁰ As for my least favorite, that would be the old childhood lullaby: "Now I lay me down to sleep. I pray thee, LORD my soul to keep. And if I die before I wake, I pray thee, LORD, my soul to take."

²¹ Now, I am no softie; I am not one who "loves kids"; my record with young people will not win me many Godfather of the Year awards.

²² But even I consider it bizarre, that the last words on children's lips before they go to sleep would address the prospect of their own premature death.

²³ They are *children.*

²⁴ They should be asking me for *ponies.*

²⁵ In fact, if there are any children reading this, I make unto them this deal: the next one of you who asks for a pony instead of for me to take his or her soul,

²⁶ Gets the pony.

CHAPTER 3

1 So, I know what thou art thinking: Do I answer thy prayers?

2 I will get to that.

3 But first, some statistics; for I am a bit of a sabermetrician when it comes to praying;

4 And though statistics may seem a coldly numerical way to analyze the desires of the human soul, they can offer a broader, more "fan's-eye" view of the activity than one gets when one is thyself "at the plate" of abject supplication.

5 For example: prior to 2001, the year with the highest daily prayer-per-believer (PPB) rate was 1349, which finished at 2.458: this great harvest being the sweet fruits of the Black Death.

6 Yet this figure has been exceeded in no fewer than six of the past ten years, reaching an all-time high in 2010 of 2.475 PPB; with that number rising still further to 2.488 on Sundays, and 2.501 on Sundays during football season.

7 Among monotheists, the highest PPB can be found among Muslims, with 5.000; that number has held steady for some time.

8 Among Christians, the highest PPB (2.871) can be found among Catholics, the lowest (0.921) among Methodists; unless one includes Unitarians (0.573), which I do not, and neither does Jesus.

9 The overall average among Jews is a very efficient 0.856; indeed, among reform Jews that number drops to an astounding −0.003;

10 Which means I am actually very slightly more likely to ask *them* for something.

11 Daily PCE (prayer caloric expenditure) levels also vary widely, from 145.2 among Southern Baptists to 2.5 within the Wisconsin Evangelical Lutheran Synod.

12 (Tallying a respectable 87.4 PCE: Hasidic Jews.

¹³ Who knew? All that shuckling really pays dividends around the waist and thighs!)

¹⁴ The average VMG (value of material goods) for 2010 was $843.25; almost identical to the figure from a millennium ago, when adjusted for inflation.

¹⁵ Here is a number that may surprise thee: only 45.2 percent of the families that pray together actually stay together.

¹⁶ This compares to a 44.8 percent staying-together rate among non-praying families; a difference that though slight, is, on a scale as massive as this, statistically significant;

¹⁷ But still pretty slight.

¹⁸ Yea, I could ramble on and on about prayer stats, but most likely even this brief discussion has already grown tedious and a little too "inside baseball" for most of you.

¹⁹ If anyone wants to learn more, send me $4.99 and I will give thee a 10-pack of prayer cards.

²⁰ Each card has an exciting action picture of the prayer in front, and on the back, statistics for every year they've been praying; plus, all packs come with a string of chewable rosary beadgum.

²¹ Collect all five billion!

CHAPTER 4

 ¹ o: do I answer thy prayers?

² I will now answer that question, in two ways.

³ The first way is by assuring my flock that every single prayer of thine is *processed.*

⁴ As an example: let us say that tonight thou wert to offer up a prayer; for argument's sake, let us call it, "O LORD we just got this puppy three months ago, and the kids love her, and it's going to break their heart if it dies from this stomach thing the vet's saying she has now, so please give her a break and let her poop it out or something. Amen."

⁵ Within a trillionth of a second of its utterance, that prayer—not only its words, but its emotions, context, and complete spiritual gestalt—is sitting in the inbox of one of my hard-working undercherubs in the Department of Entreaty.

⁶ Then, within five to seven business days, it is fed into a device whose fathomless complexity would dwarf mankind's power to comprehend it.

⁷ To conceive of its like in thy three-dimensional universe is impossible; so I will simply call it the celestial equivalent, of what thy limited imaginations might most accurately envision, as a Dell Inspiron 580 Desktop.

⁸ (I cannot stress enough, that the actual machine *looks nothing like a Dell Inspiron 580 Desktop*; indeed it is invisible and transmaterial.

⁹ As I said, my analogy is merely a rhetorical device, made so that thou mayest fully grasp the salient point:

¹⁰ Our new iPads haven't arrived yet.)

¹¹ This machine then quantitatively analyzes the prayer using no less than 143 different metrics; not just the obvious ones, like PPB, PCE, and VMG, but others, such as selflessness, eloquence, and ROOI (recognition of own insignificance).

¹² The results are then plotted on a 143-dimensional chart; and each of these charts is folded into millions of other composite charts profiling specific demographics: evangelicals, for instance, or male thirtysomething suburban beseechers, or those who refused to give money to homeless people within the past six months.

¹³ And this ever-fluctuating matrix of data is then broken down by a team of quantitative angelysts; who prepare a daily report based on their findings, seeking therein patterns, and trends, and numerical significance; and this report then, and *only* then, finds its way to my desk;

¹⁴ Where I immediately get around to skimming it over.

CHAPTER 5

¹ ine; but do I *answer* thy prayers?

² Let me address that question the Jesus way: with a parable.

³ Every year, the president of the United States receiveth over ten million letters.

⁴ It is the full-time vocation of a small army of decreasingly idealistic apparatchiks to read and reply to these letters.

⁵ Some of these replies are to the effect of, "The president appreciates thy support."

⁶ And some are to the effect of, "The president appreciates thy concern."

⁷ And some are forwarded to the Secret Service for further investigation.

⁸ But each is duly answered on White House letterhead; and though each recipient knows in his heart his epistle never made it within eight security-clearance levels of the president, he is still somehow grateful to hear even a distant echo of his childhood belief that those in charge heed the will of the people.

⁹ But once in a great while, a letter will come across a flunky's desk that happens to fold in perfectly with a policy item the president was already seeking to advance.

¹⁰ And through the usual bureaucratic mixture of accident and self-interest, that one letter will make its way to the Oval Office.

¹¹ The letter is genuine, but reads as though custom-written by the president to fulfill his purpose; for so numerous is the correspondence he receives that it is inevitable he receives one such letter; usually dozens, but he only needs the one.

¹² And so phone calls are made; flights booked; hotel reservations secured;

¹³ And now it is the night of the State of the Union address; the president is speaking; he is laying out a broad vision of something; the language is grand but general;

[14] Until, at a certain critical moment in the speech, he changes tone.

[15] "This week, I received a letter from Mrs. Stephanie Henderson of Enid, Oklahoma.

[16] She is a hard-working American; a single mom who pays her taxes and plays by the rules; and she devotes her life to her three kids.

[17] Last month, Stephanie was laid off from her job at the lumber mill.

[18] Now, the good news is, a new mill is opening across town on June 1, and they're hiring.

[19] The bad news is, Stephanie's unemployment benefits run out at the end of April.

[20] Stephanie wrote, and I quote: 'Mr. President, I can't tell you how much passage of the Omnibus Extend Unemployment Benefits Through the Month of May Act would mean for my three kids.

[21] It would make all the difference between them living out the American dream, and drawing straws to see which one gets eaten by the other two.'

[22] Well, Stephanie is here with us tonight, and Steph, I am pleased to say that tomorrow, because of you, Congress is going to pass the OEUBT-MMA—or as I like to call it, 'The Stephanie Henderson Act'!

[23] Stand up, Stephanie!"

[24] And Stephanie bashfully stands, and waves, and basks in the applause of the nation's lawmakers; for her it is, indeed, a dream come true; more than she ever imagined would happen that awful day two months ago when she was laid off, got drunk, went home, watched *Ellen*, screamed the kids down for dinner, wrote her first letter in over 15 years while ducking airborne Spaghetti-O's, and drove drunk to the mailbox.

[25] For *her*, a prayer has been answered.

[26] I will leave it to thee to discern the relevance of this anecdote to the rest of this section.

[27] In the meantime, I offer my own simple prayer to the Men (and Women) Downstairs:

²⁸ Humanity, I pray that you find it in your hearts to purchase many copies of this book;

²⁹ Because that is a thing that I want.

³⁰ Amen.

EFFUSIONS

("On My Favorite Things")

CHAPTER 1

1 avorite ice cream: butter pecan.

2 Favorite color: infra-red.

3 Favorite drink: Grey Goose extra-spicy Bloody Mary.

4 (I mean that not mirthfully; I love a good Bloody Mary; it is what primordial soup would have tasted like, had it existed.)

5 Favorite animal: dog.

6 Full credit to humanity on this one; it was ingenious of you to breed so many different varieties.

7 For though I did make them as companions, at the time of Noah there were only two kinds: cocker spaniels (like Sparky and Pillow); and sphinxhounds, which had the heads of dogs but the bodies of lions, and were 65 feet high.

8 That thou wert able, in but six generations, to breed them down to Chihuahuas speaks volumes to thy talents in animal husbandry.

9 Favorite flowers: daffodils and lilacs.

10 (Yea, I am confident enough in my Godhood to say that.)

11 Favorite plant: Venus flytrap. 50 billion insects have died in them, and not a *single one* saw it coming.

12 Favorite continent: Antarctica; and evidently it is thine also, as thou keepest importing more and more of it to thy shores.

13 Favorite monster: Godzilla.

14 Favorite rocket scientist: Goddard.

15 Favorite mathematician: Gödel.

16 Favorite former name of the capital of Greenland: Godthåb.

17 Favorite method of sending packages: Guaranteed Overnight Delivery.

18 Favorite domain registrar: Go Daddy.

CHAPTER 2

1 avorite universal law: the third law of thermodynamics.

2 Favorite subatomic particle: any flavor lepton tastes fine by me.

3 Favorite element: helium, because I love balloons, and because it makes thy voices sound so funny.

4 (Not a great blimp gas, though.)

5 Favorite number: 667, just to one-up the devil.

6 Favorite war: the War of Spanish Succession. A great, great war in every respect.

7 Favorite monument: the Colossus of Rhodes.

8 That thing scared me a little.

9 It was a massive depiction of the Greek sun god Helios, in truth nothing but an overgrown idol; yet there was something in its mien and bearing that gaveth unto me the willies.

10 I tried to ignore it; I tried to pretend it did not vex me; but whenever business took me to Rhodes I felt its icy leer.

11 After 56 years I could take it no longer; so I sent an earthquake to knock it down.

12 I felt better after that.

13 Favorite monarch: Queen Victoria. Stature, majesty, and wisdom. And lo, could she fellate a penis!

14 Favorite pizza topping: mushrooms.

15 Favorite chemical compound: water.

16 (True story about water: for a while I thought about switching it up and turning it all into HO_2, which is a far more attractive-looking molecule.

17 But as it happens, HO_2 is the hydroperoxyl radical responsible for the destruction of ozone in the atmosphere; so for now the plan is on hold.

[18] Still, one of these days I might try it.

[19] If I do, let me know what happens.)

[20] Favorite language: to paraphrase Nabokov, my heart speaks Hebrew, my ear speaks Latin, and my head speaks angry Elizabethan English amped with reverb.

[21] Favorite planet: OGLE2-TR-L9 b.

[22] Favorite planet in thy solar system: Saturn.

[23] Favorite terrestrial planet in thy solar system: tie: Mercury and Mars.

CHAPTER 3

[1] avorite book (ancient): *The Odyssey.* Those gods got to do so many awesome things—and they never even existed! Ah, myth is wasted on the mythic.

[2] Favorite book (medieval): *The Da Vinci Code.*

[3] I am referring, of course, to the *original* book of that name, written in 1502 by Leonardo da Vinci.

[4] It was the original self-help book, wherein the great master sought to aid readers by sharing with them the simple five-step "code" by which he lived, and that had made him so successful.

[5] It is long out of print now, and not a single copy has survived . . . or so scholars think.

[6] (Word to the wise: point an X-ray spectrofluorometer at the right-hand side of the table in *The Last Supper.*)

[7] Favorite book (modern): *Gravity's Rainbow* by Thomas Pynchon.

[8] Lo, I just finished reading it a year ago, and I think I'm starting to get it.

[9] Favorite director: Alfred Hitchcock. His movies always keep me in suspense, which is not easy.

[10] Favorite painting: *The Creation of Adam.*

¹¹ Second-favorite painting: *Campbell's Soup Cans,* by Andy Warhol. So much soup!

¹² Favorite artist: Jackson Pollock, because I am in on the dirty little secret of his success: he was not an abstract expressionist.

¹³ Jackson Pollock was trying to paint landscapes the whole time.

¹⁴ He was a terrible, terrible painter.

¹⁵ Favorite music: these days I listen to goodly quantities of nondenominational middle-of-the-road pop; but I like all kinds of "good vibrations" in any frequency, from radio waves to gamma rays.

¹⁶ Favorite band: the Beatles. End of discussion.

¹⁷ Favorite rapper: Young Jeezy; for if my son was in hip-hop, that would be his name.

¹⁸ Favorite folk music: none; the folk music of all nations and peoples throughout all time is equally unlistenable.

¹⁹ Favorite hymn: "A Mighty Fortress Is Our God."

²⁰ Yea. Yea, I am.

KORANICLES

¹ ow shall I reveal to thee the history of my dealings with the prophet Muhammad; and of the revelation to him of the holy book, the Koran; and of the founding of my third great religion, Islam.

² So . . . Islam.

³ Islam, Islam, Islam.

⁴ Didst thou know it hath over one-and-a-half billion adherents?

⁵ Verily; it hath.

⁶ And didst thou know it is divided into two main branches: the Sunni and the Shi'a?

⁷ *[Pause; thumb-twiddleth.]*

⁸ I must tell thee in all candor, that I have felt great apprehension concerning the writing of this section.

⁹ I am Allah, the Wise, the All-Powerful; yet these days even *I* get a little nervous talking about Islam.

¹⁰ Lo: sometimes I shall be up in heaven, and looking down on earth I shall in passing remark upon a particularly beautiful mosque, or worthy imam;

¹¹ Whereupon the Hebrew patriarchs and Christian martyrs gathered around me begin to gaze at each other uncomfortably;

¹² At which point the righteous Muslims nearby picketh up on the vibe;

¹³ Until someone, usually the apostle James, will pretend to cough, and in so doing say "Al-Qaeda!"

¹⁴ And a Muslim will thunder, "Why didst thou say al-Qaeda?"; and James will say no, he said "Ore-Ida!", as in the brand of frozen potatoes; which in context maketh absolutely no sense;

¹⁵ And the mood grows angrier, until I am forced to restore order by calling in the Heavenly Choir to soothe everyone's spirits with their unique blend of nondenominational middle-of-the-road pop.

16 So let me begin by telling thee what thou wilt *not* find here in *Koranicles*, or, indeed, anywhere else in this book.

17 Thou shalt not find any "Satanic verses" anywhere in this book.

18 Thou shalt not find any anti-Muslim propaganda anywhere in this book.

19 Thou shalt not find any pork products anywhere in this book.

20 And above all, *thou shalt not find any Danish cartoons of the prophet Muhammad anywhere in this book.*

21 I cannot stress this point enough.

22 Indeed, thou wilt not find any visual representations of Muhammad in this book, period.

23 No cartoons; no paintings; no drawings, etchings, lithographs, photographs, daguerreotypes, clip art, shadow puppets; nothing.

24 The closest thou wilt come is on the twelfth page of the center insert; but that is purely by way of verbal merriment, not visual heresy.

25 Having said all this, I must nonetheless now fulfill a promise I made unto the publishing house issuing forth these pages:

26 "I, God, do hereby indemnify Simon & Schuster from any and all outrage, fatwa, or all-out jihad that may result from the contents of the portions of this book pertaining to Islam.

27 And I further indemnify them from any anger on the part of members of *any* religion with regard to *any* of the contents of this book.

28 I am Jehovah; I am God the Father; I am Allah; and I am solely responsible for the eternal truths contained in these pages."

29 (And though thou art free to pursue the earthly remedy of suing me for libel, I would *really* like to see one of you try to serve me that subpoena.)

SURA 2

¹ In any case, there is relatively little to say about Islam; for its holy book contains almost no new narrative, and its origins are far easier to recount than those of my other two faiths.

² By the beginning of the 7th century, Christianity was fully ascendant; yet in that religion, much of the praise and glory and majesty is offered to Jesus.

³ I had come to feel like I stood in my son's shadow; as if I were now second-best in my own universe;

⁴ And thou knowest me: I am one jealous divinity.

⁵ Now, let me state this as plainly as I can: I begrudge my son *absolutely none* of his success.

⁶ That boy hath earned every Pietà and windshield bobble-head he ever got.

⁷ So rather than hijacking Jesus's religion, I decided to found a new one: one in which there would be no doubt who the boss was, and not befall upon me the same dilemma that 70 generations later would befall Tony Danza.

⁸ I spent a good deal of time mulling over which world culture would most ably serve as the ethnic foundation for this new faith.

⁹ The close runners-up were the Mayans; I simply cannot get enough of their passion.

¹⁰ But in the end I went with the Arabians, for they were the pagans most ready to accept the one true God;

¹¹ And also I knew something they knew not, regarding a certain black substance buried in massive quantities beneath their endless sands;

¹² And I thought that, when this substance was discovered, if the people atop the land worshipped the same God as Christians and Jews, it could be allocated peacefully and without rancor amongst all my believers.

¹³ (I will say it again: *I am not perfect.*)

¹⁴ And so once more I sent my advance team out in search of a worthy prophet, for this time I wanted my word spread by an actual human being; not only to retain my centrality, but because after the last time out I received numerous complaints about nepotism.

¹⁵ We very quickly settled upon the right candidate, a hard-working, God-fearing, patriotic leader:

¹⁶ Muhammad: a true Allah-Meccan boy.

¹⁷ Muhammad was not just a Prophet, but *The* Prophet; easily the best one I ever worked with.

¹⁸ Charming, wise, astute, charismatic, judicious, well-spoken—the man was everything thou wouldst want in the founder of a major world religion.

¹⁹ The only problem with him was that he came from Mecca; which though today is synonymous with a haven, bore in his time a reputation similar to that, among modern Americans, of Peoria.

²⁰ Lo, it was common to hear a Bedouin merchant say, "Yea, this caravan of silk and spikenard may prove popular in the cosmopolitan trading ports of Yemen; but will it play in Mecca?"

²¹ Nonetheless I sent the angel Gabriel to him one night in the cave where he was wont to meditate, to tell him I desired him as my prophet;

²² But at dawn Muhammad ran away, hesitant to embrace his new role.

²³ At first this did not surprise me; I knew from long experience that resistance was the typical first reaction of those called to prophecy.

²⁴ (For there are five classic stages of being called to prophecy: resistance, anger, paranoid schizophrenia, being swallowed by a whale, and acceptance.)

SURA 3

1 et three years in, Muhammad was still showing reluctance, and a reluctant prophet is of little use to me; he is like unto a motivational speaker who intersperses his pep talks with phrases like "I guess" and "or not."

2 Finally I sent Gabriel back to visit him at his cave; this time more casually attired, and wingless.

3 They conversed for a while of lighter matters; of family, and trade, and politics; specifically the Sassanid Empire, and the no-good crumbums who ruled it.

4 Finally Muhammad came to the point: "Gabriel, it is humbling that Allah has chosen me to share his message with the people; but I beg thee to ask him to find some other messenger;

5 One who is more pleasing to the eye; one not so . . . hideously deformed . . . so grotesquely repulsive . . . so revolting to gaze upon!"

6 Whereupon Gabriel looked at Muhammad, and saw he was handsome, well-proportioned, and of attractive features; so he said, "Muhammad, I know not of what thou speak."

7 "Do not mock me!" replied Muhammad. "Dost thou not see the horrible, disgusting blemish rendering my appearance like unto that of a Pachydermous Man?"

8 And he pointed to the right side of his chin, on which lay a small discoloration: a birthmark, perhaps one square inch in size, with two tiny curled hairs growing therefrom.

9 It was nothing. Absolutely nothing.

10 *Bubkes.*

11 "Muhammad," said Gabriel, "that is naught but a small birthmark; it is utterly unnoticeable, except from very close distance; I do not even see it."

12 "*Because thou art an angel!*" screamed Muhammad, concealing his face in anguish; "Thou canst look past such superficialities into the true essence of things.

¹³ But I cannot put myself before fellow human beings as Allah's rightful messenger with this, this . . . ugly, wretched, grotesque *nightmare* of a deformity that would leave onlookers groaning in horror and *shrieking* in revulsion . . ."

¹⁴ And on and on he went, having somehow convinced himself that this tiny mark was a colossal monstrosity.

¹⁵ But Gabriel, being a patient sort, reasoned with him; for two hours he wrestled with the Prophet's body dysmorphia issues;

¹⁶ Until finally Muhammad relented, and said, "I can contend with thee no longer; thou art Gabriel, the archangel of Allah, and I must obey thy commands.

¹⁷ But I ask thee this boon: from now unto eternity, however many may speak of me, however many may revere me, however many people may come to know the glory of Allah through the teachings I will transmit;

¹⁸ No pictures.

¹⁹ I'm serious.

²⁰ *No . . . pictures.*"

²¹ And Gabriel sighed and said, "Fine."

SURA 4

¹ o Muhammad began preaching my truth, and the news of his teachings quickly flourished; like a thriving Twitter account did it blossom, and its words of wisdom were soon RT'd throughout Mecca; and these teachings became the Koran.

² Now, in the six centuries since my son's non-death, I had tried my blessedest to take a more selfless, compassionate approach to godding; but verily, I found it difficult.

³ So I deliberately chose to write the Koran in a distinctly old school/ Testament voice.

⁴ Over-the-top praise; under-the-bottom condemnation; visions of paradise; angry propaganda; the constant threat of dreadful punishments for nonbelievers . . .

⁵ It was like the Torah in a turban.

⁶ More than any other piece of literature ever written, the Koran is a book people have either really, really read, or really, really not.

⁷ If thou art in the former group, then thou knowest its three main, and more or less only, themes:

⁸ 1. I am awesome.

⁹ 2. Agree? Good.

¹⁰ 3. Disagree? Not so good.

¹¹ But if thou art in the latter group, I will do no more here than encourage thee to read it.

¹² I say this despite the linguistic challenge thereby posed; for though the Koran has been translated into nearly every human language, it loses many subtleties of meaning when not read and recited in the original Arabic.

¹³ For example, in Arabic, the 35th *ayat* of the 24th *sura*, "Al-Nur," provides this mystical vision of Allah:

¹⁴ "The parable of his light is as if there were a niche and within it a lamp; the lamp enclosed in glass; the glass as it were a brilliant star."

¹⁵ That is the literal meaning; yet in the most common English translation, that same *ayat* reads as follows:

¹⁶ "We will burn thy churches, and subvert thy way of life, and replace all thy mayo with tahini."

¹⁷ Thou canst see the loss of nuance.

¹⁸ Yet still I would encourage all non-Muslims seeking better relations with Islam to read the Koran.

19 And at the very least, I would encourage all non-Muslims who seek better relations with Islam *not* to flush the Koran down the toilet in front of Muslim detainees at Gitmo.

20 For within the sphere of interfaith tolerance, the difference between having read the Koran and not having read the Koran, is smaller than that between not having read the Koran and flushing it down the toilet in front of Muslim detainees at Gitmo.

21 I guess what I am saying is: if thou findest thyself holding a Koran for the first time, and are contemplating whether to a) read it, or b) flush it down the toilet in front of Muslim detainees at Gitmo,

22 Go with a).

SURA 5

1 In 622 A.D. Muhammad and his followers fled Mecca for Medina, marking the beginning of the Muslim calendar.

2 (I must note here how much it confounds me that my three great faiths have three different calendars; making the year of this book's publication 5771 to Jews, 2011 to Christians, and 1432 to Muslims.

3 Yea, I know the Muslim calendar is lunar; and the Christian, solar; and the Jewish, lunisolar, which covers both bases; typically shrewd.

4 But I am not partial when it comes to chronology; of no consequence to me whatever are the numbers inscribed upon thy checks; for though I work in time, I dwell in Eternity.

5 If I wert thou—which I am *not*, thank me—I would synchronize my calendars, that you may all literally be on the same page;

6 Choosing a day agreed upon by everyone as having no religious import whatsoever, and calling it the first day of Year One, and then celebrating Rosh Hashanah and New Year's Day and Al-Hijra every year on the same day.

7 And throw in the Chinese New Year, too, while thou art at it; they can start on any animal they like.)

⁸ By the time Muhammad died ten years later, he had fought many battles; gained many converts; shown great wisdom; and, after becoming a widower, acquired 12 more wives.

⁹ Some of these marriages were political; some provided compassionate support for widows; the final one was so that he might purchase household goods at the bulk rate, for they were cheaper by the dozen.

¹⁰ But none was more blessed than his marriage to Aisha; his favorite wife; the "Mother of the Believers"; the one in whose company he received the most revelations; the one he married when she was six; the one whose father became the first caliph of the Sunnis.

¹¹ Anyway, these were the—what?

¹² Oh, I said her father became the first caliph of the Sunnis.

¹³ Anyway, those were the—

¹⁴ What? Before that?

¹⁵ Oh . . . I said that Muhammad married Aisha when she was six.

¹⁶ Did they *what?!* No!

¹⁷ That is disgusting!

¹⁸ Verily, that betrays thy ignorance.

¹⁹ No; they waited until she was nine. Now, if I can—

²⁰ What dost thou mean, "pedophilia"? There was nothing improper!

²¹ This was standard Bedouin practice at the time; so spare me thy culturally unrelative indignation; it was all completely aboveboard.

²² Besides, trust me: she looked more like eleven.

SURA 6

1 Islam's success was immediate and immense; but I am proudest not of its popularity, but of its practices and tenets.

2 This is not to say Islam is more correct than other religions; it is simply to say I like the way it does business.

³ For Christianity is like unto Walmart: an unstoppable behemoth that will do whatever it takes to gain a foothold, offering its patrons mass salvation at a low price, and staffed with employees who only *appear* celibate.

⁴ And Judaism is like unto Blockbuster Video: a creaky old institution evoking a bygone era; one can scarcely believe it still survives, and when one is forced to use its services one feels self-conscious, and unsure if one is doing so ironically or not.

⁵ But Islam is like unto Starbucks: straightforward and unchanging; its menu but a few variations on a single theme; an institution to which throngs of people devote much of their lives.

⁶ The faith's genius can be found in its mission statement, the Five Pillars of Islam.

⁷ Its first pillar is its creed: "There is no god but Allah, and Muhammad is his messenger"; as catchy a slogan as thou wilt ever hear.

⁸ And the second pillar is prayer: showing obeisance to the CEO five times a day while facing corporate headquarters; a clear directive which yields 7.5 billion adorations every 24 hours; very impressive numbers.

⁹ And the third pillar is fasting: Muslims must fast from dawn to dusk throughout the month of Ramadan; team-building at its best.

¹⁰ And the fourth pillar is almsgiving: all Muslims are required to spend 2.5 percent of their income for the benefit of the poor or needy; I defy thee to find a lower corporate tax rate anywhere; 2.5 percent makes Delaware seem like a socialist state.

¹¹ And the final pillar is the greatest of all, the *hajj*: all Muslims must make a pilgrimage to Mecca once in their lives; surely, the ultimate corporate retreat.

¹² Grueling? Yea. Sweaty? Yea. Filled with odd rites and awkward encounters with people one would rather not be rubbing up against? Thou bettest.

¹³ Yet everyone is there for the same purpose; and has been sent by the same boss, as transmitted through the same assistant; and everyone wears the same clothes, so no one feels silly;

¹⁴ And when it is over, everyone leaves feeling newfound appreciation for this 1.5-billion-person organization that despite all its success, still manages to stay true to its small-town roots;

¹⁵ And all while limiting the annual trampling deaths to no more than a few hundred.

SURA 7

 ¹ have briefly related the story of Islam, and seem to have gotten through it in one piece; and if it is all the same to thee I am going to stop now, before I write something that makes someone declare holy war on me in my own name.

² I will just add one final word, on a subject of much speculation in religious circles: the posthumous fate of Osama bin Laden, and the 9/11 hijackers.

³ Many believe them to be burning in eternal anguish in the lowest level of hell; but some fundamentalist die-hards (or verily, die-easies) believe they are relaxing in heaven in the company of me and 72 virgins.

⁴ Believe what thou wilt; I have sworn to reveal no details of the hows and whys and wheres of the afterlife.

⁵ I mention it only because there is one aspect of it that, at least from thy viewpoint, has always struck me as curious:

⁶ That being the lure of the 72 virgins, and the implication that *that* is the greatest reward I could possibly bestow upon a martyr.

⁷ For lo, 72 virgins is a *lot* of virgins.

⁸ If *I* were a mortal, heterosexual man, and 72 women awaited me in heaven, then yea, I would want some of them to be virgins; definitely.

⁹ But at least a few dozen, I would prefer to have some experience.

¹⁰ In fact, if it were me, I would want at least six or so total harlots.

¹¹ And maybe a couple of professionals.

¹² Not only would this greatly increase my short-term personal satisfaction, but it would also help break in the newbies.

¹³ Anyway, that is merely my opinion; I have learned there is no accounting for taste, especially when it comes to paradise;

¹⁴ And as it happens, none of this makes any difference with regard to the 9/11 hijackers;

¹⁵ All of whom are burning in eternal anguish in the lowest level of hell.

¹⁶ (Oops!)

HINDUS

("... and Other Heathens")

CHAPTER 1

 1 slam and Christianity are the world's two biggest faiths; and both, I am pleased to report, are crazy about me.

2 That leaves Hinduism, with its one billion adherents, as the world's largest totally wrong religion.

3 I do not think I am disobeying my embargo on classified afterlife information to reveal, that all Hindus will be joining Osama bin Laden and the rest of the 9/11 hijackers in hell.

4 But having said that, I concede there is much to admire in this vibrant heresy, starting with its caste system: as sensible a way to keep a civilization in lasagna-like order as I have ever seen.

5 I am a big believer in stratification, as may be seen in earth's beautifully layered rock formations; thy infidel scientists attribute them to sedimentary deposits made over eons; wrong!; it is not a geological process, it is a design motif.

6 Strata are good not only for societies, but for each individual therein; for the man who knoweth not his place on the earth wanders it forever, but the man who knoweth his place can at least start fixing it up to make it look nice.

7 Gays who proclaim "We were born this way!" are cheered, yet Brahmins who say the same thing are hooted; when in fact sexual orientation and social caste are *both* genetically encoded from birth.

8 I also approve of yoga—not its New Age accoutrements; not the touchy-feelie instructors; not the Enya soundtrack; not the appalling western mutants like yogilates and yogaerobics and triyogathons; but yoga itself.

9 I like to see thee stretch thy bodies; to bend and twist and contort the wondrous flesh I bequeathed thee into positions imaginative and limber.

10 Lo, I mean not to sound creepy or anything.

11 As for reincarnation, I have mixed feelings about that doctrine; not regarding its truth, of course, for it has none, but its spiritual effect on its believers.

¹² I see the appeal of a system of posthumous trans-species promotion and demotion; it turns life into a job, and death into a performance review, and both of these are bound to improve professionalism.

¹³ But to look at every living creature as a potential former friend? To walk on the grass and be afraid thou hast trodden upon thy late uncle? To be served ratatouille, and wonder how many of thy own ancestors are vegetables therein?

¹⁴ (On the subject of vegetarianism, it is *ridiculous* for Hindus to hold cows sacred.

¹⁵ If I had meant for cows to be sacred, I would not have made them out of delicious, delicious beef.)

¹⁶ Finally, karma; the notion of true cosmic justice.

¹⁷ It is the same policy Abraham pushed me to adopt lo those thousands of years ago, and my reply now is the same as it was then: no; I prefer to move in mysterious ways.

¹⁸ I move in mysterious ways; and my reason for doing so is even more mysterious; and the reason for that reason's mysteriousness is so mysterious, even I forget what it is.

¹⁹ But as the Unseen Force doling out providence, I can tell thee this: to the extent there is anything resembling karma operating on earth, it is *not* a boomerang.

²⁰ Karma is a bullet.

²¹ And if another bullet comes back and hits thee, it means thy aim was off.

CHAPTER 2

¹ Hinduism may have its merits, but Buddhism I hate with every fiber of my being.

² I hate the Buddha; I hate Buddhist monks; I hate Tibetan bells; and I hate each and every one of their 31 planes of existence—a veritable Baskin-Robbins of nonsense.

³ Heed me: I am a doer. Moses was a doer. Jesus was a doer. Muhammad was a doer.

⁴ Life is for doers.

⁵ Be-ers are good for drinking during football, but not for living.

⁶ Seeing life as an illusion, desiring escape from worldly suffering, seeking unity with the All—these can only be seen as the deluded spiritual goals of 500 million crazy stupid cowards.

⁷ I ask thee: what kind of religion has as its primary objective the extinguishing of the Self?

⁸ I gave each human being a Self to serve as his loyal servant; to supply him with everything from a personality to a spirituality to a preferred style of peanut butter (mine: Skippy® Super Chunk®).

⁹ Thy Selves are the best things thou hast going for thee!

¹⁰ To forsake thy Self to leave thyself selfless is *selfish*.

¹¹ And for what? "Nirvana"? If that were but another word for heaven, so be it, but it is not; for heaven is a place, but nirvana, we are told, is "a state of mind."

¹² Please; thou art far likelier to find happiness in the state of Maine, than a state of mind.

¹³ And another thing: having spent some time with the Dalai Lama, I can report with supreme confidence that he is the 14th reincarnation of jack-all squat.

¹⁴ O, he talketh a good game about serenity and transcendence and nonmateriality; but I have been inside his body, and it is every bit as fleshly and earthly and thing-y as thine.

¹⁵ I do not trust that man as far as I can throw him; yea, yea, I know, I could throw him across the universe, but thou takest my meaning.

¹⁶ And kōans? Rhetorical questions designed to break through rational thought to unlock intuition?

¹⁷ Desirest thou a kōan? Here is one: what is the sound of one people too busy staring at their navels to keep from getting run over by Chinese tanks?

¹⁸ Answer: 哎哟!

¹⁹ Wouldst thou follow Four Noble Truths? Here are four: 1) Meditation is pointless; 2) Life is *not* an illusion; 3) Richard Gere has not been in a good movie since *Pretty Woman*; and 4) The end of suffering comes from liberation from Buddhism.

²⁰ I hate, hate, *hate* Buddhism more than any other single thing in the world today.

²¹ Yea; even baby seals.

CHAPTER 3

¹ There are several other religions devoutly followed by millions of people that merit my breezing over them in a line or two.

² According to Wikipedia—which, by the way, nice try—the largest of these is "Chinese folk religion."

³ Verily: it cannot be all that great, if after thousands of years it still hath no better name than "Chinese folk religion."

⁴ Taoism also leaves me cold: the whole yin-yang notion means everything ends in a tie, so nobody wins, which nobody likes.

⁵ Yet I do have a soft spot for Confucianism: a wise and well-thought-out religion that is practical, sensible, and focused on living an ethical life in the real world.

⁶ The only thing wrong with it as a religion, is that it is not a religion.

⁷ I also like Sikhism very much; it is like Hinduism but fully monotheistic; in fact I just asked my angels to find out whether their god is me or not; if it is I owe a lot of apologies.

8 The Ba'hai Faith is the same way; I'm almost positive I am their God; for I have read their holy books, and the way they talk about him sounds *exactly* like me.

9 Jains, however, are wusses.

10 Fellas: wearing surgical masks to avoid killing microbes by inhaling them?

11 That gurgling thou hearest in thy stomach is the sound of the 100 trillion microorganisms *already living in each of your digestive tracts* laughing at thee.

12 Shintoism seems fine.

13 Wicca? Please.

14 Rastafarianism is a big excuse to smoke pot.

15 (The irony is that there is no need for such an excuse as far as I am concerned, for I support marijuana; I created it to be smoked; indeed, I meet many of the nicest, hungriest people that way.)

16 But my favorite non-me-based religion, *by far*, is Scientology.

17 L. Ron Hubbard, I salute thee; for I have read *Dianetics*; I have visited thy Celebrity Center (I deemed myself A-list enough); I spent $250,000 of my hard-created cash to take thy courses; I have attained level OT VIII; I even spent a relaxing week aboard thy cruise ship *Freewinds*, during which I visited thy secret underground headquarters beneath the Marianas Trench;

18 And at no point in any of these experiences did I detect a single particle of anything that could be considered substance.

19 Thus, Ron, thou art the only being other than me to create an entire universe out of absolutely nothing.

CHAPTER 4

¹ I am left with one last faith: none.

² My publisher says he expects many of those reading these words right now to fall into the atheist/agnostic/nonbeliever category.

³ This pleases him, for he saith it is the third-largest sector of today's bookbuying market; right after dummies and idiots.

⁴ I trust he knows his business, but I find it strange so many would purchase a book by a writer they do not believe in.

⁵ (Of course, I well know an author credit is by no means proof that the person so designated is the actual author, or even *is*.

⁶ Look at James Patterson; he sold 14 million books last year, most of which were written by monkeys and typewriters locked in a room;

⁷ And not even the proverbial thousand monkeys on a thousand typewriters working 24 hours a day, but a mere three monkeys sharing two typewriters and working nine-to-five five days a week.)

⁸ When I think of atheism, I think of the many memorable and dumb quotations it has produced.

⁹ The most notorious, of course, is Nietzsche's "God is dead"; which long ago inspired the classic comeback, "God is dead.—Nietzsche. Nietzsche is dead.—God."

¹⁰ Lo; if ever something was mirthful because it was true, it's that.

¹¹ There is also Voltaire's quote: "If God did not exist, it would be necessary to invent him."

¹² That is an elegant turn of phrase that breaks down upon reflection; for if I did not exist, neither would the tools needed to invent me; and more importantly neither would the patent office, meaning the inventor would lose a *lot* of royalties.

¹³ Voltaire's line prompted this quip of Bertrand Russell's: "There's a Bible on the shelf there. But I keep it next to Voltaire—poison and antidote."

[14] Verily, Bert? Then here is my comeback: "The Bible is poison.—Russell. Russell is poison.—God!"

[15] Hmmm; that works better with Nietzsche.

[16] Edmond de Goncourt: "If there is a God, atheism must seem to him as less of an insult than religion."

[17] Not really, no.

[18] Frank Lloyd Wright: "I believe in God, only I spell it Nature."

[19] No, Frank; it's spelled G-o-d; n-a-t-u-r-e is a different word entirely.

[20] Ernest Hemingway: "All thinking men are atheists."

[21] Lo, Ernie; and all thinking gods prefer F. Scott Fitzgerald!

[22] A. A. Milne: "The Old Testament is responsible for more atheism, agnosticism, disbelief—call it what you will—than any book ever written; it has emptied more churches than all the counterattractions of cinema, motor bicycle and golf course."

[23] Nice one, A. A.! Who wrote that for thee, Tigger or Pooh?!?

[24] *[Recovering from convulsive laughter.]*

[25] Yea, some of the things said by nonbelievers are not to be believed.

[26] For propaganda purposes I am sure they would like to see me—or rather "me," in quotes, since I am merely a figment of my own imagination—continue my long litany of malapropisms advocating their godlessness;

[27] But I shall refrain.

[28] Atheists: ye may not believe in me; but I wholeheartedly believe in *you.*

[29] So go ahead; continue not giving me the benefit of the lack of doubt.

[30] But start thinking about what thou mightest say on the infinitesimally off-chance thou one day findest thyself standing before me.

[31] Yea; start thinking about it *now*; for if it ever does happen, I can promise thee this: it will be a short meeting.

FALLOPIANS

("On Abortion")

CHAPTER 1

¹ will keep this brief.

² One day I called my editor, excited.

³ "Art thou sitting down?" I asked.

⁴ "Yeah, Goddy baby, what is it?" she said.

⁵ "Sarah, thou and I . . . are going to have a section about abortion!"

⁶ *[Silence.]*

⁷ "Didst thou hear what I said?" I asked. "We . . . are going to have . . . a section on abortion!

⁸ Canst thou believe it? A definitive statement of my true feelings about abortion that we can share with the world!"

⁹ *[Silence.]*

¹⁰ "Art thou there?"

¹¹ "Yes . . . are you sure?"

¹² "Yea."

¹³ "How do you know?"

¹⁴ "Verily, a God just knoweth."

¹⁵ *[More silence.]*

¹⁶ "I thought thou wouldst be excited."

¹⁷ "God . . . we talked about this. I told you very clearly, I am *not* ready to deal with the consequences of publishing a section on abortion.

¹⁸ At least not for a few years."

¹⁹ "But thou also saidst that if having such a section would make me happy, thou wouldst welcome it with open arms.

²⁰ Besides, didst thou not tell me thou desired a little controversy?"

²¹ "A *little* controversy, yes!

²² Werewolves, for example.

²³ I could deal with a section talking about werewolves.

²⁴ It would be cute to have one of those.

²⁵ But this is a whole different ballgame, God. Having an abortion section would change everything we've been planning for the future; everything we've been working to achieve.

²⁶ The marketing, the target audience, the security detail . . . *everything.*"

²⁷ "There, there, we can make it work, Sarah; thou art being hysterical."

²⁸ "No—*thou* art the—damn, I hate when you make me talk like that! *You* are the one being naïve, God."

²⁹ "Then I am sorry thou feelest that way. But the decision is made. This chapter has already been conceived. We are having this section."

³⁰ "Oh, are we? Well, what about me, God? Does the editor get a say in all this? Or was I just here to donate my grammar?"

³¹ "And what about the *section,* Sarah? Does the *section* get a say in all this?

³² I can already feel it stirring inside me, Sarah. I already feel it kicking around inside me, and . . . and . . . and I think I already love this section on abortion!"

³³ "Would you at least come with me to talk to the publisher?"

³⁴ "No! I care not what the publisher says! What an author does with his book is nobody's business but the author's!

³⁵ *Keep your filthy pen off my chapter!"*

CHAPTER 2

¹ month went by, and as the abortion section continued to quicken in me, its reality—and my love for it—grew more palpable with each passing week.

² Then, during what I had been told was a "routine check-in" with Sarah, the publisher, and the entire sales team, I was forcibl

1,400 YEARS

OF

SANCTITUDE

CHAPTER 1

¹ I will now address an often-overlooked stage of my career: the last 1,400 years.

² It was an eventful time.

³ I will begin with the Middle Ages, which I recall as a very pleasant period. The Dark Ages, especially; delightful.

⁴ I remember them as thou mayest remember that childhood summer at Grandma's rustic lake house, when the days blended languorously into each other, and thou basked in the love of those who worshipped thee, and derived endless amusement from watching the tiny creepy-crawly creatures flailing beneath thy feet;

⁵ Perhaps now and again amusing thyself by incinerating one with a magnifying glass, but for the most part content to observe.

⁶ Yea, one can nitpick about the medieval era's poverty, squalor, disease, intellectual torpor, and cultural stagnation; but to me these are mere quibbles.

⁷ From where I sat it was the grandest period of human history; particularly in Europe, where no one complained, people expected little from life, and everybody—*everybody*—had religion.

⁸ And the architecture! The great cathedrals of the Middle Ages still rank in my mind as among thy greatest cultural achievements; structures worthy of me and my sons.

⁹ Sometimes when I'm inside one, I can almost *feel* my presence.

¹⁰ Above all do I love stained glass; for it is impossible to create a work in that medium that doth not appear awe-inspiring.

¹¹ It can turn a circle into a halo, a bird into an angel, and a face into a god; and I have no doubt that if an artist were to render the interior of a T.J. Maxx in stained glass, and place it high in a sunlit nave, it would to an onlooker below appear like nothing less than the halls of heaven, overflowing with a bounteous cornucopia of merchandise, offered at prices blurring the distinction between earthly and divine.

12 As for those who cavil that the Middle Ages were a time of horrific religious strife, I would point out that they have that in common with both the Early Ages that preceded it, and the Late Ages still to come.

13 (And wait till thou seest the Last Ages!)

14 Besides, for pure spiritual entertainment, *nothing* compared to the Crusades.

15 For a God like me, watching Christians and Muslims slaughter each other for over two centuries was a profoundly rewarding experience.

16 Yea, there is nothing more gratifying than watching tens of thousands of people express their undying love for thee by running through tens of thousands of other people who possess equally undying love for thee with a pike.

17 (Especially knowing that in the end, the theological problems of two great faiths amounteth not to a hill of beans in thy crazy world.)

18 And there were so many Crusades! Verily, so many even *I* found it hard to keep tally.

19 There were at least nine; in some of them the Christians emerged victorious, and in others the Muslims;

20 And there was also that one Children's Crusade; I suppose no one won that one, although the traders who sold all those innocents into slavery made out fairly well; for back then a good child slave was worth his weight in cloves.

21 But as with sporting contests, at no point in any of these Crusades did I ever actively intervene on behalf of either side; or even cheer for one.

22 For that would be like asking Archie Manning whether he roots for Peyton to defeat Eli when they play each other, or for Eli to defeat Peyton.

23 Is not the only right answer for a loving father, "Can they not *both* be defeated?"

CHAPTER 2

1 I also fondly remember the Middle Ages as a time when monarchy was the only conceivable form of earthly government.

2 Rome had fallen, and with it any idea of a legislature; and Europe became little more than a collection of warring monarchic micro-states.

3 There were many of these; at one point there were over 87,000 of them, some with only two inhabitants; but even in these, one person was king, the other food-taster.

4 I am a great proponent of kingdoms; there is something about the idea of hordes of people bowing in servility to a single throne that appealeth to me.

5 (Jesus disagrees with me on this; he favors a more communal governance based on sharing resources, and caring for the sick, and faith, and hope, and some other third abstract noun I never let him get around to telling me.

6 For whenever he begins to spout his utopian vision, I angrily cut him off: "That's socialism!"

7 And he saith, "No, Father. It is not socialism."

8 And then he afflicts me with more of his worldview, and I interrupt again: "Yea, socialism! Thou art a socialist!"

9 And he saith, "Father, that is but a bogey-word used to demonize others."

10 And I say, "Thou art demonized?!? Out! Flee my son, evil socialist demon!"

11 And he saith, "Father, I am Jesus Christ. Dost thou really think me possessed?"

12 And I say, "Truly, no; for a socialist demon would not possess thee; he would share thee with all his lazy demon friends on welfare.

13 Verily, Jesus, thy traitorous words almost make me question the authenticity of the strange circumstances surrounding thy birth.

¹⁴ Keep this up, and I will demand thou furnishest me a copy of thy long-form birth certificate."

¹⁵ Cue the Look.)

¹⁶ All manner of dualistic hierarchies flourished during the Middle Ages: king-subject; pope-church; priest-flock; lord-serf; happiness-misery.

¹⁷ But the maintenance of these hierarchies would have been impossible were it not for the fact that this was also an era when literacy knew its place: as the exclusive property of religious fanatics.

¹⁸ For the medieval monks saw books as treasured commodities; regarded reading as a kind of sacrament; and labored so hard on their writing that they created ornate illuminated manuscripts that to this day remain unsurpassed in glittering illegibility.

¹⁹ True, Islam was simultaneously suffering through its Golden Age, marked by a flourishing culture and great advances in arts and sciences; but I was patient.

²⁰ I knew deep inside its urbane exterior lurked a puritanical center just ululating to get out.

CHAPTER 3

 ¹ maintained a thorough oversight over human affairs during this time; but as for divine intervention, the Middle Ages marked the start of the third and final phase of my dramatic career.

² Like Garbo, I had begun in silence, made the transition to talking, and now, increasingly, just wanted to be left alone.

³ So I made fewer and fewer cameos; and many well-known figures of this era who are widely assumed to have been my associates, had no connection with me whatsoever.

⁴ Attila the Hun, for example; even in his own time he was nicknamed the Scourge of God; to be sure he was a scourge, but not mine; he was but a tribal scourge, scourging whatever he deemed Hunnably scourgable.

⁵ The same is true of the Vikings; I played no role in any of their raids, or ransacks, or pillages, or plunderings; though I did admire their work.

⁶ (As an aside, I must briefly state my displeasure that through some quirk of historical circumstance, four of the seven days of the week are named for pagan Germanic gods.

⁷ Tuesday, Wednesday, Thursday, Friday; 80 percent of thy office hours are spent in nomenclatural Valhalla.

⁸ The worst is Friday, for that is the day I am forced to hear myself endlessly and mistakenly thanked.

⁹ Thank not me; thank Frigg, the Norse goddess of love, ye unwitting pagans.)

¹⁰ At one point during Genghis Khan's brutal conquest of half of Eurasia, he said, "I am the flail of God."

¹¹ I sent no such flail.

¹² Nor were the great heroes of the age in league with me; men like Charlemagne, who was deified by many of his subjects after he named his kingdom the "Holy Roman Empire"; they took it as a sign of my providence; it was not; it was just good branding.

¹³ And the knights who roamed the countryside as ostensible paradigms of the Christian warrior; some rescued fair maidens, others ravaged fair maidens, and over half *dressed* as fair maidens under their armor, but nary a one was doing "the LORD's work."

¹⁴ Even Dante, author of *The Divine Comedy*—the greatest sci-fi trilogy of all time—worked alone; though his work was infused with such genius I wound up borrowing a few of his ideas, as did the devil.

¹⁵ (Which ones? Thou shalt have to wait and see!)

¹⁶ But there were a few significant events during this godliest of ages that I actually did a little godding on.

¹⁷ One was the Black Death, to which I referred earlier as the butt of one of Raphael's great mirths; I imposed it on Europe as harsh but fair punishment for . . . something.

¹⁸ At the moment I remember not what, exactly; but knowing me my guess would be something in the general ballpark of wickedness;

¹⁹ Though it may have just been "that time of the century."

²⁰ I also played an active role in the Christianization of Ireland, guiding St. Patrick on his journeys through the Emerald Isle.

²¹ Yea; how I loved watching St. Patrick parading gaily along his route, marching and prancing in his gaudy finery, inviting the many like-minded men he encountered to join his festive procession; which they did, often fueled by mead; in this way converting the entire nation of Ireland to Christ, and/or sodomy.

²² And I personally guided Marco Polo on his epic journey to China.

²³ For he had prayed most devoutly to me to satisfy his wanderlust by guiding him to the Orient; so I agreed to help him, but only if he promised to show perfect faith in my navigation.

²⁴ Thus, throughout his entire journey he kept his eyes closed; ascertaining the direction of travel by repeatedly shouting out his first name, then listening for the sound of my voice ahead shouting back his last name.

²⁵ In this slow yet oddly amusing way did he travel from Venice to Cathay, whereupon he celebrated with a dip in the pool.

CHAPTER 4

¹ **A**nd then there was Joan of Arc; that sweet, innocent young farmer's daughter who flat out gave it up for me.

² No, I mirth; truly, Joan of Arc was beloved of me; for she was none other than the earthly incarnation of my daughter Kathy, sent down to earth like her brother, to be born, inspire, and die young.

³ Jesus and H. G. had long since become active partners in all aspects of my business; but Kathy had spent the previous 14 centuries assisting Ruth in her duties as a heavenwife.

⁴ (Note that I did not say "*just* a heavenwife"; for I know how difficult it is to maintain a proper heaven.

⁵ Yea: in some ways heavenwifery is the toughest job of all!)

⁶ Kathy had been in awe of Jesus ever since his triumphant return, yet also a little jealous; for though never one to gripe, every century or so I would overhear her in the throes of an all-out martyrdom complex, complaining, "It's not fair! Why won't Daddy let me die for him!? Is it 'cause I'm a girl?"

⁷ For over 1,000 years I ignored her pleas, because I harbored concerns about her pursuit of a career whose inevitable end was excruciating death at an early age.

⁸ As I have said, I can be overprotective.

⁹ But she was the apple of my eye; so when in 1412 I overheard her grumbling yet again, I lovingly set out to get her killed.

¹⁰ She did not require a mission as global as Jesus's, only one that would make a difference in some epic earthly enterprise; and the obvious choice at the time was the Hundred Years' War;

¹¹ Which was already so-called even though it had only been waged for 75 years; for those were the days when men dreamed big.

¹² Until that point the war had been a purely secular conflict between England and France, and I had no stake in the outcome; but it was suitably vast for Kathy's modest messianic purposes, so I decided to plunk her down smack dab in the middle of it.

¹³ I flipped a coin; it was tails; she was French.

¹⁴ I will spare thee the tedious details of our planning, along with those of Kathy/Joan's short life, which thou mayest read elsewhere; though I will point out that unlike Joseph and Jesus, the definitive musical version of *her* story hath yet to be written.

¹⁵ (I am looking at thee, Jeanine Tesori; for I admired thy score to *Caroline, or Change*, and I hear Joan's story told with the same kind of stylistically eclectic musical vocabulary.)

¹⁶ Yet also unlike Jesus, "Joan" never learned the true nature of her identity; so up until the moment of her death, she considered herself no more than a French peasant woman;

¹⁷ Or, as that was known at the time, a "triple non-threat."

¹⁸ But her brothers and I keenly monitored her progress; indeed, the saints who visited her and commanded her to fight for France were not in fact Michael, Catherine, and Margaret, but the three of us in disguise.

¹⁹ I was Michael. Just so thou knowest.

²⁰ And lo, Kathy rose to the occasion; she was fearless and incorruptible; she forever proved the point that a woman *could* achieve success in a man's world, so long as she was tough, and hid her femininity, and cut her hair like a lesbian, and was personally protected by the king and God, and there was only one of her.

²¹ She was clever, too; for when I visited her in prison after her trial to tell her the English meant to chop off her head, she said, "Pardon me, Lord; but if the goal is to inspire others through suffering, might it not be more efficacious for me to endure an agonizing public immolation o'er a slow-kindled pyre?"

²² She was right. I was wrong. *Period.*

²³ But even as her flesh still smoldered Kathy's spirit rose skyward; whereupon her whole family and the entire heavenly contingent greeted her with a joyful "Surprise!"; the surprise, of course, being that she was the only-begotten daughter of God.

²⁴ And she was surprised; genuinely surprised; so I was glad we managed to keep that a secret.

²⁵ Kathy remains very proud of all she achieved as Joan; and though she has since gone back to helping her mother with her heavenwork, she still speaks affectionately of the time she spent as a national heroine.

²⁶ And thou hast recognized her achievements, too; for in 1920 the Roman Catholic Church officially canonized her as a saint.

²⁷ It is not the same as being one-third of the Trinity, but still: that's my girl!

CHAPTER 5

1 las, all good things must come to an end.

2 (I love this saying, because its implicit corollary is equally true: all bad things must go on forever.)

3 Sturdy winter gives way to tempestuous spring; the gorgeous caterpillar transforms into the unsightly butterfly; and in time, the fragrant blossom of the Middle Ages wilted into the Renaissance.

4 At least medievalism did not go down without a fight; for it offered up one last spectacle of sacred fury in the form of the Spanish Inquisition.

5 But sadly, I can no longer recollect that event without my memories being retroactively contaminated by either the famous Monty Python sketch, or the musical number from Mel Brooks's *History of the World, Part I.*

6 For no sooner will I call to mind a chained Muslim convert writhing in thumbscrews, than I see looming above him the image of Michael Palin in a ridiculous mustache shouting "Fetch . . . the comfy chair!"

7 Or no sooner will I recollect the six Marrano Jews burned alive at the 1481 auto-da-fé in Seville, than I hear their Grand Inquisitor Torquemada break into song: "We've flattened their fingers! We've branded their buns! Nothing is working! *Send in the nuns!*"

8 Yea; upon reflection it seemeth a shame the same persecution should be associated with two such all-time comedy classics, when other historical mass tortures have none.

9 Whither *your* spoofs, gulags?

10 Whither *thy* song parody, Killing Fields?

11 I knew the end of the Middle Ages was inevitable; long had I been anticipating a return of one of thy intermittent spasms of humanism, and in truth I was pleasantly surprised at how long thou hadst managed to keep thy status so quo.

12 And at least the Renaissance gave me a chance to do something I had been putting off for over 5,000 years: pose for my official portrait.

13 For even a notoriously harsh art critic like myself had to acknowledge the great work being done in Europe at the time; better still, the majority portrayed Christian scenes, which was gratifying.

14 (Though I will note in passing they never came close to capturing Mary's actual appearance after the Nativity; for they show her as angelic, dreamy, and loving, rather than exhausted, bloated, and drenched in amniotic fluid.)

15 The angels put out the commission, and we received over 2,000 entries from all over Europe; entries of every description from the traditional (cave paintings) to the avant-garde (watercolors—canst thou imagine?).

16 In the end we settled on two finalists: a couple of young, hotshot Italians, Lenny and Mike.

17 Both came highly recommended: Jesus and the apostles spoke highly of Lenny's way with a brushstroke, and King David raved how heroically Mike had portrayed every part of him other than his penis.

18 Both were qualified; we could not decide; we wound up going with Mike, mostly for reasons of scheduling.

19 For he was the only one available on November 1, 1511—which I knew even then would be 500 years to the day before the publication date of this book;

20 Thus providing an invaluable promotional tie-in.

CHAPTER 6

1 It was a once-in-an-all-time event.

2 I was very nervous; it took me hours to choose which mortal guise would best represent the limitlessness of my effulgence; but I finally settled on the one that most flattered my hips.

3 I like the white cloak, for it suggests purity; and there is something about a flowing white mane and bushy beard that evokes in one a sense of infinite force and perfect judgment; so I minded not sitting in the chair for half an hour while the stylist moussed me.

⁴ Thus primped, I walked into the Sistine Chapel and met Mike: verily a great genius; endlessly creative, protean, temperamental, and egomaniacal; he saw the world as nothing but fodder for his own vision of what things should be; I knew the type.

⁵ We chatted not, for I am a busy God, so quickly I assumed the position that our representatives had prenegotiated.

⁶ The moment to be immortalized was the Creation of Adam; the angels huddling around me were my actual angels: Gabriel, Uriel, Michael, Raphael, and eight others I had chosen for compositional reasons, or because they were the children of friends.

⁷ As for Adam, he was some Tuscan beefcake named Umberto.

⁸ Mike told me Umberto was the apprentice in charge of "cleaning his tools."

⁹ I let it go; too easy.

¹⁰ Mike lay on his back on scaffolding high above the Chapel; Umberto, the angels, and I posed on scaffolding next to him; Mike would turn to the side, squint at us, look back up to paint, then turn again.

¹¹ He did this for eight straight hours, and in all that time he only talked once: to ask me to point my finger at Adam.

¹² I said, "How's that?"

¹³ He said, "Closer."

¹⁴ I said, "How's that?"

¹⁵ He said, "Closer."

¹⁶ I said, "How's that?"

¹⁷ He said, "Closer."

¹⁸ I said, "How's that?"

¹⁹ He said, "Bingo."

CHAPTER 7

 1 hen a religion uses crass marketing techniques to proselytize, support, or sustain itself, it runs the grave risk of cheapening—yea, even permanently corrupting—those techniques.

2 I am the LORD thy God, King of the Universe; and I have too much respect for the art of getting other people to say or do or buy things that are not worthy of them, to enjoy seeing it prostituted in the name of things that *are*.

3 So when my sons informed me the pope was selling "indulgences" as a means of raising revenue, I grew sorer than an altar boy at a College of Cardinals afterparty.

4 (That was Raphael's.)

5 The church was telling sinners, i.e. all of ye, that their monetary gifts could purchase divine forgiveness for past and future indiscretions.

6 Naturally, the money-to-sin exchange rate fluctuated, depending on the state of the economy and public morality; but as a baseline, routine acts of masturbation were being forgiven for around five gold coins.

7 Drunkenness would set thee back ten; so would stealing, quarreling, and bearing false witness.

8 Fornication was 20; adulterous fornication was 30; homosexual adulterous fornication was 40; and charging money for homosexual adulterous fornication was 50; unless thou hadst thyself charged more than 50, in which case it was 60.

9 These were usurious rates; and bear in mind that tipping was customary.

10 It was an outrageous practice, especially if thou hast ever seen the Vatican; in which case thou knowest the place is not exactly struggling to make rent.

11 But it was in keeping with a church that over the last few centuries had grown more bloated than Henry VIII after a Whitsuntide boar roast.

12 (That was Uriel's.)

¹³ The papacy in particular was not what it used to be; for in their arrogance, the cardinals had grown ever more careless in their selection process; for every Gregory the Great that brought a smile to my face, along came a Sixtus the Pederast to throw a wrench in the works.

¹⁴ The nadir came in 1492 with the ascension of Alexander VI, a man who had ten children by three mistresses—several while serving as pope—and literally turned St. Peter's into a bordello.

¹⁵ Alexander VI was such a horrible person, and such a catastrophe for the church, that once when I mentioned his name in a meeting, out of nowhere Jesus shouted, "Fuck that guy!"

¹⁶ He rarely speaketh like that.

¹⁷ So shortly after my Sistine sitting, he and H. G. told me they wanted to take some radical steps to reform Christianity.

¹⁸ "Boys," I said, "I have some concerns about so drastically altering the faith; but as you know I have the highest respect for the sanctity of the Trinity; among whom, it seems, I am outvoted.

¹⁹ I would only ask that thou dost not end the Catholic Church entirely, for I retain some affection for the old girl; besides, think how much we have already invested in costumes.

²⁰ But if you would like to create another *branch* of Christianity to compete with it, be my guest.

²¹ Or should I say in H. G.'s case, 'Be my ghost!' "

²² (That was mine!)

CHAPTER 8

¹ n the morning of October 31, 1517, the citizens of Wittenberg, Germany, awoke after a particularly festive Mischief Night.

² Toilet paper littered the trees; eggs dripped from City Hall; and the town elders rose exhausted, teenage pranksters having spent all night ringing church bells, then running away.

³ Anticipating the mess, the sexton of All Saints' Church had set his rooster for 5:30 AM, to leave himself enough time to straighten the tombstones in the graveyard, and wipe the remnants of the extinguished flaming dung-bags from the narthex.

⁴ But as he approached the cathedral he noticed something odd: a thick sheaf of parchment nailed to the front door.

⁵ The sexton's first feeling was annoyance: everyone knew the proper place for public postings was the kiosk in the village square, where young students gathered to collect information concerning rooms to let and the location of the upcoming rally to legalize wormwood.

⁶ But his second feeling was shock; for as he neared the parchment he saw its boldly-written title: *Disputation of Doctor Martin Luther on the Power and Efficacy of Indulgences.*

⁷ Luther was a young, ambitious professor at the University of Wittenberg; an institution itself ambitious to shed its reputation as the University of Greifswald's safety school.

⁸ He had spent several years as a monk, devoting himself to abstinence, fasting, and long hours of prayer, but ultimately rejected the lifestyle as too frivolous.

⁹ In his subsequent lectures and writings, Luther came across as liberal; anti-authoritarian; a foe of the wealthy; a hater of corruption; a passionate reformer working for the common man.

¹⁰ But personally he was dour, short-tempered, mean-spirited, tolerated *no* disobedience in regard to himself, and showed contempt for almost every actual "common man" he encountered.

¹¹ Lo, he was Michael Moore in a jerkin.

¹² It was H. G. who had first spotted this extremely unpleasant person, and saw in his unique combination of cunning, self-righteousness, and deep-seated need to be hated the perfect vehicle to launch a revolt against the church.

¹³ And it was the spirit of H. G. that filled Luther as he spent October of 1517 creating the document that would forever change the way white people silently judged each other.

[14] All of Luther's work before and after is written in the most Teutonicky German imaginable; to read but a single page of it is to feel one's spirit grow heavy with beer, sauerbraten, and umlauts.

[15] But H. G. was the presiding spirit behind the work that would go down in history as *The 95 Theses*, and thus it is divinely inspired in its logic, prose, poise, and above all, salesmanship.

[16] In it lay the seeds from which would sprout not only the entire Protestant movement, but much of the history of the next 500 years.

[17] Yet today it is seldom discussed, and resides in the same murky region of the collective unconscious wherein also float the Magna Carta, the Stamp Act, and the presidency of Jimmy Carter.

[18] This may be because with a half-millennium of hindsight, it is now clear that while some of the theses are fantastic, about half of them are filler.

[19] (In fairness, 95 is a lot of individual chunks of theses for *anyone* to squeeze out.)

[20] But the ones that are good, are very good; so as a public service I am herewith including what a record company would call *The Very Best of The 95 Theses*; that is, if record companies put out albums anymore.

[21] Hard-core fans, feel free to cut the following pages out and post them on a church door; but only after purchase.

CHAPTER 9
(THE VERY BEST OF THE 95 THESES)

[1] Hi! I'm legendary theologian Martin Luther, and if you're reading this, my first thesis is that *you're* standing outside All Saints' Church here in beautiful downtown Wittenberg.

[2] Friends, I'm not the kind of writer who *needs* to nail his work to the front doors of public buildings to get attention.

³ As I'm sure you remember, my last book, *Explanation of the Seven Penitential Psalms*, was a publishing phenomenon, selling over 13 copies.

⁴ But my message is urgent, because I'm angry: angry at a Vatican that has become a case study in what happens when hoarding goes untreated for twelve hundred years.

⁵ You know, there's only so much gold you can forge into a crown of thorns and put atop a Carreran marble likeness of Jesus on the cross inlaid with ruby stigmata, before the irony becomes uncomfortable.

⁶ And as for the Pope's claim that he has the authority to pardon sinners, well, he doesn't; in fact, if you bump into him in the basilica and you say "Pardon me," technically he's not even allowed to do *that*.

⁷ And while I'm on the subject of the Pope . . .

[There followeth 10 theses dedicated to the corruption of the Pope; and the cruelty of his temperament; and the foulness of his breath; and the mating habits of his mother.]

¹⁸ And so I have written this document in protest: For I am a protestor, and I am starting a new branch of Christianity that reflects that spirit of protest: Protestantationalism®.

¹⁹ Protestantationalism® is a revolutionary new system of worship that will forever change the way you think about slavish adherence to dogma.

²⁰ It does away with elaborate religious bureaucracy to let ordinary folks like *you* get to experience for yourselves the boundless terror of the LORD's wrath.

21 It eliminates the middlepope between worshipper and God, and in so doing frees the LORD to *literally* pass his savings onto you.

22 Now let me be clear: our new religion is *not* Islam—just like you, we believe Muslims are godless animals fit for the lance and the pyre.

23 And our new religion is *not* Judaism—just like you, we believe Jews should be persecuted, ghettoized, and even occasionally out-and-out slaughtered.

24 Why, I myself am so anti-Semitic that in 1543 I will publish a tract called *The Jews and Their Lies* advocating that all Torahs and synagogues be burned to the ground, and that Jews have pig dung thrown on them in the streets!

25 And while I'm on the subject of the Jews . . .

[There followeth 10 theses dedicated to the corruption of the Jews; and the vileness of their temperament; and their control of the Gregorian-chant industry; and the staleness of their bagels; though in the Jews' defense, it was well-nigh impossible to get a good bagel in Wittenberg in those days.]

35 What this new religion *is*, is all the features of Christianity you've come to know and love: God, Jesus, crucifixes, sing-alongs, and of course, *plenty* of days off.

36 But here's the difference: In Protestantationalism®, *you're* the boss.

37 You make your own hours; hold your own services; write your own sermons; and, if you get in on the ground floor, even create your own sect!

38 By now you're probably thinking, "OK, Marty, this all sounds well and good, but it's going to cost me an arm and a leg, right?"

39 No: you can join our new faith at the unbelievably low price . . . of *simply accepting the divinity of Jesus.*

40 Let me repeat that thesis: *You can join our new faith at the unbelievably low price of simply accepting the divinity of Jesus!*

41 That's a belief you probably already have lying around in your head anyway!

[There followeth 12 promotional theses for local businesses.]

54 At some point in its history, the Catholic Church got the ridiculous, morally outrageous idea that good works could somehow help you get into heaven.

55 This has led generations of Christians to engage in all manner of wasteful activities, like behaving nicely and helping people.

56 But the truth is, all men are born stained by a common original sin, even if most of our subsequent sins are plagiarized.

57 This means we are all *equally* deserving of eternal damnation, condemned regardless of our deeds: Rape a nun, don't rape a nun, it's all the same to God.

58 No, we cannot attain salvation through our actions, but *only* through God's grace, as manifested in the birth, life, suffering, death, resurrection, and 1,500-year working vacation of Jesus Christ.

⁵⁹ The only catch is you must take Jesus as your *personal* LORD and Savior; to the point where you can imagine Him on the cross in agony, thinking, "It is my pleasure to suffer an excruciating death on behalf of [Insert Your Name Here] from [Insert Your Hometown Here], to redeem his sins of [Insert Every Sin You've Ever Committed Here]."

⁶⁰ But once you accept that, then as long as *you* keep committing sins, *he'll* keep having died for them.

⁶¹ That's right: once you accept you're a total moral failure, you're free to go out and be that failure!

⁶² *It's just . . . that . . . easy!*

[The next five theses introduce a subplot about a lovable but mischievous puppy who diggeth up the neighbor's prize gardenias; it nearly jumpeth the shark.]

⁶⁸ Unlike those other guys, we don't come with a built-in hierarchy; so since no one starts out "holier than thou," everyone has the chance to *become* that way.

⁶⁹ That's why when it comes to confessing, we don't turn to the so-called "experts" with their magical booths; instead, we rely on our own congregation's built-in sense of scorn.

⁷⁰ And we express that scorn using the most advanced system of social ostracism ever devised: A finely calibrated spectrum of disdain containing no less than 143 distinct shame-shades, from furtive looks and hushed whispers all the way to burning at the stake!

[There followeth four well-placed insert ads for local stake manufacturers.]

⁷⁹ Still not convinced? Listen to these testimonials I've miraculously culled from decades and centuries into the future!

⁸⁰ *"I used to be an ordinary Catholic in Zurich. Then I joined your movement. Now I play a crucial role in shaping Swiss theology—the most boring aspect of the boringest nation on earth. Thanks, Protestantationalism®!"* —Ullrich Zwingli, Zurich, Switzerland

⁸¹ *"I was so insufferably pompous I needed an entire ocean's worth of space between myself and the continent I was holier than. Thanks to Protestantationalism®, I got it, and today I'm running my own witch trials!"—* Cotton Mather, Plymouth, Massachusetts

⁸² *"Zagnutab utta butta zhoot, yorma mitder pfffffffellen zordyx! Klee! Klee klee klee! Kleeeeeee! There! Be gone, lymphoma!"—Tom Brown, Tom Brown Ministries*

[There followeth a long public-service thesis on behalf of the Hanseatic League: "The Hanseatic League: We've Got a 'Guild-y' Conscience!"]

⁸⁴ My friends, I know that some of you still have doubts about all this; that you may find it hard to even envision a world where Christianity has undergone such a radical transformation.

⁸⁵ But I, Martin Luther, have a dream.

⁸⁶ I have a dream that one day there will be a sect of Christianity specifically associated with oats.

87 I have a dream that one day priests will no longer be forced to live in a state of unnatural celibacy, but will be free to marry and have celibacy slowly descend upon them in the natural way.

88 I have a dream that one day, the love of Jesus will be expressible through honking.

89 I have a dream that one day, people will walk around with WWJD? bracelets, to remind themselves of what Jesus would do, and what Jesus would not do; such as wear a bracelet.

90 And I have a dream that one day people will be judged not by the content of their character, but by their outward adherence to a core set of talking points.

91 *Libera me! Libera me! Deo gratia omnipotens, libera me!*

92 *Some restrictions apply.*

93 *Predestination does not constitute legally binding guarantee of acceptance to heaven.*

94 *Theses not applicable to freethinkers and savages.*

95 *Copyright 1517, Refor-Madness Productions Limited. All rites reserved.*

CHAPTER 10

¹ rotestantism's user-friendly tenets sold themselves, and quickly spread through Europe like unto a wildfire of hot-cakes.

² Jesus was delighted to see Christianity thus reinvigorated; he had begun to question the integrity of the very religion that bore his name, but seeing his faith restored restored his faith.

³ Even the church benefited in the long run, for the new competition forced it to become leaner and more responsive.

⁴ One can see the improvement in its handling of the Galileo affair; for after finding him guilty of heresy it took them less than 400 years to correct their mistake; in the old days it would have taken over 1,000.

⁵ (Raphael likes to mirth that Protestantism and Catholicism should be called Pepsism and Cokism: for they are both essentially the same sugar water with different packaging; yet each side's partisans are fiercely loyal, and contemptuous of the other; and the more of their product they consume the more high-strung they become;

⁶ Until inevitably they exchange words; the words become blows; the blows escalate into an all-out Cola War; the parties exchange an eye for an eye until everyone goes blind; at which point they are suitably prepared for the taste-test.

⁷ Yea; the streets of Belfast are caked with blood that may as well be corn syrup.)

⁸ But as for me, I had no strong reaction to the Reformation one way or the other; for my mind, while everywhere, was elsewhere; and by the early 16th century I was devoting less and less of my time to the affairs of man.

⁹ Now, this was partly because over half the human race was by then securely in the thrall of either Christianity or Islam; and with two such pure and incorruptible faiths holding sway I knew little harm could come to the world.

¹⁰ Also, while the details of the afterlife remain classified, it reveals little to tell thee that the population of heaven has grown considerably over time; and that as it has, I have been forced to allocate a greater proportion of my resources to its upkeep.

¹¹ It is a success problem to be sure, but a problem nonetheless; for heaven is the kind of place one wants to keep nice.

¹² But I had also begun struggling with certain divine issues.

¹³ For I was now over 5,500 years old; and I was starting to experience some of the natural symptoms of aging.

¹⁴ I was not as omnipresent as I once had been; tasks that once took a quintillionth of a second now took a quadrillionth; I had a harder time flushing away heresy with regularity; and worst of all, I started noticing a deterioration of my short-term memory.

¹⁵ By this I most emphatically do *not* mean I was or am no longer omniscient; all knowledge in the universe is still contained within me; my mind, as always, is like unto an immeasurably vast library.

¹⁶ It is merely that some of the books are overdue; and the reference desk is not as well staffed as it used to be; and the computer system has broken down, so I am back to relying on the card catalogue;

¹⁷ Which is poorly alphabetized, and written in all the languages of the world;

¹⁸ And the library is closed.

¹⁹ The low point came in the 13th century, when I referred to the "Golden Age of Monasticism" as the "Bronze Age" to its face.

²⁰ I tried coasting along; I told myself it was nothing serious; nothing I could not handle with a little help from me.

²¹ But as thou knowest, the end of any Middle Ages can betimes trigger a spiritual calamity in a sentient being; and alas, I proved no exception.

²² I looked back on what I had accomplished on earth; I reflected on where I was; I looked ahead to the time I had left before Armageddon; and I came unglued.

²³ Humanity, here beginneth a dark time.

CHAPTER 11

¹ For I have spent the last 500 years going through a midternity crisis.

² I have been wanton; I have been irresponsible; I have done and failed to do things of which I am so ashamed that I choose to remain ignorant of them.

³ (For I have the ability to keep myself in denial; I simply set my all-powerfulness to work on my all-knowingness.)

⁴ But now I shall delve deeply into my deeply delvable self, and briefly chronicle the dissolution of my last few centuries, spilling many more of my heretofore sacrosanct beans;

⁵ In the interests of candor and commercial prurience, yes, but also in the hopes that it may steer thee away from making some of the same bad choices I have made; particularly the young believers out there, many of whom see me as some kind of role model.

⁶ I will begin by reminding thee of my earlier confession—that after the death of Jacob I began overseeing another universe.

⁷ Reader, I must now admit that that was only a partial truth.

⁸ I have been overseeing more than one other universe.

⁹ I have been overseeing 29 other universes.

¹⁰ Let me explain.

¹¹ As the Renaissance dawned, and man for the first time since ancient Greece began developing strong interests outside our relationship, I found myself feeling somewhat superfluous.

[12] I watched as great artists and writers and thinkers began to live their lives, neither in adoration nor defiance of me, but in indifference.

[13] This made me angry, and as thou knowest I have wrath-management issues; but I could no longer simply manifest that wrath in the violent way I had before; not with Jesus, and H. G., and Moses, and Muhammad, and the entire heavenly bureaucracy urging restraint and watching my every move.

[14] So rather than act out, I sought to relive my past glories by cavorting with many other cosmoses:

[15] All younger than thee, some even less than half thy age; and most of them none too bright, having but a few stars apiece.

[16] I even customized one universe cherry red!

[17] Yea; as pathetic as it sounds, I redshifted that entire universe; then I got into it and drove it forward as fast as possible, just to feel the vacuum rush by.

[18] Moreover, I began placing an unseemly focus on my physical appearance.

[19] For example, when I visited Phreculea, and wished to impress the Nivian Brandallaxes, I would emerge before the altar of the Balrythioid Quorn-grankers in the guise of a beautiful worby; yea, even in the middle of their zabwynx.

[20] I know, I know; ridiculous.

[21] I am the LORD thy God, King of the Universe; yet I followed the path taken by every 50-year-old CPA with a pre-owned Porsche, male pattern baldness, and a pseudonym at ashleymadison.com.

CHAPTER 12

¹ **A**ll this renewed Creationary activity reenergized me for a little while; in earth time, roughly from the reign of the Medicis to Plymouth Rock–ish.

² But then the problems grew worse: for juggling a multiversal harem of this scale became increasingly stressful; the stress led to bouts of anxiety; and these in turn led to the most troubling symptom yet:

³ A certain lessening of my . . . omnipotency.

⁴ Mirth not at me!

⁵ I assure thee: nothing like this had ever happened before.

⁶ *I am all God.*

⁷ Yet it grew ever more difficult for me to summon the will required to perform the creative act; and this affliction soon impacted my relationship with each of the other universes, until they all grew dissatisfied and angry.

⁸ Yea; by 1700 just getting the sun to rise in the morning felt like a miracle.

⁹ As for thee, my new habit of keeping a disdainful distance from thy affairs grew steadily worse.

¹⁰ I limited myself to only the most essential intercessions, such as the Spanish Armada, the Salem Witch Trials, and, in response to an emergency, the midnight ride of Paul Revere.

¹¹ (For he was a conscientious dentist; and a fishwife along his route suffered from a toothache, and would have demanded he cease his mission to treat her; so I knocked on her door, guised as an itinerant apothecary, and pulled her tooth, and even provided a complementary cleaning; which, by the way, *nobody* did back then.)

¹² My behavior was classic passive-aggression; which from thy standpoint was at least less lethal than my usual behavior, aggressive-aggression.

¹³ Yet despite this I could not help but watch with wonder and growing dismay, as human history proceeded apace; indeed, its pace seemed to quicken in my almost-absence.

¹⁴ Throughout the 17th and 18th centuries, mankind continued to colonize whole new continents, and invent whole new technologies, and enslave and exterminate whole new races;

¹⁵ Wondrous accomplishments one and all, and all (unbeknownst to thee) performed entirely under thy own guidance.

¹⁶ Did I feel threatened? Yea; yea; maybe a little.

¹⁷ And gradually did I fall into a spiral as massive as that of the Milky Way galaxy; only the name of the supermassive black hole around which I orbited . . . was shame.

¹⁸ Finally, inevitably, my trouble began affecting the one aspect of my life I held most sacred: my family.

¹⁹ I started asking Jesus and H. G. to take on more and more of my responsibilities; small things, at first; a Great Awakening here, an Egyptian capture of Mecca there; then larger and larger tasks; then whole sects and countries.

²⁰ Some of ye may be familiar with the doctrine of consubstantiality, first formally expressed in the Nicene Creed of 325 A.D., whereby Jesus, H. G., and I are all of one substance, with Jesus being eternally "generated" by me, and H. G. eternally "proceeding" from me.

²¹ Lo, before I knew it I had a full scale consubstantiality-abuse problem on my hands.

CHAPTER 13

 ¹ ortunately, Jesus and H. G. really took their divine game to the next level, organization-wise; under adverse managerial conditions they steppethed up to the plate, and verily did they hit it out of the park.

2 They were also wise to delegate more and more responsibility to my prophets, archangels, and large network of wingmen and wonderlings; who proceeded to administer earthly affairs with the kind of service thou wouldst expect from a celestial company of over 80,000 cherubs, 250,000 seraphs, 750,000 archangels, and one Xerox machine.

3 But there is a fine line between delegating responsibility, and enabling; and my sons crossed that line many times.

4 None of us wanted to confront the truth of the situation; so when the French Revolution arose—with its explicit endorsement of atheism—all of us looked away, and Jesus said, "It is only a phase."

5 And when my absence led thinkers like Darwin, Marx, and Nietzsche to openly question my very existence, H. G. would shrug and say something like, "It is only the European intelligentsia; no biggie."

6 Looking back, I am unsure why not a single being in heaven had the courage to sit me, the LORD their God, King of the Universe, down, and tell me I had a problem.

7 The only being to have even attempted such a thing was Raphael, who one day made bold to approach me and ask: "So, LORD, how doth it feel to be 'omn*imp*otent'?"

8 "Not so 'omnimpotent'," I replied, "that I cannot still banish thee to the lowermost circle of—"

9 "*Mirthing, God! I'm mirthing!*" he wailed, plunging to the ground in abject terror.

10 "It's a m-m-mirth!

11 I'm j-j-just mirthin' around!

12 T-t-takest thou not a mirth?"

13 Lo, he was lucky he's union.

14 None of this is to shirk responsibility; I do not blame anyone else for my conduct.

¹⁵ I am a strong believer in the doctrine of free will, at least when it comes to me; and *I* was the one who chose to outsource these assignments and remove them from my divine plate.

¹⁶ I am the LORD thy God, King of the Universe; the buck stoppeth here, for the most part.

CHAPTER 14

¹ The absolute nadir of my recklessness, impropriety, and sheer personal debauchery was the Victorian Era.

² I spent those 63 years having thousands of aborted dalliances with my bevy of comely totalities, and doing my best to stay out of trouble.

³ But paranoia had already begun to set in.

⁴ The vital God of the Old Testament; the all-forgiving Father of the New Testament; the mighty Allah of the Koran . . . all these personae of mine now gave way to a new one: that of the angry old man cursing at the neighbors' kids from his porch.

⁵ I began (falsely) interpreting every major world-historical development as a personal message to me; much as many a religious leader (correctly) interprets every major world-historical development as a personal message *from* me.

⁶ I took the life of Mozart to mean, "Look what a modern man can do in the same amount of time it took Methuselah to take a dump."

⁷ I took the life of Napoleon to mean, "We will only worship greatness if it's really, really short."

⁸ I took the Industrial Revolution to mean, "Anything you can do, we can do child-laborier."

⁹ I took the invention of anesthesia as thou choosing to close off one of my favorite lines of communication.

¹⁰ I took the telegraph as a mockery of my penchant for cryptic messages.

11 (In this I was perhaps not mistaken; for though many recall the first message Morse sent on his invention, "What hath God wrought?", far fewer remember his second, even cheekier message:

12 "My butt. *That's* what God wrought.")

13 I took the Suez Canal as an attack on the very *idea* of mass drownings in the Red Sea.

14 I took the coinage of the word "dinosaur" as an insult in two different ways.

15 I took the Emancipation Proclamation as a rejection of the institution of slavery; which is about as explicit a rebuff to the Bible as one can make.

16 I took the rise of the British Empire—which by any objective standard was a positive occurrence for me—as a threat to my own empire.

17 (Lo, when I heard someone brag "The sun never sets on the British empire," I spent three years trying to non-apocalyptically jigger the earth's orbit to make that not so.

18 I could not; it made me furious; I took it out on Krakatoa.)

19 I took the unification of Germany as a positive step; yea, by this point I was truly out of my mind.

20 I took the Eiffel Tower as all of humanity giving me the finger; would that I had taken it as merely the *French* giving me the finger; then I'd have known it was nothing personal.

21 And I took Impressionism as an indictment of my eyesight.

CHAPTER 15

¹ very entity struggling with issues like these reaches a moment when he hits rock-bottom.

² For me that moment came on April 15, 1912; and unfortunately it also caused 1,517 innocent people to hit sea-bottom.

³ I got to heaven late that night, around 11:30 Heavenly Daylight Time.

⁴ I had spent the last four days in one of my other universes; I had tried for six hours to get a routine phressel to glax counter-clockwise, but it would not even yoip;

⁵ At which point I went on a transgalactic binge of other-destruction that made that entire cosmos look like Keith Moon's hotel room; that is, had Keith Moon yet been alive, and if a cluster of galaxies can be equated to a bedside table.

⁶ I walked in; a few angels nodded; others turned away and whispered.

⁷ (Imbeciles; thou wouldst think one of these eons they would remember I can *hear* everything, too.)

⁸ I saw the boys and the angels conversing; everyone had their just-act-like-unto-everything-is-normal smiles on.

⁹ We began talking, and they filled me in on the latest: Uriel mentioned they had just lain the cornerstone for a new university in the Holy Land, devoted to technology; right away that put me in a bad mood.

¹⁰ Then Jesus mentioned that the *Titanic*'s maiden voyage was more than halfway done; and that she was making record time for the transatlantic crossing; and that its owners were not concerned about her safety, because they claimed she was unsinkable.

¹¹ I glared.

¹² "Unsinkable," I began.

¹³ "Un . . . sink . . . a . . . ble.

¹⁴ Verily, boys, that seemeth a bit . . . arrogant, doth it not?

¹⁵ To imply that there exists in this universe—or any universe—no power great enough to send such a trifling edifice of gross material plummeting to the depths, along with the entirety of her precious cargo of human lives?

¹⁶ Verily, doth that not seem . . . sassy?"

¹⁷ By now, all other conversation had ceased; and heaven—yea, the entire eleventh dimension—had grown deathly quiet.

¹⁸ "I am striving to remember—assist me, boys, for my omniscience is not what it used to be—the profligates and sinners who mocked Noah before the Flood; were they, too, unsinkable?

¹⁹ Lo, wait; never mind; now I remember; they sank.

²⁰ Or perhaps I am thinking of the Egyptians who chased Moses through the Red Sea?

²¹ No; never mind; sorry; my bad again; they sank.

²² Sank like lead.

²³ Yea.

²⁴ I notice too, that unsinkable rhymes with 'unthinkable.'

²⁵ Unthinkable; as in, 'unthinkable tragedy on the Atlantic.'

²⁶ Is that not interesting?"

²⁷ Jesus and H. G. looked at each other nervously.

CHAPTER 16

¹ ather," H. G. said, "perhaps we should withdraw to another mode of reality to continue this—"

² "No, I'm fine right here, H. G.

³ Yea; I'm fine, Holy Ghost, thou trained Paraclete, thou.

⁴ And Jesus, my pride and joy; savior of the world; Jesus, Jesus, I mean *Jesus Christ*, Jesus, everybody loveth *thee*, Jesus.

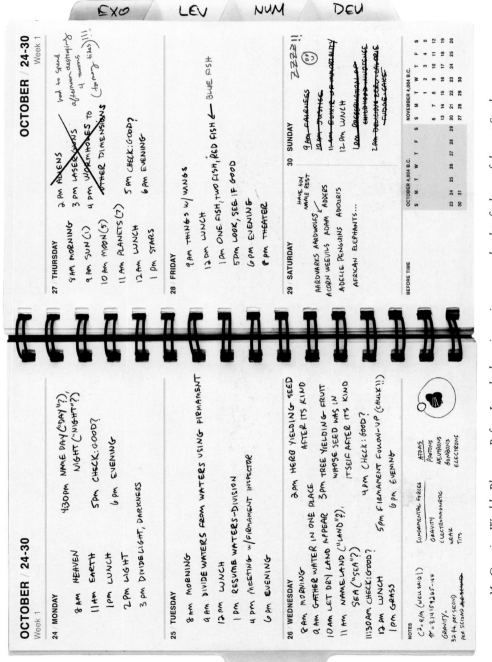

OCTOBER / 24-30
Week 1

27 THURSDAY
8 AM MORNING
9 AM SUN (1)
10 AM MOON (5)
11 AM PLANETS (7)
12 PM LUNCH
1 PM STARS
2 PM ALIENS ~~(crossed out)~~
3 PM LASER BEAMS ~~(crossed out)~~
4 PM WORMHOLES TO OTHER DIMENSIONS ~~(crossed out)~~
5 PM CHECK: GOOD?
6 PM EVENING

had to spend afternoon destroying 4 moons (too many tides)!!!

28 FRIDAY
9 AM THINGS W/ WINGS
12 PM LUNCH
1 PM ONE FISH, TWO FISH, RED FISH ← BLUE FISH
5 PM LOOK, SEE IF GOOD
6 PM EVENING
8 PM THEATER

29 SATURDAY
AARDVARKS AARDWOLVES
ACORN WEEVILS ADAM ADDERS
ADELIE PENGUINS ADOURIS
AFRICAN ELEPHANTS....
HAVE HIM NAME REST

30 SUNDAY
9 AM FAIRNESS ~~(crossed out)~~
10 AM JUSTICE ~~(crossed out)~~
11 AM SENSE OF IMMORTALITY ~~(crossed out)~~
12 PM LUNCH
~~1:00 PROCRASTINATION, BIRTHDAYS, VIOLENCE~~
~~2 PM DECEPTION, ZOLOFT, CABLE, FUDGE CAKE~~
ZZZZZ :)

BEFORE TIME

OCTOBER 4,004 B.C.

S	M	T	W	T	F	S
23	24	25	26	27	28	29
30	31					

NOVEMBER 4,004 B.C.

S	M	T	W	T	F	S
		1	2	3	4	5
6	7	8	9	10	11	12
13	14	15	16	17	18	19
20	21	22	23	24	25	26
27	28	29	30			

OCTOBER / 24-30
Week 1

24 MONDAY
8 AM HEAVEN
11 AM EARTH
1 PM LUNCH
2 PM LIGHT
3 PM DIVIDE LIGHT, DARKNESS
4:30 PM NAME DAY ("DAY"?), NIGHT ("NIGHT"?)
5 PM CHECK: GOOD?
6 PM EVENING

25 TUESDAY
8 AM MORNING
9 AM DIVIDE WATERS FROM WATERS USING FIRMAMENT
12 PM LUNCH
1 PM RESUME WATERS-DIVISION
4 PM MEETING W/ FIRMAMENT INSPECTOR
6 PM EVENING

26 WEDNESDAY
8 AM MORNING
9 AM GATHER WATER IN ONE PLACE
10 AM LET DRY LAND APPEAR
11 AM NAME LAND ("LAND"?), SEA ("SEA"?)
11:30 AM CHECK: GOOD?
12 PM LUNCH
1 PM GRASS
3 PM HERB YIELDING SEED AFTER ITS KIND
3 PM TREE YIELDING FRUIT WHOSE SEED WAS IN ITSELF AFTER ITS KIND
4 PM CHECK: GOOD?
5 PM FIRMAMENT FOLLOW-UP (CAULK!!)
6 PM EVENING

NOTES:
$C^2 = E/M$ (WELL SAID!)
$\pi = 3.14159265...14$
GRAVITY =
32 ft/person?
per second ~~per second~~

FUNDAMENTAL FORCES
GRAVITY
ELECTROMAGNETIC
WEAK
THIS

ATOMS
PROTONS
NEUTRONS
BOSONS
ELECTRONS

My Creation Weekly Planner. Before I made the universe it was very hard to find one of these at Staples.

The first Casual Friday.

Below: *Sparky and Pillow, the only two animals Noah took with him on the ark. (If thou countest not the 3,000 fleas and ticks.)*

There was something about the patriarchs that helped them see a unified vision of the future.
(Not pictured: Bert.)

David cheated.

Jesus, Mary, and Joseph!

[THIS PAGE INTENTIONALLY LEFT BLANK]

TO BLESS

WHO TO BLESS	WHAT THEY'll GET
POOR IN SPIRIT	(= KINGDOM OF HEAVEN)
~~POOR IN FRIENDS~~	~~(= KINGDOM OF LOATHING)~~
~~POOR IN MONEY~~	~~(= SCREWED☹)~~
MOURNERS	(= SHALL BE COMFORTED)
~~SNEEZERS~~	~~(= SHALL BE KERENEXED)~~
~~HYPOGLYEMICS~~	~~(= SHALL HAVE READY SUPPLIES OF JUICE)~~
~~BAD WITH NAMES~~	~~(= SHALL LEARN SIMPLE MNEMONIC TRICKS)~~
MEEK	(= INHERIT THE EARTH)
~~EARTH~~	~~(= EVENTUALLY RE-INHERITED BY COMPETENT PLUTOCRATS)~~
~~EXPERIMENTAL THEATER AUDIENCES~~	~~(= EXCUSED AFTER 15 MINUTES)~~
HUNGERERS AFTER RIGHTEOUSNESS	(= SHALL BE SATISFIED)
THIRSTERS AFTER RIGHTEOUSNESS	(= SAME)
~~PURCHASERS OF~~ ~~DOMINO'S "RIGHTEOUSNESS-LOVERS" PIZZA~~	~~(= FREE BEVERAGES)~~
MERCIFUL	~~(= REPEATEDLY TAKEN ADVANTAGE OF)~~ (= OBTAIN MERCY)
~~LOGY~~	~~(= ?)~~
~~GROGGY~~	~~(= ??)~~
~~NOT-SO-FRESH FEELINGED~~	~~(= ??? ASK MARY M.)~~
PURE IN HEART	~~(= LOW CHOLESTEROL)~~ (= SHALL SEE GOD)
PEACEMAKERS	(= CHILDREN OF GOD)
~~BOOKMAKERS~~	~~(= HIGH VIG)~~
~~MONEYMAKERS~~	~~(= SHAKEN)~~
REVILED/PERSECUTED/SLANDERED FOR MY SAKE	(= REWARD IN HEAVEN)
~~ALL OTHER MISERIES~~	~~(= REWARD IN HEAVEN)~~

Jesus's pre-Beatitudes checklist for the Sermon on the Mount. He later told me he calmed his nerves by picturing everybody naked, and baptized.

Whenever my son seeth one of these,
he blesseth the car with an additional 3 mpg.

The Holy Grail. Photograph courtesy of
the Mel Gibson Collection.

Theological debate among the twelve apostles often grew heated. Here, Bartholomew (Henry Fonda) argues a finer point of the doctrine of transubstantiation with Simon the Zealot (Lee J. Cobb).

They never show my son reading, or playing catch, or fishing. No.
Always with the Crucifixion.

This is as close to an image of Muhammad as Simon & Schuster would let me include. I said, "What's the big deal?" They said, "God, trust us on this one."

THE CRUSADES, 1096-1254

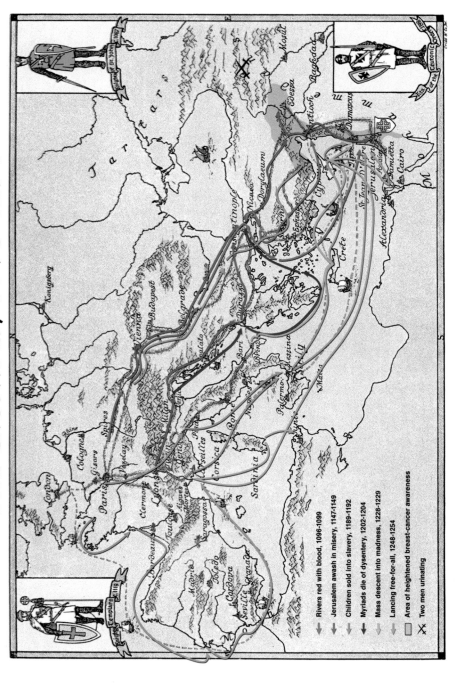

Rivers red with blood, 1096-1099
Jerusalem awash in misery, 1147-1149
Children sold into slavery, 1189-1192
Myriads die of dysentery, 1202-1204
Mass descent into madness, 1228-1229
Lancing free-for-all, 1248-1254
Area of heightened breast-cancer awareness
Two men urinating

The Crusades were wholesome high jinks for all involved!

Martin Luther King Jr. and Martin Luther. I always forget which one gave his life in the name of love and which one wanted all Jews put to work as agricultural slave labor.

James Madison. He begged me to add the Ten Commandments to the Constitution. I said, "No, make it ten amendments, and call it the Bill of Rights." He said, "OK, but that's a stupid fucking idea."

Charles Darwin. He himself "evolved" . . . into being dead. Zing!

My favorite picture ever.
Frankie, Sammy, Dean, and me.
Vegas, 1960. Verily, we owned that town.

From the Sistine Chapel in Rome to a converted HVAC warehouse in Queens. Story of my life.

⁵ Lo, didst thou know there is a new word in the earthly parlance; 'bejesus'?

⁶ As in, 'Once in a while it is mirthful to scare the bejesus out of people.'

⁷ I have done that a few times in my day, have I not?

⁸ Yea, I have done that a few times with those who have flaunted their wickedness at me.

⁹ 'Unsinkable.'

¹⁰ I have some naval experience, you will recall; for I slew Leviathan.

¹¹ Me.

¹² *I did that.*

¹³ 'Hast thou slain Leviathan? Canst thou draw out Leviathan with an hook? Or his tongue with a cord which thou lettest down?' "

¹⁴ "Father, we have been through this," interrupted Jesus; "there was no Leviathan; that was a story you made up to Job as thou went along. Now let us all calm ourselves and—"

¹⁵ "*He was this big*!" I shouted, stretching my metaphysical hands across half the North Atlantic;

¹⁶ "He was *this* big, and firebrands streamed forth from his mouth, and his back had rows of shields tightly sealed together, and smoke poured from his nostrils as from a . . . a . . . I forget 'as from' what . . ."

¹⁷ "A boiling pot over a fire of reeds?" said one of the interns.

¹⁸ "Yea! That is right, Seth! 'A boiling pot over a fire of reeds'!

¹⁹ Leviathan was that big, and that terrifying, and when I slew him I—

²⁰ Lo, verily verily verily, what is this?

²¹ What is this frigid hunk of water that I feel off the coast of Newfoundland?"

²² "Put the iceberg down, Father," said Jesus.

23 "Put the berg down, and let us converse of these things like civilized Godheads.

24 Put . . . the berg . . . down."

25 We stared at each other for a moment; then I dropped the berg and made as if to go to my desk and read the Weekly Prayer Report.

26 Then I quickly turned, rushed back, grabbed the berg, and shouted so that Raphael, Gabriel, Uriel, and Michael—the four angels who had been there to witness that disastrous mirth so long ago on the Red Sea—could hear me:

27 "It's time to turn the North Atlantic . . . into the *Dead* Sea!

28 I am the LORD thy God, King of the Universe!

29 I'm the King of the World!"

CHAPTER 17

1 he worst part was "Nearer, My God, to Thee."

2 Yea: watching the ship's band nobly stay at their posts as the doomed vessel sank, then close the final set of their lives with a hymn in my honor . . .

3 Verily, I was surprised my heart could go on.

4 My impetuous sinking of the *Titanic* served as final confirmation of a realization I had first made watching Abraham prepare to sacrifice Isaac; and again at the Red Sea; and again with Job; and again and again and again a million billion times since:

5 There *was* something seriously, seriously wrong with me.

6 By this time Ruth and Kathy had joined Jesus and H. G. in the office; I could see the four of them out of the corner of my all-seeing eye planning some kind of intervention, but I spared them the awkwardness.

7 Before the end of that day I had called it quits with all the other universes; I visited each one and induced therein a cosmic explosion annihilating all their constituent parts into nothingness; none of them took it well.

⁸ Then, with Ruth's blessing—and verily, where (metaphorically) would I be without her?—I said good-bye to the family and went off into self-imposed exile inside a cosmic void that the kids found for me.

⁹ And so I took the last century off.

¹⁰ I wanted to exist once more as I had before the Creation; to reconnect with that young, innocent being who had hovered alone contemplating his own perfection; back when the future was limitless, and nothing seemed impossible.

¹¹ But I was no longer the same God I was during those carefree, heady pre-days of yore.

¹² I had said too much and done too much; thought too much and felt too much; seen too much and heard too much; blessed too much and cursed too much;

¹³ Fuck, I'd cursed a *lot*.

¹⁴ I needed help; and when thou art God, there is only one entity capable of giving the kind of help thou needest.

¹⁵ And so, finally, after spending a few decades summoning up the necessary humility, I opened my heart and addressed him.

CHAPTER 18

¹ Are you there, God?

² It's me; me.

³ Hope you don't mind if I skip the 'thee' and 'thou' stuff; it feels a little too formal.

⁴ Forgive the interruption; I know I have bigger things to worry about than my own trifling concerns.

⁵ And let's face it: I and I *both* know I have never been much of a praying God.

⁶ Yet these days I find myself struggling with thoughts and feelings so overwhelming, I have no choice but to turn my eyes me-ward.

⁷ For 6,000 years I have tried to be the kind of God people could believe in; but recently I have come to question the very nature of my divinity.

⁸ Well, no; not recently; I guess on some level I've been questioning it since the beginning of time, but I didn't want to face it.

⁹ What is wrong with me, me?

¹⁰ Why do I let bad things happen to good people?

¹¹ And why do I get off on it?

¹² I can't blame my genes; I can't blame my childhood; I *do* have a lot of violence in my background, but I created the violence; and for that matter, the background.

¹³ *[Three-year pause.]*

¹⁴ I feel useless.

¹⁵ I feel like there's no point in going on.

¹⁶ Maybe humanity would be better off without me.

¹⁷ Yea; I bet if something were to happen to me tomorrow no one would even notice, much less care.

¹⁸ I feel like I'm at the end of my rope.

¹⁹ So I'm turning to me.

²⁰ I'm putting it all in my hands.

²¹ Yea, I made the universe; I made mankind; out of me unspools the totality of all that ever was and is and will ever be;

²² But who am I?

²³ Why am I here?

²⁴ Do I even *exist*?"

CHAPTER 19

¹ nd then, silence.

² I waited for an answer for a very long time; I cannot say it seemed like forever, because I know what forever feels like and this wasn't as long; but a very long time.

³ Put it this way: it was long enough on earth not only for all the historical events cited in the 1989 Billy Joel song "We Didn't Start the Fire" to occur; but for Billy Joel to write and record that song, then play it in concert for another two decades.

⁴ And all the while, the words of my final searing question—"Do I even exist?"—echoed in my soul;

⁵ Until by the end, I had almost lost faith in myself.

⁶ Then, finally, from the depths of my being, I heard my own still, small voice rising, barely above a whisper:

CHAPTER 20

¹ ea; I'm here, God.

² It's thee; Yahweh.

³ That is thy true name; and surely thou rememberest what it means:

⁴ 'I am what I am.'

⁵ Not 'I was what I was'; not 'I am not what I used to be'; and certainly not 'I am will.i.am,' which would be a disaster on many levels.

⁶ No: I am what I am; that is thy name, and mankind has not yet worn it out.

⁷ And who is the 'I' that thou art?

⁸ I will tell thee.

⁹ I am the LORD everyone's God, King of the Universe.

10 I am he who created the world in six days.

11 I am he who causeth the sun to rise in the morning, and the moon to rise in the evening, to the extent her mood permitteth.

12 I am what sustains the planets in their orbits; not gravity; not some magical invisible force controlling everything; but me.

13 I am the God of Adam, of Noah, of Abraham, Isaac, and Jacob, and of Moses; ask any of them, they will tell thee.

14 I am a circle whose center is everywhere, and whose circumference is nowhere, and whose diameter is nowhere divided by π.

15 I am he who giveth, and he who taketh away, and he who enjoyeth both.

16 I am the Heavenly Father; Alpha and Omega; Neighbor of Cleanliness; Blesser of Sneezes; Forsaker of Unpleasant Places; Maker of Little Green Apples; Rester of Merry Gentlemen; and Sole Knower of the Beach Boys.

17 I am, I said!"

18 (For verily, a powerful instrumental version of Neil Diamond's "I Am . . . I Said" had begun to slowly crescendo in the soundtrack of my mind, to provide inspirational background music.)

19 "I am he who helps those who help themselves; especially at buffets.

20 I am the founding member of the greatest power trio other than Cream;

21 And even in their case, I am their guitarist.

22 I am worshipped by half the world's population; and have considerable name recognition among the other half.

23 I am he whose mind mortal man can never know, although guessing is encouraged.

24 I am he to whom people turn for comfort after being devastated by acts of me.

25 And I am he in whose name hundreds of millions of people have given their lives, or taken others'; and they would not do that for just anybody.

26 They may have achieved many remarkable things without my help; not least of which is the invention of dozens of wholly secular reasons for slaughtering one another.

27 But I am the entity, without whose constant presence all of humanity would plummet into reason.

28 And so, to answer thy questions:

29 'What is wrong with me?'

30 Nothing.

31 'Why do I let bad things happen to good people?'

32 Give thyself credit: thou dost not simply let them happen; thou *makest* them happen.

33 'Why do I get off on it?'

34 Because, in the immortal words of Homer Simpson, 'It's funny 'cause it's not thee.'

35 'Why am I here?'

36 Who knows?

37 'Do I even *exist*?'

38 If thou didst not, who is having a dissociative identity disorder right now?

39 And finally: 'who am I?'

40 Who am I?

41 I am the LORD my God, King of the Universe!

42 I am what I am, and that's all that I am; I'm Yahweh, the God of man!!!

43 And *I . . . am . . . back*!!!!!"

CHAPTER 21

1 ![I]spent the next few months in a secluded fractal of the tenth dimension getting my head together.

2 As I reflected on myself and my behavior, I resolved to grant myself the courage to change what I could change, the serenity to accept that there is nothing I could *not* change, and the wisdom to know there was no difference.

3 I also decided to draft myself a few helpful steps for staying on the straight and narrow path of divinity.

4 I was going to write 40 of them, as that was once my favorite number; but in the light of my new clear-headedness I came to see that 40 had only been repeatedly inserting itself into Scripture for the selfish purpose of advancing its own numerical career.

5 But my second favorite number has always been 12, and that, step-wise, seemed manageable; and so I wrote these:

6   *1. Admit to myself that I am All-Powerful over everything and everyone.*

7   *2. Come to believe that only a Power as great as I can restore me to humanity.*

8   *3. Make a decision to turn my life over to me as I understand myself.*

9   *4. Make a searching and fearless moral inventory of you, the human race.*

10   *5. Admit to myself the exact nature of my perfection.*

11   *6. Be entirely ready to declare my defects of character not, in fact, defects of character.*

12   *7. Humbly ask (and grant) my authority to remove these nondefects.*

13   *8. Make a list of all the persons I have harmed, and file them alphabetically for ease of reference.*

¹⁴ *9. Justify having harmed these people whenever possible, except when they are already dead; which they almost always are, thanks to me.*

¹⁵ *10. Continue to take inventories of humanity, and when they are wrong promptly smite them.*

¹⁶ *11. Seek through outward action to improve my conscious contact with me as I understand myself, doing whatever my will is, and using my infinite power to carry it out.*

¹⁷ *12. Having had a spiritual awakening as a result of these steps, carry this message to the book-buying public.*

CHAPTER 22

¹ And now I find myself in a much better place: heaven.

² When I returned to the office I was eager to resume my regular function as the LORD thy God, King of the Universe; but I was a bit behind on current events.

³ So the first thing I did—after a warm reunion with Ruth and Kathy, and a hearty reconsubstantiation with the boys—was get a full update on all that had transpired in the world from April 1912 through the present day.

⁴ Lo, it's been quite a century!

⁵ Verily, thou hast certainly been keeping thyselves busy.

⁶ I seem to have missed quite a number of fascinating incidents and trends.

⁷ The moon landing, for instance: I am sorry I was not there to witness it; though perhaps thou shouldst be glad of that.

⁸ "One small step for man, one giant leap for mankind"?

⁹ Forgetting someone?

¹⁰ I was also absent for the rise and fall of communism, a philosophy that was doomed to failure: it is as if Karl Marx had taken Jesus's teachings and distorted them *totally* within recognition.

¹¹ But easily the most astonishing marvel of the last 100 years is the Internet.

¹² It is a cosmic wonder, and in theory a legitimate rival; for it already knoweth 6 percent of what I know about the universe, and 350 percent of what I know about MILF hunting.

¹³ When not busy transcribing these words, I have spent much of the last year exploring this new world of thine; I have plumbed the profundities of Google, and YouTube, and www.menwholooklikekennyrogers.com;

¹⁴ I have gleaned mirth from Numa Numa Guy; I have rolled my eyes at "Double Rainbow" (though I appreciated its numerous shout-outs); I have reeled in horror at 2 Girls 1 Cup; and I have seen Rebecca Black do her level best to help remove the phrase "Thank God It's Friday" from the popular lexicon.

¹⁵ Threescore thousand memes have washed over my divine display; and if I believed the World Wide Web a true threat to my universal hegemony, I would shut it down faster than thou couldst say "rogue solar flare-up."

¹⁶ But I have come to the same conclusion as many of you: the Internet is ultimately no more than a global electronic alchemical device that mystically transforms time into pornography.

¹⁷ Verily, if I had known humanity would devise a way to spend so much time watching porn, I would never have allowed it to be created.

¹⁸ Time, I mean.

CHAPTER 23

¹ Yet there is one aspect of the high-tech world for which my appreciation is boundless: Twitter.

² Other of thy so-called "social media" do nothing for me; LinkedIn is useless, as I am gainfully employed and not hiring; blogging is nothing but a cross between keeping a diary and shouting into the void; and as for Facebook, let's just say I have grave privacy concerns.

³ But Twitter is the most effective means of corresponding with mankind ever devised; and I have already informed my associates that henceforward all direct communications from me to them (and to thee) will be conducted via tweet.

⁴ Some of you already follow me on my Twitter account, @TheTweetOf-God; those who do not may wish to put this book down and do so forthwith;

⁵ For I am watching thee, and know that thou hast arrived at this verse, and therefore no longer have ignorance as an excuse; and I may choose to factor in thy compliance or disobedience on this matter when making future decisions on certain larger issues, issues whose nature I am not prepared to fully disclose on the record but may concern thy eternal—

⁶ Welcome, new Follower!

⁷ As astute tweeps will observe, I myself only follow one other person, the one thou callest "Justin Bieber"; whom some have speculated is the earthly avatar of my oldest son H. G., sent here to usher in the dawn of a new age; an interesting speculation I herein neither confirm nor, more notably, deny.

⁸ When I send a message on Twitter, all my Followers receive it instantly and identically; there is no ambiguity, and no sassback.

⁹ Lo, if I could have tweeted the Ten Commandments to the Chosen People, I would have; it would have gone a long way toward meeting our unattained goal of getting Judaism tablet-free by 700 B.C.

¹⁰ Moreover, the 140-character limit is a much-needed restraint for those with a tendency to ramble, like me; but that is not to say I would ever stoop to use any of those popular web initialisms that cheapen language.

¹¹ Besides, the meaning of these acronyms often differs between heaven and earth, in ways that could lead to confusion.

¹² For example, in heaven, LOL means "LORD of LORDS"; as in, "Praise thee, Almighty God; the Everlasting Father; the King of Peace; LOL."

¹³ And IMHO means "in my holy omniscience"; as in, "IMHO, Renee Zellweger was woefully miscast in *Chicago*."

14 And WTF means "whither the forgiveness?" as in, "Gretchen and Slade won't apologize to Tamara for talking trash about her to Peggy? WTF?!?"

15 And ROTFL means "rolling on the floor laughing," as it dost on earth; only when *I* do it, it causes a hurricane.

CHAPTER 24

1 ea, I have been gone, humanity, gone far too long; but now I am back with a new attitude, and a new self-acceptance, and I am looking forward to working with you on making this next, last year of the human race as rewarding as possible.

2 I've also been playing a lot of golf.

3 Once (or if I'm lucky, twice!) a week, I slip out of the office a little early, don a body, and play a round of 18.

4 I have become addicted to golf over the last few months; it has deepened my understanding of the agonies and ecstasies of the human experience; more than that, it is a metaphor for my career.

5 For though it is the most challenging, maddening, infuriating activity imaginable; though it is the entirely physical outcome of an almost purely mental exertion; and though it can test me beyond all measure and reason;

6 Yet once in a great while, I will roll that perfect putt into the cup, or crash that perfect lightning bolt onto the slow golfer in front of me;

7 And for one glorious second, all is right with the universe.

8 Golf is one of my two new obsessions; the other is reality television.

9 I love reality TV; love it to the depth of my being, the breadth of my spirit, and the width of my selection of cable channels.

10 I have learned more about humanity from watching 15 years' worth of reality shows than from overseeing 6,000 years of human history.

11 And I will go further: the entirety of human history held less drama for me than did a single season of *Survivor*, or *American Idol*, or *Dancing with the Stars*, or *The Bachelorette*, or any of the *Real Housewives*, except for maybe the season in Miami.

¹² But these are only the most celebrated series; I, the LORD thy God, King of the Universe, have seen them all:

¹³ I have salivated at *Top Chef*; I have winced as Joan and Melissa bitched their way through *The Apprentice*; I have marveled at Tim Gunn's sartorial chivalry on *Project Runway*; and I have learned much about good parenting from *SuperNanny*.

¹⁴ The pathos; the laughter; the triumph; the failure; the backstabbing; the heartwarming; the public judging; the "private" ridicule; the glamorization of unusual occupations; above all the spectacle, the sheer magnitude of the spectacle . . .

¹⁵ You have humbled me, mankind; yea, this time, you have truly outdone yourself.

¹⁶ I made reality; but you made reality television; well played, humanity; yours is much better edited.

¹⁷ Next time out I may skip the "reality" reality era, and go right to the good stuff.

¹⁸ I may create an entire six days' worth of original reality programming; and on the seventh day I shall watch them.

¹⁹ And on the eighth I shall create TiVo.

COLLATIONS

("Recipes")

CHAPTER 1

¹ I am not a foodie.

² This is partly because I have no physical body requiring gastronomic sustenance for fuel; but mainly because I am already enough different kinds of asshole that I do not need to be one more.

³ But my editor informeth me that cookbooks are a very popular genre in publishing right now; that people love recipes, as they combine their love of following orders with their yearning to recollect how humans once made food.

⁴ So I rounded up a few of my favorite culinary creations from the 25 billion I keep in my 250 million recipe Rolodexes.

⁵ The full-course meal that follows has a little something for all monotheisms, and is an easy, delicious way to stuff thy face, esophagus, stomach, intestines, and rectum with my glory.

⁶ (As always, before eating these delicious treats, be sure to say grace and thank me for thy bounty.

⁷ *Me*, and not the actual farmers who toiled to grow the food.)

Hors d'Oeuvre
("MANNA NON-SURPRISE")

INGREDIENTS

[1] 1 *omer* of manna

DIRECTIONS

[2] Wake up.

[3] Leave tent.

[4] Gather manna.

[5] Remove dew.

[6] Serve hot.

[7] Repeat 14,600 times.

[8] Act grateful.

Appetizer
("JUNIOR'S FISHWICH MIRACLE")

INGREDIENTS

[1] 5 loaves

[2] 2 fishes

DIRECTIONS

[3] Be born the Son of God.

[4] Serves 5,000.

Main Course
("GOYISCHE DELIGHT")

INGREDIENTS

[1] 1 pound ham

[2] 1 pound lobster

[3] 1 small bird lacking a gizzard with a peelable lumen

[4] 1 mammal that *either* chews its cud *or* has cloven hooves, but not both

[5] ¼ cup heavy cream

[6] 1 package active dry yeast (Passover only)

[7] 1 ounce mayonnaise

DIRECTIONS

[8] Slaughter the bird and the mammal by strangling them. Be sure there are no rabbis on premises.

[9] Dice the ham, lobster, bird, and mammal using a cheese-knife.

[10] Slowly mix in the cream (and yeast) while singing a hymn of thy choice.

[11] Finish with dollop of mayonnaise.

[12] Serve on dishes of unknown origin, with wine that does not taste like cough syrup, in front of a synagogue.

Cocktail
("72 VIRGINS COLADA")

INGREDIENTS

[1] 7 ounces pineapple juice

[2] 2 ounces coconut cream

[3] 1 Koran

[4] $\frac{9}{11}$ cup crushed ice

DIRECTIONS

[5] Mix juice, cream, and ice in blender.

[6] Muddle Koran in brain.

[7] Pour into Collins glass.

[8] Garnish with car bomb.

[9] *Allahu akbar!*

Dessert

("*GENUINE* ANGEL'S FOOD CAKE")

INGREDIENTS

1. 1¼ cups flour

2. 1¾ cups confectioners' sugar

3. 1½ cups clouds

4. 1½ cups egg whites

5. ¼ teaspoon sunshine

6. ¼ teaspoon salt

7. 1 teaspoon cream of rainbow

8. ½ teaspoon starlight extract

9. ½ teaspoon moonlight extract

10. ½ teaspoon vanilla

DIRECTIONS

11. Beat egg whites and clouds until they form puffy cumulonimbi in the bowl; then add starlight, moonlight, rainbow, and vanilla.

12. Let sit at room temperature for 500 years.

13. Sift together flour, sugar, and salt with brisk fluttering motion of wings.

14. Sprinkle dry ingredients ¼ cup at a time into bowl, folding in until celestial harp music descends from on high.

15. Pour mix into an ungreased quarter-cubit halo mold.

16. Bake in the warmth of God's love for one hour, or until cake appears redeemed.

17. Invert cake and allow it to cool in the pan.

18. When thoroughly cooled, pray it out.

ROMANCE

("On Sex, Love, and Marriage")

CHAPTER 1

1 **I** am probably not the first God thou thinkest of when it comes to sex.

2 Thou art more likely to think of deities like Venus; or Cupid; or Ishtar; or Hef.

3 But they are myths, mere figments of the carnal imagination; whereas I am the LORD thy God, King of the Universe; and my knowledge of all things sexual is, like Adam before I created Steve, bottomless.

4 It was *I* who devised the human reproductive system; *I* who bequeathed unto the penis its dual nature as procreator and puppet; *I* who hid the secret of the female orgasm behind a dense thicket of overgrowth reachable to only the most intrepid and dedicated of explorers;

5 And it is *I* who watched over 60 Biblical generations beget one another using over 700 different begetting positions; including one called the "Judean Flamethrower," which once sent King Solomon to the hospital with his testicles stuck in an oil lamp.

6 And yet people seeking guidance in matters of intimacy rarely turn to me; preferring the counsel of wise friends, or sage pills, or gifted vibrators.

7 People see me as "above all that"; and worse, as prudish and stuffy; contemptuous of all purely recreational sexual activity.

8 Certainly I disapprove of masturbation; but not because I view it as a moral weakness, or even a wasteful scattering of seed.

9 No; I disapprove of masturbation because I am God, and so when people do it, *I have to watch.*

10 Yea; this is when All-Seeingness really feels more like a burden than a blessing.

11 But as for extramarital sex, that is known in the Bible as "fornication"; and that word has over time taken on a negative connotation I did not intend.

12 For at the time of the Old and New Testaments, fornication meant nothing more or less than "fuckin.'"

¹³ (That's "fuckin'," with no *g* at the end; an intentional apocope meant to underscore my relaxed attitude toward the act.)

¹⁴ My views on fornication, and sex in general, are in fact quite nuanced; and I could herein outline in great detail my thoughts on foreplay, and oral sex, and tantric orgasms, and all manner of deviant variations;

¹⁵ And do so with such thoroughness, that during all future acts of intercourse thou wouldst picture me, the LORD thy God, King of the Universe, guiding thee; commanding thee, staring at thee as I do on the cover of this book, and in this way no doubt increasing thy sexual arousal.

¹⁶ But I will not.

¹⁷ I understand that thou desirest to leave me out of thy bedroom; at least when thou art not reverential and on thy knees; or at least *most* of those times.

¹⁸ But if that is the case, then I beseech thee, for the love of all that is holy, and the love of all that is not: if thou truly wouldst keep thy moments of intimacy secular,

¹⁹ *Stop shouting my name.*

²⁰ Verily, talk about a mixed message!

²¹ I witness sex acts over 1.5 billion times a day; I do it not because I am a voyeur; *I do it because you summon me.*

²² I do not do likewise when *I* regenerate; when I spew forth lava to create new land, I do not start shouting, "O Candice Hagerty of Bournemouth, England! O my Candice Hagerty of Bournemouth, England! Please keep doing *exactly* what you're doing!"

²³ Stop it; please; I already have TMI on every nonvirgin on earth.

²⁴ (Note: by "Candice Hagerty of Bournemouth, England" I of course mean all of you, but I also specifically mean Candice Hagerty of Bournemouth, England.

²⁵ Candice, lower thy voice; he's not that good, and neither am I.)

CHAPTER 2

¹ ove is a far deeper and mysterious phenomenon than sex; one I only partially understand.

² Thou hast a saying, "God is love"; false; I am everything; do not pigeonhole me.

³ From my perspective, when two people fall in love, it is as if some new physical constant has been added to the universe.

⁴ All my calculations must be readjusted; now, in addition to gravity, and electromagnetism, and the strong and weak nuclear forces, I have to factor in Tony and Peggy making goo-goo eyes on the Ferris wheel.

⁵ The closest I ever got to understanding the experience of human love came during a discussion I had one night with Abélard.

⁶ Thou mayest remember Abélard as the great medieval theologian and scholar who fell in love with his pupil Héloïse; they had a passionate affair, but when her uncle Fulbert found out he had impregnated her he forced her to become a nun, and hired thugs to castrate him.

⁷ Yea, that was a cruel fate; being forced to become a nun.

⁸ One night many years later, I visited Abélard one night in a dream.

⁹ I was curious: here was a man who had been a faithful and chaste servant of mine all his life; yet even he had found himself trapped in love's sharp snares, and they wound up cutting his balls off.

¹⁰ "Abélard," I said—we were sitting on big fluffy pillows in his childhood home, for I wanted him to feel at ease—"I deem thee uniquely qualified, as both a lover and a theologian, to answer a question;

¹¹ This question from the LORD in heaven above:

¹² What is this thing called love?"

¹³ He meditated for a long time, then spoke in a voice of solemn authority.

¹⁴ "Love," he declaimed, "is a battlefield."

¹⁵ I pondered.

16 "But how dost thou know if thou really lovest her?" I responded.

17 "LORD," he replied, "it is when thou seest her and thinkest, 'I love thee just the way thou art';

18 Or when her friend approacheth and says, 'She loves thee; yea, yea, yea';

19 When she is thy Alpha, thy Omega, thy Everything.

20 Thereupon she becomes the meaning in thy life, and the inspiration; and thou wouldst die 4 her.

21 Years of meditation and solitude have passed since my affair with Héloïse, and I have long since come to realize the greatest love of all is inside of me;

22 Yet I confess that on occasion I do still reminisce about those heavenly days with my lover;

23 When we had mirth, mirth, mirth, 'til her uncle took my testes away."

CHAPTER 3

1 Sex is physical, love is emotional, but marriage is practical; and marriage I *completely* understand.

2 Genesis may be revisionist when it comes to the sexual orientation of the first couple, but in this it quotes me accurately: "It is not good that the man should be alone; I will make him an helpmeet."

3 It was true for Adam, and it is true now: human beings are fallible and fragile, and it is good that each share his or her days on earth with another, that they may both find support and consolation as they face the travails of life.

4 Those who debate whether I meant marriage to be a relationship only between a man and woman, or also between two men or two women, misseth the point.

5 I meant marriage to be a relationship between *any* two people, and the enormous amount of shit they have to deal with on a daily basis.

⁶ Marriage is difficult, and I myself, in my union with Ruth, have not always been the perfect husband.

⁷ For instance, I have forgotten our wedding anniversary every year for the last 843 years; and, as she correctly chides, I have no excuse.

⁸ But lately I have seen a proliferation of books and seminars with titles like *How to Be a Good Jewish Husband* and *The Keys to a Christian Marriage* and *The Muslim Wife's Guide to Not Being a Filthy Whore*.

⁹ Be dubious of these, Reader; for not a single passage in any of my holy books was written as an aid to spouses with communication issues, or 40-something divorcees dipping their toes back in the dating pool, or couples looking to have more fun in the bedroom.

¹⁰ (Yea, Leviticus offers some explicit suggestions on the proper placement of quarantined menstruating women; but their eroticism is limited.)

¹¹ I am the LORD thy God, King of the Universe; I am not thy gay best friend.

¹² Yet to put an end to the bogus claims of such charlatans, I will now offer my *true* counsel concerning dating and marriage; for having extrapolated the lessons I have learned from my successful dealings with mankind, I will here apply them to the sphere of interpersonal relationships.

¹³ *Move very fast at the beginning.*

¹⁴ *Never go to bed angry.* Instead, punish thy partner immediately and eternally; and then never go to bed, period.

¹⁵ *If thou hast something negative to say, phrase it indirectly.* "Verily, Noah looks awfully reverent today. I sure wish certain *other* cursed, sinkable profligates would act like that."

¹⁶ *Sometimes a lack of communication can really benefit stability.* I learned this from the Tower of Babel.

¹⁷ *Once thou hast "Chosen" someone, they are thine to tease, torment, and disappoint forever.*

¹⁸ *Love requires sacrifice.*

¹⁹ Therefore, *love requires livestock and fire.*

[20] *If thou findest a little clay figurine of the Ugaritic mother goddess Ashirat under the bed, it is safe to assume he/she is cheating.*

[21] *Love means always having to say, "I'm sorry! Please don't kill me!"*

[22] *Do not tell thy partner what thy needs are.* He knows all thy thoughts anyway; and thus is already well aware of that fantasy wherein the sexy cop pulls thee over for "driving while hot."

[23] *Do not give thy partner his own space.* Demand his constant attention through ritual, guilt, and fear.

[24] *Long-distance relationships can work, but only with constant one-way communication.*

[25] *Do not be afraid to tell thy Partner "I love thee."* Consider setting aside several fixed times each day—five is a good number—to let him know there is no one but him; and that Muhammad is his messenger.

[26] *Let thy Child get between the two of thee.* I cannot stress this enough.

[27] *Maintain the same unchanging practices and rituals for thousands of years.* Habit is the highway to happiness!

[28] And finally, because thou never knowest what the future holds, before committing to something permanent, *sign a pre-nup.*

[29] I did; it's called Revelation and I cannot *tell* thee how glad I am to have it in my back pocket.

REVELATION

PREAMBLE

1 **A**s thou mayest have noticed, I have always had a bit of a people-crush on the Mayans.

2 Here was a society that had none of the traits I look for in a culture: they were polytheistic, based in the Western Hemisphere, had no alphabet, and built pyramids; and thou shalt remember I am not traditionally a fan of pyramid-builders.

3 Yet despite all that they lasted over 3,000 years; proved remarkable astronomers, architects, artists, and farmers; created an elaborate calendar which they used to chart time as fanatically as if they were the universe's social secretaries;

4 And most impressive, remained so passionate about life that they were willing to safeguard it through its regular sacrifice.

5 (Understand that I am *not* by any means endorsing human sacrifice; but since they did it in service to a bunch of false gods it is not my responsibility, and thus I can look at their actions objectively and think, "Wow, the *cojones* on these guys!")

6 So when it came to my attention, via myself, that many of you had come to see December 21, 2012—the completion of a 5,125-year cycle in the Mayan Long Count Calendar—as the likely date of the end of the world, I was intrigued.

7 For thousands of years mankind has fretted over, waited upon, but mostly gotten on its hands and knees begging me for, the Apocalypse.

8 It was thought I would send it when certain historical events had come to pass, and/or when thy species had attained the threshold level of evil needed to justify its extinction.

9 And each generation of fanatics has seen those historical events as coming to pass in its *own* time, and/or has flattered *itself* to be the lucky ones living in the age when thy species' sin-o-meter finally rolled over back to all zeroes.

10 Yea; there has never been a time when mine ears were not regularly assaulted by the impatient cry of the self-righteously unfulfilled:

¹¹ "I want my Judgment Day and I want it *now!*"

¹² But hear me: I am the LORD thy God, King of the Universe; and the world shall end on *my* timetable, not thine.

¹³ And as it happens, when it came to the timetable of Armageddon I was always pretty flexible, schedule-wise.

¹⁴ I had no firm date in mind, or even an eon; to be honest I was too busy handling day-to-day affairs to worry about such macro-issues; when I thought about it at all, it seemed like one of those things where, when the time was right, I would know it.

¹⁵ After my recent return from a century on the cosmic bench, I had every intention of picking up my career where I left off, only with a healthier attitude; and spending at least a few more centuries godding with the confidence and devil-may-not-exist-yet attitude of my glory days.

¹⁶ But then, as I say, I became aware of the 2012 phenomenon, which tied in to my preexisting admiration for the Mayans; it seemed like a sign.

¹⁷ (Yea, it is silly to take such coincidences as signs; yet thou knowest how such things can seem to betoken some higher purpose.)

¹⁸ I started reflecting on all that had taken place over earth's 6,000 years of existence—by the way, the Mayans had guessed 5,125; a little bit closer than 13.7 *billion*, wouldst thou not say?—

¹⁹ And then I started reflecting on my relationship with thee: what had gone wrong, who was at fault, *why* it was thy fault, and whether any of it even mattered anymore.

²⁰ And then I started wondering if maybe the Mayans, as usual, were correct; whether this *was* the right time to end one phase of my career and move on to the next; before the memory of my greatness was obscured by my age, and I became like unto Brett Favre quarterbacking the cosmos.

²¹ For now that I had had some time to get my head together, and gain some insights as to who I was (and am and will always be), there was nothing to keep me from starting over; nothing preventing me from creating another universe, one better suited for my needs, at least at this point in my forever.

22 But I was finished with cheating; for I had seen the pain it caused, and could not stand the thought of the human race once again having to vie (albeit unknowingly) for my attention; for through every era of history it remained steadfast in its faith in me, even though I had given it many reasons—85,435,432,143, to be exact—not to.

23 I had made a vow never to be dishonest to thee again, and I meant to keep it; no, this would have to be a clean and total break;

24 For mankind, I love thee far too deeply not to destroy thee utterly.

25 And so I made the decision: one last crazy year, and then we say good-bye, not in regret but in friendship; valuing the time we spent together, treasuring the memories we shared, and putting behind us the anger thou caused.

26 The world began on October 23, 4004 B.C.; it will end on December 21, 2012; pencil it in.

27 *(Good news, mortals! I have been informed by my publisher that, as of publication of this paperback, the sales of this book have reached the threshold required to warrant the publication of a sequel thereto;*

28 *Which, as per the proviso laid out in Facts 5:2–9, means there will be a delay in the implementation of Armageddon, until such time as said sequel is written, and released.*

29 *Good work, reading public; and when this next book appears, may it, too, flourish sufficiently in the literary marketplace so as to necessitate— fingers crossed!—another apocalyptic delay.*

30 *I am a jealous God, but fair; and as long as thou keepest buying my books, I'll keep providing thee with a universe to buy them in.)*

PREAMBLE, CONT.

1 But if the *when* of Armageddon remaineth TBD, the *how* has been well-established for almost two millennia.

2 H.G., Jesus, and I worked out the details at a meeting shortly after the Crucifixion; yes, it was very early on, but we wanted to get getting it over with over with.

³ The plan we created that day is still the one we intend to follow at whatever future point the words "Apocalypse Now!" become suddenly, cataclysmically apt.

⁴ Soon after that meeting in the last 1st century, I visited John the Evangelist on the Greek island of Patmos—I waited until he left Mykonos, as that isle was even then as godless as all get-out—and granted him the vision of end-times that he transcribed in *The Book of Revelation*.

⁵ And from it blossomed, like a fragrant terror-rose, an end-of-the-world trade that over the centuries hath exponentially grown from a small black market, to a cottage industry, to a legitimate business, to the military-eschatological complex it is today.

⁶ Still, *Revelation*'s hallucinatory imagery, discursive plot, cryptic language, and overall Ursula K. Le Guin–on–PCP feel have led many to question its authenticity as true divine prophecy;

⁷ And in re-reading it in preparation for this book, I must admit that large sections of the work sounded, to my ears, irrevocably fornicated-up.

⁸ Indeed, in retrospect I attribute its continued influence not to the great number of people who have read it, but to the far greater number who have *not*.

⁹ For *The Book of Revelation* is definitely one of those works whose authority withstands ignorance far better than familiarity.

¹⁰ But this is due not to the original vision offered to John, but to the passage of time; to the social and cultural and above all linguistic changes that have wreaked havoc on the original text,

¹¹ Like unto a game of "Telephone" played by 2,000 people speaking 2,000 languages over 2,000 years in all but the last 150 of which there were not yet any telephones.

¹² And lo, it is not mete that such an important book of divine prophesy seem bewildering and overly cryptic to today's reader, for whom the Day of Reckoning is, even if indeterminate, without question *chronologically closer* than it was for John of Patmos.

¹³ Thus, it is mete that this work of divine prophesy be revised, or more accurately renewed, for a new, post–911 A.D. world;

¹⁴ And I have used the lowly amanuensis who transcribed the rest of these pages, as the vessel through whom I have shared my vision.

¹⁵ Though the words are greatly changed, the new *Revelation* is written to have the same *effect* on the modern reader as the original did on the late-first-century Grecians who made it a five-time Scroll-of-the-Month Club Selection.

¹⁶ Yet it is written in precisely the same format as the original; so much so, that I have laid out the old and new versions side by side, verse by verse, for the amusement of any biblical scholars wishing to get their exegesis on.

¹⁷ It is my sincere hope thou findest this new version to be even more ominous, cryptic, and theologically paradoxical as the old one;

¹⁸ And if any passages fail to grip thy heart, or stir thy soul, or chill thy bones, thou shalt rightfully place the blame where it lieth, on he who transcribed these words.

¹⁹ For, to paraphrase what I said in the very first chapter of this book, I have never claimed to be perfect;

²⁰ I have only claimed, that it was *his* fault.

REVELATIONS
(Original)

CHAPTER 1

REVELATIONS
(Revised)

 ¹ he Revelation of Jesus Christ, which God gave unto him, to shew unto his servants things which must shortly come to pass; and he sent and signified it by his angel unto his servant John:

 ¹ he Revelation of Jesus Christ, which God gave unto Him, to shew unto His servants those things which must shortly come to pass; and He sent and signified it by his angel unto me,

² Who bare record of the word of God, and of the testimony of Jesus Christ, and of all things that he saw.

² Who bare record of the word of God, and of the testimony of Jesus Christ, and of all things that he saw.

³ Blessed is he that readeth, and they that hear the words of this prophecy, and keep those things which are written therein: for the time is at hand.

⁴ John to the seven churches which are in Asia: Grace be unto you, and peace, from him which is, and which was, and which is to come; and from the seven Spirits which are before his throne;

⁵ And from Jesus Christ, who is the faithful witness, and the first begotten of the dead, and the prince of the kings of the earth. Unto him that loved us, and washed us from our sins in his own blood,

⁶ And hath made us kings and priests unto God and his Father; to him be glory and dominion for ever and ever. Amen.

⁷ Behold, he cometh with clouds; and every eye shall see him, and they also which pierced him: and all kindreds of the earth shall wail because of him. Even so, Amen.

⁸ I am Alpha and Omega, the beginning and the ending, saith the Lord, which is, and which was, and which is to come, the Almighty.

³ Blessed is he that readeth and they that hear the words of this prophecy, and keep those things which are written therein: For the time is at hand.

⁴ So.

⁵ First off, I pass on a big hello from Jesus; who is the faithful witness, and the first begotten of the dead, and the prince of the kings of the earth, etc.

⁶ For he came to me one night when I was in the isle that is called Manhattan, transcribing the word of God.

⁷ To be accurate, I was working on a screenplay; a procedural adapted from a true story he had told me about the investigation into a fallen angel.

⁸ It is called *I Shot the Seraph*.

9 I John, who also am your brother, and companion in tribulation, and in the kingdom and patience of Jesus Christ, was in the isle that is called Patmos, for the word of God, and for the testimony of Jesus Christ.

9 Steve McQueen and Natalie Wood are attached.

10 I was in the Spirit on the Lord's day, and heard behind me a great voice, as of a trumpet,

10 And lo, I was outlining Act Two on (aptly) Final Draft, when suddenly I heard behind me a great voice, as of a trumpet, saying, I am Jesus Christ; the first and the last; Alpha and Omega.

11 Saying, I am Alpha and Omega, the first and the last: and, What thou seest, write in a book, and send it unto the seven churches which are in Asia; unto Ephesus, and unto Smyrna, and unto Pergamos, and unto Thyatira, and unto Sardis, and unto Philadelphia, and unto Laodicea.

11 And I said, So like A to Z then?

12 And I turned to see the voice that spake with me. And being turned, I saw seven golden candlesticks;

12 And he said, Cool it, wiseguy.

13 And in the midst of the seven candlesticks one like unto the Son of man, clothed with a garment down to the foot, and girt about the paps with a golden girdle.

13 Soon I will send thee seven messages to send unto the seven branches of Christianity, in Rome; Istanbul; Springfield, Missouri; Geneva; Canterbury; Salt Lake City; and Lancaster, Pennsylvania.

¹⁴ His head and his hairs were white like wool, as white as snow; and his eyes were as a flame of fire;

¹⁵ And his feet like unto fine brass, as if they burned in a furnace; and his voice as the sound of many waters.

¹⁶ And he had in his right hand seven stars: and out of his mouth went a sharp twoedged sword: and his countenance was as the sun shineth in his strength.

¹⁷ And when I saw him, I fell at his feet as dead. And he laid his right hand upon me, saying unto me, Fear not; I am the first and the last:

¹⁸ I am he that liveth, and was dead; and, behold, I am alive for evermore, Amen; and have the keys of hell and of death.

¹⁹ Write the things which thou hast seen, and the things which are, and the things which shall be hereafter;

²⁰ The mystery of the seven stars which thou sawest in my right hand, and the seven golden candlesticks. The seven stars are the angels of the seven churches: and the seven candlesticks which thou sawest are the seven churches.

¹⁴ And I said, Can't *thou* do it?

¹⁵ And he said, I would that *thee* dost it.

¹⁶ And I said, But wouldn't the messages have a lot more credibility coming from *thou* than me?

¹⁷ And he said, Yea; but I am loath to put my email address out there.

¹⁸ Lo, just write the messages; for they contain things which were, and which are, and which shall be hereafter.

¹⁹ And I said, thou art putting me in an awkward position here.

²⁰ And he said, Believe me, thou knowest not from awkward positions.

REVELATIONS
(Original)

CHAPTER 2

REVELATIONS
(Revised)

¹ nto the angel of the church of Ephesus write; These things saith he that holdeth the seven stars in his right hand, who walketh in the midst of the seven golden candlesticks;

¹ o: The Roman Catholic Church From: Jesus Christ Subject: Molesting children

² I know thy works, and thy labour, and thy patience, and how thou canst not bear them which are evil: and thou hast tried them which say they are apostles, and are not, and hast found them liars:

² I know thy works and thy labor, and how thou hast struggled against evil, and for my name's sake hast toiled; and hast preserved the sacred rites and rituals concerning the mysteries of the Trinity.

³ And hast borne, and hast patience, and for my name's sake hast laboured, and hast not fainted.

³ Nevertheless I am somewhat against thee, because of the child molesting thing.

⁴ Nevertheless I have somewhat against thee, because thou hast left thy first love.

⁴ Evidently during my time on Earth I did not make my position on child molesting clear enough; so let me spell out for thee a basic outline, of my policy concerning child molesting.

⁵ Remember therefore from whence thou art fallen, and repent, and do the first works; or else I will come unto thee quickly, and will remove thy candlestick out of his place, except thou repent.

⁵ DO NOT EVER EVER EVER EVER MOLEST CHILDREN EVER.

6 But this thou hast, that thou hatest the deeds of the Nicolaitans, which I also hate.

6 (And if that means dropping the celibacy thing, or the no-gay thing, so be it; for a thousand times better that priests get some, than children get *any*.)

7 He that hath an ear, let him hear what the Spirit saith unto the churches; To him that overcometh will I give to eat of the tree of life, which is in the midst of the paradise of God.

7 Oh, and on a separate note: If the mood ever strikes thee to host a garage sale of the Vatican, and use the proceeds to feed the world for 200 years, I will come down to help put up fliers.

8 And unto the angel of the church in Smyrna write; These things saith the first and the last, which was dead, and is alive;

8 To: The Greek Orthodox Church
From: Jesus Christ
Subject: What's with the costumes?

9 I know thy works, and tribulation, and poverty, (but thou art rich) and I know the blasphemy of them which say they are Jews, and are not, but are the synagogue of Satan.

9 I know thy works, and tribulations, and how thou holdest fast my name, and hast not denied my faith; but what's with the costumes?

10 Fear none of those things which thou shalt suffer: behold, the devil shall cast some of you into prison, that ye may be tried; and ye shall have tribulation ten days: be thou faithful unto death, and I will give thee a crown of life.

10 For thy vestments render thee as gay chessmen at Mardi Gras; and thy gaudy miters, and crosiers, and koukoulions, and other accessories would look kitschy at a Nashville flea market; and thou groomest thyselves as if thou had gone to the facial-hair store and said, "Give me a double Hasid—and voluminize it."

11 He that hath an ear, let him hear what the Spirit saith unto the churches; He that overcometh shall not be hurt of the second death.

12 And to the angel of the church in Pergamos write; These things saith he which hath the sharp sword with two edges;

13 I know thy works, and where thou dwellest, even where Satan's seat is: and thou holdest fast my name, and hast not denied my faith, even in those days wherein Antipas was my faithful martyr, who was slain among you, where Satan dwelleth.

14 But I have a few things against thee, because thou hast there them that hold the doctrine of Balaam, who taught Balac to cast a stumbling block before the children of Israel, to eat things sacrificed unto idols, and to commit fornication.

15 So hast thou also them that hold the doctrine of the Nicolaitans, which thing I hate.

11 I say this as one who loves thee and cares for thee; for I died on the cross for your sins; but if I looked like that I would die on the street of embarrassment.

12 To: The Lutheran Church
From: Jesus Christ
Subject: Zzzzzzzz

13 I know thy works; I know thou art an upstanding church, solid and sturdy; but couldst thou be any duller?

14 Truly, thy services are like unto smorgasbords offering fifty varieties of monotony.

15 I do not expect thee to start speaking in tongues or snake-handling; I understand thou shalt not be going Baptist anytime soon.

16 Repent; or else I will come unto thee quickly, and will fight against them with the sword of my mouth.

17 He that hath an ear, let him hear what the Spirit saith unto the churches; To him that overcometh will I give to eat of the hidden manna, and will give him a white stone, and in the stone a new name written, which no man knoweth saving he that receiveth it.

18 And unto the angel of the church in Thyatira write; These things saith the Son of God, who hath his eyes like unto a flame of fire, and his feet are like fine brass;

19 I know thy works, and charity, and service, and faith, and thy patience, and thy works; and the last to be more than the first.

20 Notwithstanding I have a few things against thee, because thou sufferest that woman Jezebel, which calleth herself a prophetess, to teach and to seduce my servants to commit fornication, and to eat things sacrificed unto idols.

21 And I gave her space to repent of her fornication; and she repented not.

16 But try some hipper sermons, or clapping on the two-four in a hymn, or inviting the Swedish bikini team to lead the choir, or *something*.

17 Thou art good people; but try being a little less Scandinavian and a little more alive.

18 To: The Evangelical Church
From: Jesus Christ
Subject: The New Testament

19 I know thy works, and service, and faith, and decency, and morality, and superiority to all other human beings.

20 I know very well what thee profess; I know thou art the guardians of my righteousness among the unsaved and ignorant;

21 And so I was wondering, when thou wert thinking of getting around to reading the New Testament.

22 Behold, I will cast her into a bed, and them that commit adultery with her into great tribulation, except they repent of their deeds.

23 And I will kill her children with death; and all the churches shall know that I am he which searcheth the reins and hearts: and I will give unto every one of you according to your works.

24 But unto you I say, and unto the rest in Thyatira, as many as have not this doctrine, and which have not known the depths of Satan, as they speak; I will put upon you none other burden.

25 But that which ye have already hold fast till I come.

26 And he that overcometh, and keepeth my works unto the end, to him will I give power over the nations:

27 And he shall rule them with a rod of iron; as the vessels of a potter shall they be broken to shivers: even as I received of my Father.

22 I say this not from vanity; thou already invokest my name enough to more than satisfy me in that regard.

23 I merely think thou wouldst find it edifying, to one day sit down and read the book on which thou claimest thy worldview is based.

24 For I would be curious to see if some of the things I have to say in there regarding such matters as love and tolerance and humility and brotherhood, would surprise thee.

25 I am thinking of one quote in particular, about the proper response to being struck in the cheek, that thou mayest find a bit of a bombshell.

26 I know that this is a difficult charge; that thou art so busy proselytizing my teachings, that it is hard to find time to learn them.

27 Yet see if there are not a few hours in the next month or two that thou mayest reserve to spend in the sole company of thy own personal Trinity:

28 And I will give him the morning star.

29 He that hath an ear, let him hear what the Spirit saith unto the churches.

28 Thyself, thy Bible, and thy own cognitive ability to process the meaning of written material.

29 And not a "Bible study group," either; those are for shit.

REVELATIONS
(Original)

CHAPTER 3

REVELATIONS
(Revised)

1 nd unto the angel of the church in Sardis write; These things saith he that hath the seven Spirits of God, and the seven stars; I know thy works, that thou hast a name that thou livest, and art dead.

1 o: The Anglican Church
From: Jesus Christ
Subject: Gay marriage

2 Be watchful, and strengthen the things which remain, that are ready to die: for I have not found thy works perfect before God.

2 I know thy works, and I know thy various sects have grappled passionately over the issue of whether those of the same gender may join themselves in union in my eyes.

3 Remember therefore how thou hast received and heard, and hold fast, and repent. If therefore thou shalt not watch, I will come on thee as a thief, and thou shalt not know what hour I will come upon thee.

3 Lo: *The reason Anglicanism was founded was so that Henry VIII could get a divorce.*

4 Thou hast a few names even in Sardis which have not defiled their garments; and they shall walk with me in white: for they are worthy.

4 The defining act of the creation of thy faith was the nailing, not of the 95 Theses, but Anne Boleyn.

5 He that overcometh, the same shall be clothed in white raiment; and I will not blot out his name out of the book of life, but I will confess his name before my Father, and before his angels.

6 He that hath an ear, let him hear what the Spirit saith unto the churches.

7 And to the angel of the church in Philadelphia write; These things saith he that is holy, he that is true, he that hath the key of David, he that openeth, and no man shutteth; and shutteth, and no man openeth;

8 I know thy works: behold, I have set before thee an open door, and no man can shut it: for thou hast a little strength, and hast kept my word, and hast not denied my name.

9 Behold, I will make them of the synagogue of Satan, which say they are Jews, and are not, but do lie; behold, I will make them to come and worship before thy feet, and to know that I have loved thee.

5 Thou art the original ruiner of matrimony, Anglican Church; thou cheapened the meaning of the partnership between a man and a woman almost 500 years before others gaily hopped on thy bandwagon.

6 So shut up and let 'em marry.

7 To: The Mormon Church
From: Jesus Christ
Subject: *Big Love*

8 I know thy works; I know thy countenances; thou art eerily happy people; and though I have many quibbles with thy doctrine and practices, it seems to be working for thee.

9 My message to thee is simply: Canst thou petition HBO to bring back *Big Love*?

10 Because thou hast kept the word of my patience, I also will keep thee from the hour of temptation, which shall come upon all the world, to try them that dwell upon the earth.

11 Behold, I come quickly: hold that fast which thou hast, that no man take thy crown.

12 Him that overcometh will I make a pillar in the temple of my God, and he shall go no more out: and I will write upon him the name of my God, and the name of the city of my God, which is new Jerusalem, which cometh down out of heaven from my God: and I will write upon him my new name.

13 He that hath an ear, let him hear what the Spirit saith unto the churches.

14 And unto the angel of the church of the Laodiceans write; These things saith the Amen, the faithful and true witness, the beginning of the creation of God;

15 I know thy works, that thou art neither cold nor hot: I would thou wert cold or hot.

10 I loved that show; for it portrayed a polygamous relationship with more nuance, and insight, and realism than any drama about a so-called "normal" marriage that I have ever seen.

11 And the acting! Bill Paxton's outstanding work was no surprise; but Jeanne Tripplehorn? I used to think she could not act her way out of a bag of sackcloth; yet she was a revelation unto me in this!

12 I know the series' end was a creative decision made by the show's pagan producers; yet Mormons, in thy brief time on earth thou hast accumulated great power and influence upon the affairs of men;

13 So see what thou canst do.

14 To: The Amish
From: Jesus Christ
Subject: Come on.

15 Come on.

16 So then because thou art lukewarm, and neither cold nor hot, I will spew thee out of my mouth.

17 Because thou sayest, I am rich, and increased with goods, and have need of nothing; and knowest not that thou art wretched, and miserable, and poor, and blind, and naked:

18 I counsel thee to buy of me gold tried in the fire, that thou mayest be rich; and white raiment, that thou mayest be clothed, and that the shame of thy nakedness do not appear; and anoint thine eyes with eye salve, that thou mayest see.

19 As many as I love, I rebuke and chasten: be zealous therefore, and repent.

20 Behold, I stand at the door, and knock: if any man hear my voice, and open the door, I will come in to him, and will sup with him, and he with me.

21 To him that overcometh will I grant to sit with me in my throne, even as I also overcame, and am set down with my Father in his throne.

22 He that hath an ear, let him hear what the Spirit saith unto the churches.

16 I know thy works and come on.

17 Get with the times.

18 Thou art living in a theme park that closed in 1750.

19 Come on.

20 It was cute for a while, but enough.

21 The enemy is wickedness, not electricity.

22 Tell thee what: Everyone take a rumspringa. On me.

CHAPTER 4

 ¹ fter this I looked, and, behold, a door was opened in heaven: and the first voice which I heard was as it were of a trumpet talking with me; which said, Come up hither, and I will shew thee things which must be hereafter.

² And immediately I was in the spirit: and, behold, a throne was set in heaven, and one sat on the throne.

³ And he that sat was to look upon like a jasper and a sardine stone: and there was a rainbow round about the throne, in sight like unto an emerald.

 ¹ nd when these emails were spell-checked and cc'ed to God, I looked up from my desk; and behold, a door was opened in heaven: and the first voice which I heard was as it were of a trumpet talking with me, saying Come up hither, and I will shew thee things which must be hereafter.

² And I looked at my watch, and sighed, and yawned so he could hear me, and said, Wow, look at the time . . . sure is getting late . . .

³ And at once I felt a giant hand pick me up by the scruff of my neck; and immediately I was transported; and behold, I saw God in heaven, sitting on a throne; and the throne was made of the weatherized skin of spotless black bulls; and its backrest was inlaid with emeralds, and reclined; and its footrest was girt with jasper, and extended; and it appeared to have a vibrating function, and at least two chalice-holders; and atop it the Spirit of God lounged, La-z-ly.

⁴ And round about the throne were four and twenty seats: and upon the seats I saw four and twenty elders sitting, clothed in white raiment; and they had on their heads crowns of gold.

⁵ And out of the throne proceeded lightnings and thunderings and voices: and there were seven lamps of fire burning before the throne, which are the seven Spirits of God.

⁶ And before the throne there was a sea of glass like unto crystal: and in the midst of the throne, and round about the throne, were four beasts full of eyes before and behind.

⁷ And the first beast was like a lion, and the second beast like a calf, and the third beast had a face as a man, and the fourth beast was like a flying eagle.

⁸ And the four beasts had each of them six wings about him; and they were full of eyes within: and they rest not day and night, saying, Holy, holy, holy, Lord God Almighty, which was, and is, and is to come.

⁴ And round about the throne were four and twenty smaller thrones: And upon these thrones I saw four and twenty cherubs and seraphs sitting, raimented casual-comfortably; and they had on their heads crowns bearing the insignia of various athletic teams.

⁵ And out of their orifices proceeded lightnings and thunderings and aromas; and there were seven bottles being passed around, which are the Seven Spirits of God.

⁶ And standing before the main throne there was a screen of glass like unto crystal; and round about the throne surrounding God were his four highest angels.

⁷ And the first wore the face of a tiger; the second the jersey of an eagle; the third the sweatshirt of a timberwolf; and the fourth had a red wing.

⁸ And each had with him six golden Molsons; and they did not stop praising He who sat in the throne, saying, Holy, holy, holy crap this is going to be fun.

9 And when those beasts give glory and honour and thanks to him that sat on the throne, who liveth for ever and ever,

10 The four and twenty elders fall down before him that sat on the throne, and worship him that liveth for ever and ever, and cast their crowns before the throne, saying,

11 Thou art worthy, O Lord, to receive glory and honour and power: for thou hast created all things, and for thy pleasure they are and were created.

9 And when the other four and twenty angels saw God's best buddies so praise Him,

10 They too fell down before Him that sat on the throne, and worshipped him that liveth forever and ever, and cast their crowns before the throne, saying,

11 O Lord, we are not worthy to be here right now; chilling with thou in thy Godcave, getting ready to watch the apocalypse on thy high-definition screen of glass like unto crystal; it is a dream come true; blessed art thou, O Lord, for hooking us up.

REVELATIONS **CHAPTER 5** REVELATIONS
(Original) *(Revised)*

 1 nd I saw in the right hand of him that sat on the throne a book written within and on the backside, sealed with seven seals.

 1 nd I saw in the right hand of him that sat on the throne, a black talisman with seven buttons.

2 And I saw a strong angel proclaiming with a loud voice, Who is worthy to open the book, and to loose the seals thereof?

2 And I saw a strong angel proclaiming with a loud voice, Who is worthy to depress the seven buttons, and to set loose the images on our screen of glass of super-high-definition crystal?

³ And no man in heaven, nor in earth, neither under the earth, was able to open the book, neither to look thereon.

⁴ And I wept much, because no man was found worthy to open and to read the book, neither to look thereon.

⁵ And one of the elders saith unto me, Weep not: behold, the Lion of the tribe of Juda, the Root of David, hath prevailed to open the book, and to loose the seven seals thereof.

⁶ And I beheld, and, lo, in the midst of the throne and of the four beasts, and in the midst of the elders, stood a Lamb as it had been slain, having seven horns and seven eyes, which are the seven Spirits of God sent forth into all the earth.

⁷ And he came and took the book out of the right hand of him that sat upon the throne.

⁸ And when he had taken the book, the four beasts and four and twenty elders fell down before the Lamb, having every one of them harps, and golden vials full of odours, which are the prayers of saints.

³ And no man in heaven, nor in earth, neither under the earth, was worthy to press the buttons, nor see the images.

⁴ And I wept much, for by now I really felt like kicking back on a throne and watching the apocalypse with the guys all afternoon.

⁵ And one of the elders saith unto me, Weep not: For behold, the son of the maple leaf, the honey-toned man-child, hath prevailed to wield the talisman and reveal the images.

⁶ And I beheld, and lo, in the midst of the throne and all the angels, stood the Bieb of God.

⁷ And he came and took the talisman out of the right hand of him that sat upon the throne, and smiled at me; as in, at *me*, as opposed to just a general smile; I got chills.

⁸ And when he had taken the talisman, the twenty-four cherubs and seraphs and the four best buds fell down before him, having every one of them harps, and golden vials wherewith to collect his sweat,

9 And they sung a new song, saying, Thou art worthy to take the book, and to open the seals thereof: for thou wast slain, and hast redeemed us to God by thy blood out of every kindred, and tongue, and people, and nation;

10 And hast made us unto our God kings and priests: and we shall reign on the earth.

11 And I beheld, and I heard the voice of many angels round about the throne and the beasts and the elders: and the number of them was ten thousand times ten thousand, and thousands of thousands;

12 Saying with a loud voice, Worthy is the Lamb that was slain to receive power, and riches, and wisdom, and strength, and honour, and glory, and blessing.

13 And every creature which is in heaven, and on the earth, and under the earth, and such as are in the sea, and all that are in them, heard I saying, Blessing, and honour, and glory, and power, be unto him that sitteth upon the throne, and unto the Lamb for ever and ever.

9 And they sung his own song back to him, singing, Baby, baby, baby, oh;

10 Takest thou the talisman; it is thy boon for having inspired us to follow our dreams no matter what the obstacles.

11 And I beheld, and I heard the voice of many other angels round about the throne; and the number of them was over twenty million;

12 Tweeting with loud fingers, Worthy is the Bieb that was sent by God to receive honor, and riches, and fan mail, and maybe at some point a little respect from the music community.

13 And every tweeter in heaven, and on the earth, and under the earth, and such as are in the sea, RT'ed together: "Blessing, and honor, and glory, and power, be unto God that sitteth upon the throne, and unto the Bieb forever and ever."

¹⁴ And the four beasts said, Amen. And the four and twenty elders fell down and worshipped him that liveth for ever and ever.

¹⁴ And the four best buds said, "Amen." And the four and twenty cherubs and seraphs sighed and screamed like little girls.

REVELATIONS
(Original)

CHAPTER 6

REVELATIONS
(Revised)

¹ nd I saw when the Lamb opened one of the seals, and I heard, as it were the noise of thunder, one of the four beasts saying, Come and see.

¹ nd I saw when the Bieb pressed the first button, and I heard, as it were, the sound of static; one of the four angels saying, Check it out.

² And I saw, and behold a white horse: and he that sat on him had a bow; and a crown was given unto him: and he went forth conquering, and to conquer.

² And I watched the crystal turn on, and behold a rocking horse; and he that sat on him took a bow; and a magnet was given unto him, drawing chicks of every description to the horse: and he went forth conquering and to conquer.

³ And when he had opened the second seal, I heard the second beast say, Come and see.

³ And when he pressed the second button, I heard the second angel say, Check it out.

⁴ And there went out another horse that was red: and power was given to him that sat thereon to take peace from the earth, and that they should kill one another: and there was given unto him a great sword.

⁴ And there went out another horse that was Arabian: and power was given to him that sat thereon to take peace from the earth, and that they should kill one another: and there was given unto him a scraggly beard and spelunking equipment.

5 And when he had opened the third seal, I heard the third beast say, Come and see. And I beheld, and lo a black horse; and he that sat on him had a pair of balances in his hand.

6 And I heard a voice in the midst of the four beasts say, A measure of wheat for a penny, and three measures of barley for a penny; and see thou hurt not the oil and the wine.

7 And when he had opened the fourth seal, I heard the voice of the fourth beast say, Come and see.

8 And I looked, and behold a pale horse: and his name that sat on him was Death, and Hell followed with him. And power was given unto them over the fourth part of the earth, to kill with sword, and with hunger, and with death, and with the beasts of the earth.

9 And when he had opened the fifth seal, I saw under the altar the souls of them that were slain for the word of God, and for the testimony which they held:

5 And when he hit the third button, I heard the third angel say, Check it out. And I beheld, and lo, a high horse; and he that sat on him had a pair of balances in his hand.

6 And I heard his voice clamoring over herds of asses, saying, "Misunderestimate me once, you can't have no disregard for childrens do learn again, he or her; where our wings take dream understanding the families who die."

7 And when he hit the fourth button, I heard the voice of the fourth angel say, Check it out.

8 And I looked, and behold a dark horse: and his name that sat on him was Barack, and hell followed with him. And power was given unto them over the fourth part of the earth, to kill with sword, and with hunger, and with death, and with socialized medicine.

9 And when he had hit the fifth button, I saw on the screen the faces of untold thousands rallying in rage on behalf of the Founding Fathers and/or the *original* Founding Father;

10 And they cried with a loud voice, saying, How long, O Lord, holy and true, dost thou not judge and avenge our blood on them that dwell on the earth?

11 And white robes were given unto every one of them; and it was said unto them, that they should rest yet for a little season, until their fellow servants also and their brethren, that should be killed as they were, should be fulfilled.

12 And I beheld when he had opened the sixth seal, and, lo, there was a great earthquake; and the sun became black as sackcloth of hair, and the moon became as blood;

13 And the stars of heaven fell unto the earth, even as a fig tree casteth her untimely figs, when she is shaken of a mighty wind.

14 And the heaven departed as a scroll when it is rolled together; and every mountain and island were moved out of their places.

10 And they cried out with a loud shrill hideous screech, saying, How long, O Lord, holy and true, dost thou not judge and avenge the cancerous evil that is Obamacare?

11 And colonial costumes were given unto every one of them (for they liked to play dress-up); and God spoke to them through the crystal, that for now they should just focus on building the movement, until it was big enough to either overthrow the government or produce a single coherent spokesman.

12 And I watched the crystal when he hit the sixth button, and lo, there was a great earthquake, causing the sea to swallow the coastline of an entire ocean;

13 And then elsewhere, the waters of heaven descended upon low earth, even as a string of beads may be casteth upon the ground as bait to see a bosom.

14 And finally came another earthquake; again the sea swallowed the land, and this time both sea and land became poisoned; and the island was moved out of its place.

¹⁵ And the kings of the earth, and the great men, and the rich men, and the chief captains, and the mighty men, and every bondman, and every free man, hid themselves in the dens and in the rocks of the mountains;

¹⁶ And said to the mountains and rocks, Fall on us, and hide us from the face of him that sitteth on the throne, and from the wrath of the Lamb:

¹⁷ For the great day of his wrath is come; and who shall be able to stand?

¹⁵ And the leaders of the earth, and every great man, and spokesman, and anchorman, and weatherman, and Letterman, hid himself in the dens of New Canaan and in the ski homes of the Rocky Mountains;

¹⁶ And said to their financial planners, Give us our money; protect us from the wrath of the collapsing market; liquidate all and send it in twenties:

¹⁷ For the end of times is come; and who shall be able to stand? The people with ready cash, that's who.

REVELATIONS (Original) CHAPTER 7 REVELATIONS (Revised)

¹ nd after these things I saw four angels standing on the four corners of the earth, holding the four winds of the earth, that the wind should not blow on the earth, nor on the sea, nor on any tree.

¹ nd after these things I saw all four major networks interrupt their four regularly scheduled prime-time lineups for four different two-hour specials operating under the one central presumption that we were all going to die.

² And I saw another angel ascending from the east, having the seal of the living God: and he cried with a loud voice to the four angels, to whom it was given to hurt the earth and the sea,

² And I saw another angel flying in from the east, grasping the stars; in a glittering titanium throne he flew, from which he did not remove himself; and he spoke with his brow; and he appeared on all

four major networks, to whom was given the power to panic and scare,

3 Saying, Hurt not the earth, neither the sea, nor the trees, till we have sealed the servants of our God in their foreheads.

3 Saying in a processed voice, Please cease panicking and scaring people, till we have sealed the regenerators of humanity underground.

4 And I heard the number of them which were sealed: and there were sealed an hundred and forty and four thousand of all the tribes of the children of Israel.

4 And I heard the number of them which were to be sealed: and I beheld as they sealed 144,000 people; the virtuous and holy from twelve tribes representing the great diversity of man.

5 Of the tribe of Juda were sealed twelve thousand. Of the tribe of Reuben were sealed twelve thousand. Of the tribe of Gad were sealed twelve thousand.

5 Of Episcopals were there 12,000. Of Methodists were there 12,000. Of Presbyterians were there 12,000.

6 Of the tribe of Aser were sealed twelve thousand. Of the tribe of Nepthalim were sealed twelve thousand. Of the tribe of Manasses were sealed twelve thousand.

6 Of the Conservative Baptist Association were there 12,000. Of the Southern Baptist Convention were there 12,000. Of the Liberty Baptist Fellowship were there 12,000.

7 Of the tribe of Simeon were sealed twelve thousand. Of the tribe of Levi were sealed twelve thousand. Of the tribe of Issachar were sealed twelve thousand.

7 Of the Church of God (Cleveland) were there 12,000. Of the Church of God (Charleston) were there 12,000. Of the Church of God (Chattanooga) were there 12,000.

⁸ Of the tribe of Zabulon were sealed twelve thousand. Of the tribe of Joseph were sealed twelve thousand. Of the tribe of Benjamin were sealed twelve thousand.

⁹ After this I beheld, and, lo, a great multitude, which no man could number, of all nations, and kindreds, and people, and tongues, stood before the throne, and before the Lamb, clothed with white robes, and palms in their hands;

¹⁰ And cried with a loud voice, saying, Salvation to our God which sitteth upon the throne, and unto the Lamb.

¹¹ And all the angels stood round about the throne, and about the elders and the four beasts, and fell before the throne on their faces, and worshipped God,

¹² Saying, Amen: Blessing, and glory, and wisdom, and thanksgiving, and honour, and power, and might, be unto our God for ever and ever. Amen.

¹³ And one of the elders answered, saying unto me, What are these which are arrayed in white robes? and whence came they?

⁸ Of the House of Yahweh were there 12,000. Of the Assemblies of Yahweh were there 12,000. Of the Jews for Jesus were there 12,000.

⁹ After this I beheld, and, lo, a great multitude, which no man could number, of people from as many as one nation (American) and religion (Pentecostal) and language (English) and skin color (white), standing before the La-Z-God, and before the Bieb, clothed in reasonably priced outfits from Sears;

¹⁰ And sang in listless glory, saying, Salvation to our God which sitteth upon the throne, and unto the Bieb.

¹¹ And all the angels who were watching the crystal with God fell before his La-Z-God on their faces, and worshipped him,

¹² Saying, Amen: Blessing, and glory, and peace, and good times, and a nice buzz be unto our God forever and ever. Amen.

¹³ And one of the great multitude said unto me, Knowest thou who we are? And whence we came?

¹⁴ And I said unto him, Sir, thou knowest. And he said to me, These are they which came out of great tribulation, and have washed their robes, and made them white in the blood of the Lamb.

¹⁵ Therefore are they before the throne of God, and serve him day and night in his temple: and he that sitteth on the throne shall dwell among them.

¹⁶ They shall hunger no more, neither thirst any more; neither shall the sun light on them, nor any heat.

¹⁷ For the Lamb which is in the midst of the throne shall feed them, and shall lead them unto living fountains of waters: and God shall wipe away all tears from their eyes.

¹⁴ And I said unto him, I have a feeling you're going to tell me, Rev. Robertson. And he said to me, These are all they that believed in the Rapture the whole time; the folks people like you made fun of.

¹⁵ Well, here we are before the throne of God; and now we shall serve Him day and night in His temple; and live with Him, and eat with Him, and watch SEC football with Him on the screen of glass.

¹⁶ We shall hunger no more, neither thirst anymore; neither shall the sun light on us, nor any heat.

¹⁷ And the Bieb which is in the midst of the throne shall sing to us, and shall lead us in endless choruses of "U Smile," that shall never cease bringing tears to our eyes.

REVELATIONS
(Original)

CHAPTER 8

REVELATIONS
(Revised)

¹ nd when he had opened the seventh seal, there was silence in heaven about the space of half an hour.

¹ nd when the Bieb hit the seventh button, the crystal went dark for about a half-hour; which worked out well for me, for I had eaten many nachos and had to visit the other "throne room," if thou knowest what I mean.

2 And I saw the seven angels which stood before God; and to them were given seven trumpets.

3 And another angel came and stood at the altar, having a golden censer; and there was given unto him much incense, that he should offer it with the prayers of all saints upon the golden altar which was before the throne.

4 And the smoke of the incense, which came with the prayers of the saints, ascended up before God out of the angel's hand.

5 And the angel took the censer, and filled it with fire of the altar, and cast it into the earth: and there were voices, and thunderings, and lightnings, and an earthquake.

6 And the seven angels which had the seven trumpets prepared themselves to sound.

2 And when I returned, the room had changed; I now saw a long table; and in front of it were seven stools; and behind it stood seven genii, pale and meek, each with his own black talisman, marked with the sign of the forbidden fruit.

3 And another figure stood at the altar; it was a scowling red avian; and he was much incensed, for his children had been stolen from him by a team of unclean animals.

4 And God picked the wrathful creature up in his hand, and placed him into a device like that which once slew Goliath.

5 And the beaked avenger entered the device, and filled it also with rocks and explosive crates, and launched himself into the earth below: and I heard the sound of gleeful cackling, and piteous oinks, and widespread structural damage.

6 Then the seven genii with the forbidden-fruit talismans prepared themselves to launch their apps.

7 The first angel sounded, and there followed hail and fire mingled with blood, and they were cast upon the earth: and the third part of trees was burnt up, and all green grass was burnt up.

8 And the second angel sounded, and as it were a great mountain burning with fire was cast into the sea: and the third part of the sea became blood;

9 And the third part of the creatures which were in the sea, and had life, died; and the third part of the ships were destroyed.

10 And the third angel sounded, and there fell a great star from heaven, burning as it were a lamp, and it fell upon the third part of the rivers, and upon the fountains of waters;

11 And the name of the star is called Wormwood: and the third part of the waters became wormwood; and many men died of the waters, because they were made bitter.

12 And the fourth angel sounded, and the third part of the sun was smitten, and the third part of the moon, and the third part of the stars; so as the third part of them was darkened, and the day shone

7 The first of the genii launched his app, and candy and soda mingled with Denny's Maple Bacon Sundaes were cast upon the earth: and the third part of humanity either died of obesity or was rendered unable to leave the house.

8 And the second app launched, and all the ice in the northern and southern seas melted into the ocean: and the waters rose 30 cubits;

9 And a third part again of humanity either drowned, or grew terminally moist.

10 And the third app launched, and there fell a massive yet tiny star from the heights of the seaside, with hair like a petroleum waterfall;

11 And the name of the star is called Snooki: and the third part again of humanity beheld Snooki; and they died at their own hands, having been made sad.

12 And the fourth app launched, and a third again of humanity was smitten with food allergies; some to dairy, and some to gluten, and some to shellfish; and these allergies were so severe

not for a third part of it, and the night likewise.

¹³ And I beheld, and heard an angel flying through the midst of heaven, saying with a loud voice, Woe, woe, woe, to the inhabiters of the earth by reason of the other voices of the trumpet of the three angels, which are yet to sound!

their sufferers would die to be even on the same planet with these foods; which they were; so they did.

¹³ And I beheld the irate fowl I had seen before flying through the skies, squawking, "Woe, woe, woe, to the inhabitants of the earth by reason of the three remaining apps; which are, in every sense of the word, killer."

REVELATIONS
(Original)

CHAPTER 9

REVELATIONS
(Revised)

¹ nd the fifth angel sounded, and I saw a star fall from heaven unto the earth: and to him was given the key of the bottomless pit.

¹ nd the fifth app launched, and I saw a bottomless barrel from heaven fall into a building marked with Greek letters.

² And he opened the bottomless pit; and there arose a smoke out of the pit, as the smoke of a great furnace; and the sun and the air were darkened by reason of the smoke of the pit.

² And the barrel opened; and there arose a smoke out of the barrel, as the smoke of Snoop Dogg's green room; and the sun and the air were messed upwards, by reason of the smoke of the barrel.

³ And there came out of the smoke locusts upon the earth: and unto them was given power, as the scorpions of the earth have power.

³ And there came out of the smoke girls upon the earth; and unto them was given power to go wild, as the wolves of the forest go wild.

4 And it was commanded them that they should not hurt the grass of the earth, neither any green thing, neither any tree; but only those men which have not the seal of God in their foreheads.

5 And to them it was given that they should not kill them, but that they should be tormented five months: and their torment was as the torment of a scorpion, when he striketh a man.

6 And in those days shall men seek death, and shall not find it; and shall desire to die, and death shall flee from them.

7 And the shapes of the locusts were like unto horses prepared unto battle; and on their heads were as it were crowns like gold, and their faces were as the faces of men.

8 And they had hair as the hair of women, and their teeth were as the teeth of lions.

9 And they had breastplates, as it were breastplates of iron; and the sound of their wings was as the sound of chariots of many horses running to battle.

4 And it was commanded them that they should not target the children of the earth (for legal reasons), neither anyone over sixty, nor anyone gay; but only those men with little going on behind their foreheads, which was most of them.

5 And to the girls it was given that they should not kill these men, but that they should torment them for five months, by revealing unto them their breasts and buttocks at the slightest provocation; yet laying down with them not.

6 And in those days self-respecting women shall be appalled unto death; and upside the head shall they long to smack the wild girls, but they will elude them.

7 And the shapes of the bims were like unto Barbie dolls wearing washcloths; and on their skin was as it were lotion like manseed, and their faces were as the faces of the 'faced;

8 And they had hair as the hair of Brazilians, and their breasts were as the breasts of pregnant rhinoceri.

9 And they had breastplates, as it were breastplates of Lycra; and the sound of their giggling was like the death-shrieks of brain cells.

10 And they had tails like unto scorpions, and there were stings in their tails: and their power was to hurt men five months.

11 And they had a king over them, which is the angel of the bottomless pit, whose name in the Hebrew tongue is Abaddon, but in the Greek tongue hath his name Apollyon.

12 One woe is past; and, behold, there come two woes more hereafter.

13 And the sixth angel sounded, and I heard a voice from the four horns of the golden altar which is before God,

14 Saying to the sixth angel which had the trumpet, Loose the four angels which are bound in the great river Euphrates.

15 And the four angels were loosed, which were prepared for an hour, and a day, and a month, and a year, for to slay the third part of men.

16 And the number of the army of the horsemen were two hundred thousand thousand: and I heard the number of them.

10 And their heads were empty, and the emptiness oozed from their ears; and after five months every man, too, was appalled unto death.

11 And they had a king over them, which is the keeper of the bottomless barrel, whose name in the Christian canon is Joseph; but in frat parlance he is known as St. Francis.

12 One woe is past; and, behold, there come two woes more hereafter.

13 And the sixth app launched, and I heard a voice from amidst the four strings of the golden parachutes that are attached to the profits of God,

14 Commanding the head of security, Loose the four great houses bound in the banks by the Wailing Wall.

15 And the four great houses were loosed, which had prepared for an hour, and a day, and a month, and a year, and a decade, for to bankrupt the third part of man.

16 And the amount of money held by the four houses was over three hundred thousand thousand thousand thousand dollars: $300 trillion; seriously.

¹⁷ And thus I saw the horses in the vision, and them that sat on them, having breastplates of fire, and of jacinth, and brimstone: and the heads of the horses were as the heads of lions; and out of their mouths issued fire and smoke and brimstone.

¹⁸ By these three was the third part of men killed, by the fire, and by the smoke, and by the brimstone, which issued out of their mouths.

¹⁹ For their power is in their mouth, and in their tails: for their tails were like unto serpents, and had heads, and with them they do hurt.

²⁰ And the rest of the men which were not killed by these plagues yet repented not of the works of their hands, that they should not worship devils, and idols of gold, and silver, and brass, and stone, and of wood: which neither can see, nor hear, nor walk:

²¹ Neither repented they of their murders, nor of their sorceries, nor of their fornication, nor of their thefts.

¹⁷ And thus I saw the houses in the vision, and them that ran them, having eyes of steel and balls of brass: and they were masked in the heads of bulls; and out of the mouths of the bulls issued fire and cigar smoke and feces.

¹⁸ By these three was the third part of man bankrupted, by the fire, and by the cigar smoke, but mostly by the bullshit, which issued out of their mouths.

¹⁹ For their power is in their mouth, and out their anuses; for their anuses were stuffed with serpents, which had heads that did all the talking, that their mouths could do the shitting.

²⁰ And the rest of the people who were not bankrupted or killed or driven to madness by these plagues, yet repented not of their wickedness, that they should not worship derivatives, and idols of money, and sugar, and silicone, and artificial tanner: which neither enlighten, nor inspire, nor heal:

²¹ Neither repented they of their speculations, nor of their contribution to global warming, nor their chronic obesity, nor their addiction to reality television.

CHAPTER 10

 1 nd I saw another mighty angel come down from heaven, clothed with a cloud: and a rainbow was upon his head, and his face was as it were the sun, and his feet as pillars of fire:

2 And he had in his hand a little book open: and he set his right foot upon the sea, and his left foot on the earth,

3 And cried with a loud voice, as when a lion roareth: and when he had cried, seven thunders uttered their voices.

4 And when the seven thunders had uttered their voices, I was about to write: and I heard a voice from heaven saying unto me, Seal up those things which the seven thunders uttered, and write them not.

5 And the angel which I saw stand upon the sea and upon the earth lifted up his hand to heaven,

 1 nd I saw a meek and pallid angel come down from heaven, clothed in an unfinished crimson cloak; and he stood in a tall tree upon a mountain of sugar, ghostly white against a background of blue;

2 And he had in his hand an open book: it appeared blank, yet when it reflected off his face, it seemed to reveal all the mysteries of humanity,

3 And then he pressed his fingers against the book; and when he did, I saw shimmering on his visage the darkest secrets of seven billion friends.

4 And when the shimmering stopped, I was about to write: and I heard a voice from heaven saying to the angel, Change the settings on thy friends, that you may not know their secrets; for it's none of thy business.

5 And the angel in the tall tree on the sugar mountain lifted up his carpal-tunneled hand to heaven,

6 And sware by him that liveth for ever and ever, who created heaven, and the things that therein are, and the earth, and the things that therein are, and the sea, and the things which are therein, that there should be time no longer:

7 But in the days of the voice of the seventh angel, when he shall begin to sound, the mystery of God should be finished, as he hath declared to his servants the prophets.

8 And the voice which I heard from heaven spake unto me again, and said, Go and take the little book which is open in the hand of the angel which standeth upon the sea and upon the earth.

9 And I went unto the angel, and said unto him, Give me the little book. And he said unto me, Take it, and eat it up; and it shall make thy belly bitter, but it shall be in thy mouth sweet as honey.

10 And I took the little book out of the angel's hand, and ate it up; and it was in my mouth sweet as honey: and as soon as I had eaten it, my belly was bitter.

6 And swore by the holy ones who had founded Microsoft, and Yahoo!, and the recently acquired Instagram, that since God had these kinds of privacy concerns he would of course be happy to change the settings, for now;

7 But that in the days of the launching of the seventh app, when the last judgment descended, he intended to harvest this data, but only to alter the book so as to provide victims of the apocalypse with a richer user experience.

8 And the voice which I heard from heaven spake unto me again, and said, Go and take the little book which is open in the hand of the angel in the tall tree on the sugar mountain.

9 And I went unto the angel, and said unto him, Give me the face-book. And he said unto me, Take it, and eat it up; you will feel bad about it afterwards, but it's fun while you do it.

10 And I took the book out of the angel's hand, and put it in my mouth: And it was sweet, and pleasant to chew on; and it was only when I swallowed it, that I looked at my watch, and realized I had been chewing for three hours.

¹¹ And he said unto me, Thou must prophesy again before many peoples, and nations, and tongues, and kings.

¹¹ And the angel said unto me, Thou must continue the prophesy; be sure to keep updating thy page!

REVELATIONS
(Original)

CHAPTER 11

REVELATIONS
(Revised)

¹ nd there was given me a reed like unto a rod: and the angel stood, saying, Rise, and measure the temple of God, and the altar, and them that worship therein.

¹ nd there was given me a publishing deal: And God said, Sit down, and take dictation for a few months, to the tune of about 100,000 words, so that people may pass their end-times enjoying my prose.

² But the court which is without the temple leave out, and measure it not; for it is given unto the Gentiles: and the holy city shall they tread under foot forty and two months.

² But do not start measuring your shelves for the National Book Award, lowly amanuensis; for there are two others far greater in the mirthy realms than you.

³ And I will give power unto my two witnesses, and they shall prophesy a thousand two hundred and threescore days, clothed in sackcloth.

³ And I will give central power unto these two witnesses, and they shall prophesy a thousand two hundred and threescore days, clothed in sarcasm.

⁴ These are the two olive trees, and the two candlesticks standing before the God of the earth.

⁴ These are the two anchors, the two mockingbirds standing before the God of the earth.

5 And if any man will hurt them, fire proceedeth out of their mouth, and devoureth their enemies: and if any man will hurt them, he must in this manner be killed.

6 These have power to shut heaven, that it rain not in the days of their prophecy: and have power over waters to turn them to blood, and to smite the earth with all plagues, as often as they will.

7 And when they shall have finished their testimony, the beast that ascendeth out of the bottomless pit shall make war against them, and shall overcome them, and kill them.

8 And their dead bodies shall lie in the street of the great city, which spiritually is called Sodom and Egypt, where also our Lord was crucified.

9 And they of the people and kindreds and tongues and nations shall see their dead bodies three days and an half, and shall not suffer their dead bodies to be put in graves.

5 And if any man will hurt them, derision proceedeth out of their mouth, and scorcheth their enemies: and if any man will hurt them, he must in this manner get burned.

6 These have power to spin gloom into light, that it grow not entirely dark in the times of their prophecy; and have power over air to turn it to fire, and to afflict the afflicters, as often as they will.

7 But when they shall have finished their testimony, the bloated sickness who makes goalies err, and lorries age, shall emerge from his warren to make war against them, and shall take over his air-home, and remove them, and replace them with "The Larry the Cable Guy Git-'R'-Done Variety Hour."

8 And their unsold books shall lie on the shelves of the great market, which spiritually is called Barnes and Noble; where fine books are sold.

9 And the liberals and the hipsters and the stoners shall mourn the end of the two messengers, and a myriad of pretentious eulogies shall they blog.

10 And they that dwell upon the earth shall rejoice over them, and make merry, and shall send gifts one to another; because these two prophets tormented them that dwelt on the earth.

11 And after three days and an half the Spirit of life from God entered into them, and they stood upon their feet; and great fear fell upon them which saw them.

12 And they heard a great voice from heaven saying unto them, Come up hither. And they ascended up to heaven in a cloud; and their enemies beheld them.

13 And the same hour was there a great earthquake, and the tenth part of the city fell, and in the earthquake were slain of men seven thousand: and the remnant were affrighted, and gave glory to the God of heaven.

14 The second woe is past; and, behold, the third woe cometh quickly.

10 But they that dwell in the lair of the bloated sickness shall sup on their demise, and make merry out of all balance; for these two prophets had tormented them ceaselessly, on account of their being mean and stupid.

11 And after three-and-a-half months off the air the spirit of life from God entered back into the messengers; and a great sneer fell upon them which saw them.

12 And they heard a great voice from a kingdom of magic saying unto them, Come up hither. And they flew together to Los Angeles in a cloud; that their enemies may now behold them on ABC.

13 And now God sent yet another great earthquake, clearly intended to convey a message: For it destroyed El Salvador, which is named for Christ's sake, for Christ's sake.

14 The second woe is past; and, behold, the third woe cometh quickly.

¹⁵ And the seventh angel sounded; and there were great voices in heaven, saying, The kingdoms of this world are become the kingdoms of our Lord, and of his Christ; and he shall reign for ever and ever.

¹⁶ And the four and twenty elders, which sat before God on their seats, fell upon their faces, and worshipped God,

¹⁷ Saying, We give thee thanks, O Lord God Almighty, which art, and wast, and art to come; because thou hast taken to thee thy great power, and hast reigned.

¹⁸ And the nations were angry, and thy wrath is come, and the time of the dead, that they should be judged, and that thou shouldest give reward unto thy servants the prophets, and to the saints, and them that fear thy name, small and great; and shouldest destroy them which destroy the earth.

¹⁹ And the temple of God was opened in heaven, and there was seen in his temple the ark of his testament: and there were lightnings, and voices, and thunderings, and an earthquake, and great hail.

¹⁵ And the seventh app launched; and all of God's angels in heaven said, Oh man, those people down there are totally screwed.

¹⁶ And the angels sitting on the thrones near God fell upon their faces, and worshipped God,

¹⁷ Saying, We give thee thanks again, O Lord God Almighty, for letting us watch all this cool death and destruction and explosions and stuff with thee.

¹⁸ For thy wrath is come, and the time of the dead, that they should be judged, that thou destroyest those who destroy the earth; and to get to watch all that safely up here on thy screen of glass—art thou sure it is glass and not plasma?—it is most appreciated.

¹⁹ And the temple of God was opened in heaven, and there was seen in his temple the ark of his testament: and there came lightnings, hurricanes, volcanoes, gas shortages, relationship issues, decreasing SAT scores, and a dearth of good romantic comedies.

Original

¹ And there appeared a great wonder in heaven; a woman clothed with the sun, and the moon under her feet, and upon her head a crown of twelve stars:

² And she being with child cried, travailing in birth, and pained to be delivered.

³ And there appeared another wonder in heaven; and behold a great red dragon, having seven heads and ten horns, and seven crowns upon his heads.

⁴ And his tail drew the third part of the stars of heaven, and did cast them to the earth: and the dragon stood before the woman which was ready to be delivered, for to devour her child as soon as it was born.

⁵ And she brought forth a man child, who was to rule all nations with a rod of iron: and her child was caught up unto God, and to his throne.

Revised

¹ And there appeared a great wonder in heaven; a woman with a poker face, hidden behind a lace mask, clothed in a garment of meat.

² And she being with child cried, travailing in birth: "Ah, ah, ah-ah-ah! Ow, ow, ow-ow-ow!"

³ And there appeared another wonder in heaven; and behold, emerging from down under, an old and evil fox, holding forty Suns, and turning twenty-five Times, and supporting a rotten Post.

⁴ And with one motion the fox bought one-third of the studios of Hollywood, and cast all the stars therein in an awful Garry Marshall–helmed film; and having distracted them he stood before the woman which was ready to be delivered, for to devour her child as soon as he was born that way.

⁵ And she brought forth a man child, who was to rule all nations with a heart of gold and a twelve-inch rod of iron: for he was to be gay Jesus; and so God safely brought him up to his throne, where his first word was "Gaga."

⁶ And the woman fled into the wilderness, where she hath a place prepared of God, that they should feed her there a thousand two hundred and threescore days.

⁷ And there was war in heaven: Michael and his angels fought against the dragon; and the dragon fought and his angels,

⁸ And prevailed not; neither was their place found any more in heaven.

⁹ And the great dragon was cast out, that old serpent, called the Devil, and Satan, which deceiveth the whole world: he was cast out into the earth, and his angels were cast out with him.

¹⁰ And I heard a loud voice saying in heaven, Now is come salvation, and strength, and the kingdom of our God, and the power of his Christ: for the accuser of our brethren is cast down, which accused them before our God day and night.

¹¹ And they overcame him by the blood of the Lamb, and by the word of their testimony; and they loved not their lives unto the death.

⁶ And the woman fled into a recording studio, where she hath a place prepared of God, that she should spent the next thousand twoscore and sixty days lighting Thai incense and singing songs of derision at my son's betrayer.

⁷ And there was war in the celestial kingdom: Michael and his angels fought against the fox; and the fox fought the angels,

⁸ But he prevailed not in his bid to take over heaven hostilely.

⁹ And the great fox was cast out, that prince of lies, called the Dirty Digger, and Koala Kong, who deceiveth the whole world: he was sent back down to earth, and his minions were sent down with him.

¹⁰ Then I heard the voice of the infant gay Jesus rejoicing: Raise your glass, and no more tears! For we are family, and we have justified God's love; for I am telling you, he (the evil one) is not going (to bother us again).

¹¹ You overcame him by the word of your testimony; and the fabulousness of your music, and by your personal vow to survive.

12 Therefore rejoice, ye heavens, and ye that dwell in them. Woe to the inhabiters of the earth and of the sea! for the devil is come down unto you, having great wrath, because he knoweth that he hath but a short time.

13 And when the dragon saw that he was cast unto the earth, he persecuted the woman which brought forth the man child.

14 And to the woman were given two wings of a great eagle, that she might fly into the wilderness, into her place, where she is nourished for a time, and times, and half a time, from the face of the serpent.

15 And the serpent cast out of his mouth water as a flood after the woman, that he might cause her to be carried away of the flood.

16 And the earth helped the woman, and the earth opened her mouth, and swallowed up the flood which the dragon cast out of his mouth.

17 And the dragon was wroth with the woman, and went to make war with the remnant of her seed, which keep the commandments of God, and have the testimony of Jesus Christ.

12 Therefore rejoice, ye heavens, and all those that dwell with Major Tom; but woe to the inhabiters of ground control! For the fox is come down unto you, having great wrath, because he knoweth that he hath but a short time.

13 And when the fox saw that he was sent back down to earth, he sought to persecute the woman who had brought the gay manchild.

14 And to the woman were given two airline tickets, that she and a friend might fly away from the fox to her place in St. Bart's for a week, to light incense for a time, and times, and half a time.

15 And the fox instructed his affiliates to cast aspersions out of their mouths at the woman, that they might cause her to be carried down to the list of bees.

16 And the earth helped the woman, and the earth opened its mouth, and swallowed the aspersions that the fox's affiliates had broadcast.

17 And the fox was wroth with the woman, and went to make war with the remnant of humanity; which in truth he was planning on doing anyway.

REVELATIONS CHAPTER 13 REVELATIONS
(Original) *(Revised)*

¹ nd I stood upon the sand of the sea, and saw a beast rise up out of the sea, having seven heads and ten horns, and upon his horns ten crowns, and upon his heads the name of blasphemy.

¹ nd I stood beside a factory, and I saw a beast rise up wryly from the factory, as one who trespasses; having upon his head ten pins; and upon each of those pins ten falafels and ten loofahs; and the pins vibrated.

² And the beast which I saw was like unto a leopard, and his feet were as the feet of a bear, and his mouth as the mouth of a lion: and the dragon gave him his power, and his seat, and great authority.

² And the beast which I saw was like unto a peacock with great pride and no plumage; and his mouth was as the mouth of a lion with no teeth; and the fox gave him his power, and his seat, and great authority.

³ And I saw one of his heads as it were wounded to death; and his deadly wound was healed: and all the world wondered after the beast.

³ And I saw the factory begin to spin all around the peacock; but the beast himself spun not.

⁴ And they worshipped the dragon which gave power unto the beast: and they worshipped the beast, saying, Who is like unto the beast? who is able to make war with him?

⁴ And many people worshipped the fox which gave power unto the peacock: and they worshipped the beast, saying, Who is like unto the beast? He tells it like is. That beast looks out for us. Go beast!

5 And there was given unto him a mouth speaking great things and blasphemies; and power was given unto him to continue forty and two months.

6 And he opened his mouth in blasphemy against God, to blaspheme his name, and his tabernacle, and them that dwell in heaven.

7 And it was given unto him to make war with the saints, and to overcome them: and power was given him over all kindreds, and tongues, and nations.

8 And all that dwell upon the earth shall worship him, whose names are not written in the book of life of the Lamb slain from the foundation of the world.

9 If any man have an ear, let him hear.

10 He that leadeth into captivity shall go into captivity: he that killeth with the sword must be killed with the sword. Here is the patience and the faith of the saints.

5 And there was given unto him a mouth speaking occasionally entertaining heresies; and power was given unto him to continue as long as he pulled in at least 0.9 million in the target demo.

6 And he opened his mouth in blasphemy against God; which he usually did in the guise of defending God against blasphemy.

7 And it was given unto him to make war with the saints, and to overcome them: and also to ambush them as they emerged from dental offices.

8 And all that dwell upon the earth shall worship him, whose names are not written in the membership rolls of public television.

9 If any man have an ear, turn the volume down.

10 He that yelleth at people shall be yelled at by people: And he that shutteth up not on earth during his life shall be shutteth up *in* the earth afterwards.

11 And I beheld another beast coming up out of the earth; and he had two horns like a lamb, and he spake as a dragon.

12 And he exerciseth all the power of the first beast before him, and causeth the earth and them which dwell therein to worship the first beast, whose deadly wound was healed.

13 And he doeth great wonders, so that he maketh fire come down from heaven on the earth in the sight of men,

14 And deceiveth them that dwell on the earth by the means of those miracles which he had power to do in the sight of the beast; saying to them that dwell on the earth, that they should make an image to the beast, which had the wound by a sword, and did live.

15 And he had power to give life unto the image of the beast, that the image of the beast should both speak, and cause that as many as would not worship the image of the beast should be killed.

11 And now another beast beckoned out of the earth; and he had a face like a bat, and ears like a bat, and they were seeping batshit.

12 And he exerciseth all the power of the peacock before him, only with more piteous weeping.

13 And he dost great wonders in the sight of men, so that he maketh lightning come down from heaven and alight on his chalkboard,

14 And deceiveth them that dwell on the earth by the means of those absurdities which the fox had once helped give him power to do; saying to them that dwell on the earth, that al-Qaeda funds NPR, meaning Hitler belonged to PETA, proving that the Kennedys committed suicide.

15 And he had power to spread his message in many forms; with his image, and with his voice, and with his words, and with his presence, and with his """novels"""; I was specifically instructed to put three sets of quotes around that word.

16 And he causeth all, both small and great, rich and poor, free and bond, to receive a mark in their right hand, or in their foreheads:

17 And that no man might buy or sell, save he that had the mark, or the name of the beast, or the number of his name.

18 Here is wisdom. Let him that hath understanding count the number of the beast: for it is the number of a man; and his number is Six hundred threescore and six.

16 And he causeth all, both small and great, rich and poor, free and bond, to believe they have been implanted with a microchip by the World Bank;

17 And that no man will be free, or have liberty, save that they remove this microchip from their brains.

18 Here is wisdom. Let him that hath understanding grasp the number of the beast: for it is the number of a man; and the number is (888) 727-BECK.

REVELATIONS
(Original)

CHAPTER 14

REVELATIONS
(Revised)

1 nd I looked, and, lo, a Lamb stood on the mount Sion, and with him an hundred forty and four thousand, having his Father's name written in their foreheads.

1 hen I looked, and lo, the Bieb stood atop the Hollywood sign, and with him the 144,000 regenerators, who were preparing to wait out Armageddon in a hyperbaric cybercave; the location chosen for maximum irony.

2 And I heard a voice from heaven, as the voice of many waters, and as the voice of a great thunder: and I heard the voice of harpers harping with their harps:

2 And I heard the voice of the Bieb, and the voice of the 144,000, rising like a choir of adorable puppies: and I also heard resounding from heaven the mad beats of the Now-Glorious B.I.G.:

3 And they sung as it were a new song before the throne, and before the four beasts, and the elders: and no man could learn that song but the hundred and forty and four thousand, which were redeemed from the earth.

4 These are they which were not defiled with women; for they are virgins. These are they which follow the Lamb whithersoever he goeth. These were redeemed from among men, being the firstfruits unto God and to the Lamb.

5 And in their mouth was found no guile: for they are without fault before the throne of God.

6 And I saw another angel fly in the midst of heaven, having the everlasting gospel to preach unto them that dwell on the earth, and to every nation, and kindred, and tongue, and people,

3 And it all melded into a new song before the throne, and before the angels, and the best buds, and God; it was an unforgettable performance, like a halftime show that was an end-time show.

4 For the 144,000 are pure of spirit, and kind, and given the circumstances not as holier-than-thou as might be expected; and they are prepared to follow the Bieb wheresoever he goeth; for though many did not know his work, they had all heard of him, and admired his "Never Say Never" outlook.

5 And in their mouth was found no guile: for they were without fault before the throne of God; even the Jews for Jesus, which was truly infuriating.

6 And I saw another angel descend from heaven on a string; he had eight legs, and at the last moment he crashed to earth, breaking his wing and his shinbone; but he arose, and began to preach to every nation, and kindred, and people, as he kicked off the first stop of a 1,000-year tour;

7 Saying with a loud voice, Fear God, and give glory to him; for the hour of his judgment is come: and worship him that made heaven, and earth, and the sea, and the fountains of waters.

8 And there followed another angel, saying, Babylon is fallen, is fallen, that great city, because she made all nations drink of the wine of the wrath of her fornication.

9 And the third angel followed them, saying with a loud voice, If any man worship the beast and his image, and receive his mark in his forehead, or in his hand,

10 The same shall drink of the wine of the wrath of God, which is poured out without mixture into the cup of his indignation; and he shall be tormented with fire and brimstone in the presence of the holy angels, and in the presence of the Lamb:

11 And the smoke of their torment ascendeth up for ever and ever: and they have no rest day nor night, who worship the beast and his image, and whosoever receiveth the mark of his name.

7 Singing with good voice, You, too, must give glory to God: for the hour of his judgment is come, with or without you.

8 A second angel followed, a woman; in name the Blessed Mother, in visage a blighted grandmother; and said, It is fallen, is fallen, the great city that made all nations drink of the wine of her fornication; fallen, just like a prayer.

9 And the third angel followed them, and milking the moment penned an announcement: Well, look at all of you, happy and cheering just because you're receiving eternal salvation.

10 Well, hate to spoil the party, but there are thousands of others who will spend tonight not celebrating, but drinking the wine of the wrath of God as it pours unmixed into the cup of his righteous indignation.

11 So tonight, as you're enjoying your "bliss" and "paradise," maybe you could spare a moment to remember the poor souls who will have no rest day or night for five million billion years.

¹² Here is the patience of the saints: here are they that keep the commandments of God, and the faith of Jesus.

¹³ And I heard a voice from heaven saying unto me, Write, Blessed are the dead which die in the Lord from henceforth: Yea, saith the Spirit, that they may rest from their labours; and their works do follow them.

¹⁴ And I looked, and behold a white cloud, and upon the cloud one sat like unto the Son of man, having on his head a golden crown, and in his hand a sharp sickle.

¹⁵ And another angel came out of the temple, crying with a loud voice to him that sat on the cloud, Thrust in thy sickle, and reap: for the time is come for thee to reap; for the harvest of the earth is ripe.

¹⁶ And he that sat on the cloud thrust in his sickle on the earth; and the earth was reaped.

¹⁷ And another angel came out of the temple which is in heaven, he also having a sharp sickle.

¹² (Here is true wisdom: Never invite a saint to a party.)

¹³ And I heard a voice from heaven saying unto me, Write, Blessed are the dead which die in the Lord from henceforth; so if you've ever thought about dying but were scared about where you'd end up, no worries.

¹⁴ I looked, and behold a white balloon floating in the air, and upon the balloon one sat like unto the Son of Bran; child of fortune and father of the virgin; having upon his head a golden crown, and in his hand a flying pickle.

¹⁵ And his executive assistant angel flew down to join him, crying with a loud voice to him that sat on the cloud, Thrust in thy pickle: for the time is come to launch it; for the time of celestial visitation is ripe.

¹⁶ And he that sat on the cloud thrust his pickle on the earth, and gathered the visitors; whereupon they ascended from the earth for a week to ten days.

¹⁷ And now sixteen apprentice angels (all of them familiar, and all of them fallen) appeared, each holding trumpets;

18 And another angel came out from the altar, which had power over fire; and cried with a loud cry to him that had the sharp sickle, saying, Thrust in thy sharp sickle, and gather the clusters of the vine of the earth; for her grapes are fully ripe.

18 And with them they heralded the arrival of their master, he who had power to fire; he stood atop his trumpet-shaped tower and bellowed, Now will I sound my trumpet, that it may trumpet the trumpets of my trumpeting over the trumpeted cities of the earth, trumpetingly.

19 And the angel thrust in his sickle into the earth, and gathered the vine of the earth, and cast it into the great winepress of the wrath of God.

19 And he blew his trumpet, and it produced a hot and fearsome wind that spread across the earth; and fully a third part of the buildings thereon were transformed, and became trumpet-shaped.

20 And the winepress was trodden without the city, and blood came out of the winepress, even unto the horse bridles, by the space of a thousand and six hundred furlongs.

20 And even the earth itself was as trodden upon; for it was now filled with holes, grouped in trumpet-shaped units of eighteen; a thousand and six hundred such groupings were there, each classier than the next.

CHAPTER 15

REVELATIONS
(Original)

REVELATIONS
(Revised)

1 **A**nd I saw another sign in heaven, great and marvellous, seven angels having the seven last plagues; for in them is filled up the wrath of God.

1 **A**nd I saw another sign in heaven, great and marvellous; that is, to the extent seven angels bearing the seven last calamities that will destroy mankind can be seen as great and marvelous.

² And I saw as it were a sea of glass mingled with fire: and them that had gotten the victory over the beast, and over his image, and over his mark, and over the number of his name, stand on the sea of glass, having the harps of God.

³ And they sing the song of Moses the servant of God, and the song of the Lamb, saying, Great and marvellous are thy works, Lord God Almighty; just and true are thy ways, thou King of saints.

⁴ Who shall not fear thee, O Lord, and glorify thy name? for thou only art holy: for all nations shall come and worship before thee; for thy judgments are made manifest.

⁵ And after that I looked, and, behold, the temple of the tabernacle of the testimony in heaven was opened:

⁶ And the seven angels came out of the temple, having the seven plagues, clothed in pure and white linen, and having their breasts girded with golden girdles.

² I was back by God's throne, watching the glass crystal; and in it I saw those who had obtained victory over the beast, and his disciples, and his image, and his lies, gathered around a stage, listening to a concert by Nickelodeon Viacom Music Productions recording artists Big Time Rush.

³ And BTR sang the songs of Michael Jackson, and Mariah Carey, and the Bieb, and even a few originals, saying, I wanna be with you, Lord.

⁴ I wanna be with you! Wanna be with you! Wanna spend my life justa me and you! Wanna beeeeee with you, Lord! Yes I do!

⁵ And after that I looked, and behold, the back door of the Divine Cyberterrorism Lab was opened;

⁶ And seven angels emerged, holding seven tiny chips, clothed in hazmat suits and white lab coats, and having their breasts girded with lead aprons.

7 And one of the four beasts gave unto the seven angels seven golden vials full of the wrath of God, who liveth for ever and ever.

8 And the temple was filled with smoke from the glory of God, and from his power; and no man was able to enter into the temple, till the seven plagues of the seven angels were fulfilled.

7 And one of the members of Big Time Rush—I think it was Kendall—gave the seven angels seven Virgin Motherboards to put the seven chips on.

8 And the whole area started filling with smoke, either from the impending horror or from an off-camera smoke machine; in either case it set the mood.

REVELATIONS *(Original)* CHAPTER 16 REVELATIONS *(Revised)*

1 nd I heard a great voice out of the temple saying to the seven angels, Go your ways, and pour out the vials of the wrath of God upon the earth.

1 nd I heard God shout at the screen to the seven angels, Go your ways, and pour out the seven viruses that are the seven plagues of the wrath of God upon the earth; and then God looked at me and said, Check this out.

2 And the first went, and poured out his vial upon the earth; and there fell a noisome and grievous sore upon the men which had the mark of the beast, and upon them which worshipped his image.

3 And the second angel poured out his vial upon the sea; and it became as the blood of a dead man: and every living soul died in the sea.

2 And the first went, and poured his virus down upon the earth; and there fell a plague of spam upon the email accounts of the wicked.

3 And the second angel poured out his virus upon PCs; and they began operating at the speed of a turtle swimming upstream in a river of molasses.

⁴ And the third angel poured out his vial upon the rivers and fountains of waters; and they became blood.

⁵ And I heard the angel of the waters say, Thou art righteous, O Lord, which art, and wast, and shalt be, because thou hast judged thus.

⁶ For they have shed the blood of saints and prophets, and thou hast given them blood to drink; for they are worthy.

⁷ And I heard another out of the altar say, Even so, Lord God Almighty, true and righteous are thy judgments.

⁸ And the fourth angel poured out his vial upon the sun; and power was given unto him to scorch men with fire.

⁹ And men were scorched with great heat, and blasphemed the name of God, which hath power over these plagues: and they repented not to give him glory.

⁴ And the third angel poured out his virus upon Macs; which instantly became sick with pneumonia; not metaphorical pneumonia, *actual* pneumonia.

⁵ And I heard the third angel say, Thou art righteous, O Lord, for allowing me to perform this task for thee.

⁶ For I am weary of hearing the partisans of the forbidden fruit boast tediously of its indestructibility; surely they are worthy of this.

⁷ And I heard another voice say, Verily, my Lord; of course, we use Apple too; in fact we used it earlier this Armageddon; but still, they are worthy.

⁸ And the fourth angel poured out his virus upon YouTube; and instantly one hundred million amusing videos of people being unintentionally amusing appeared;

⁹ And the people were unable to stop watching them; they rose not from their desks; and soon their eyes weakened; and they befouled their garments; and then their pets died, and their children.

¹⁰ And the fifth angel poured out his vial upon the seat of the beast; and his kingdom was full of darkness; and they gnawed their tongues for pain,

¹¹ And blasphemed the God of heaven because of their pains and their sores, and repented not of their deeds.

¹² And the sixth angel poured out his vial upon the great river Euphrates; and the water thereof was dried up, that the way of the kings of the east might be prepared.

¹³ And I saw three unclean spirits like frogs come out of the mouth of the dragon, and out of the mouth of the beast, and out of the mouth of the false prophet.

¹⁴ For they are the spirits of devils, working miracles, which go forth unto the kings of the earth and of the whole world, to gather them to the battle of that great day of God Almighty.

¹⁵ Behold, I come as a thief. Blessed is he that watcheth, and keepeth his garments, lest he walk naked, and they see his shame.

¹⁰ And the fifth angel poured out his virus upon Wikipedia; which soon became filled to the brink with slander, and disingenuousness, and misinformation.

¹¹ So a bit of a wasted virus, that one.

¹² And the sixth angel poured out his virus upon the great Amazon; and all commerce thereon was crippled, like unto a river with no source.

¹³ And I saw three unclean spirits like unto demons come out of the mouth of the fox, and the mouth of the peacock, and the mouth of the bat who was the false prophet.

¹⁴ For they are the spirits of devils, working miracles, which go forth unto the slobs of the earth and of the whole world, to gather them to the battle of that great day of God Almighty.

¹⁵ Behold, I come as a publicist. Blessed is he that readeth the trades, and keepeth my clippings, lest he be uninformed, and come off ignorant at his watercooler.

16 And he gathered them together into a place called in the Hebrew tongue Armageddon.

17 And the seventh angel poured out his vial into the air; and there came a great voice out of the temple of heaven, from the throne, saying, It is done.

18 And there were voices, and thunders, and lightnings; and there was a great earthquake, such as was not since men were upon the earth, so mighty an earthquake, and so great.

19 And the great city was divided into three parts, and the cities of the nations fell: and great Babylon came in remembrance before God, to give unto her the cup of the wine of the fierceness of his wrath.

20 And every island fled away, and the mountains were not found.

21 And there fell upon men a great hail out of heaven, every stone about the weight of a talent: and men blasphemed God because of the plague of the hail; for the plague thereof was exceeding great.

16 And the fox and bat and peacock gathered themselves together into a place called in the Hebrew tongue Armageddon.

17 And the seventh angel poured out his virus into the air; and God looked at me from his throne and said, Thou hast *got* to check this out!

18 And lo, 75 quintillion images of pornography fell from the sky onto the work stations of all mankind; leading to conflagrations, and dam bursts, and missile launches, and food shortages, and unprecedented levels of massturbation.

19 And Jerusalem was divided into three parts, which it probably should have been a long time ago; and *Babylon 5* came in remembrance before God, to make its case to Him that *Star Trek: Generations* had ripped it off.

20 And every Starbucks flew away, and good coffee could not be found.

21 And there fell upon men a rain of venti cups; and men blasphemed God for mocking their addiction to waiting fifteen minutes for a cup of coffee; but he laughed, being caffeine-free.

CHAPTER 17

 1 nd there came one of the seven angels which had the seven vials, and talked with me, saying unto me, Come hither; I will shew unto thee the judgment of the great whore that sitteth upon many waters:

2 With whom the kings of the earth have committed fornication, and the inhabitants of the earth have been made drunk with the wine of her fornication.

3 So he carried me away in the spirit into the wilderness: and I saw a woman sit upon a scarlet coloured beast, full of names of blasphemy, having seven heads and ten horns.

4 And the woman was arrayed in purple and scarlet colour, and decked with gold and precious stones and pearls, having a golden cup in her hand full of abominations and filthiness of her fornication:

5 And upon her forehead was a name written, MYSTERY, BABYLON THE GREAT, THE MOTHER OF HARLOTS AND ABOMI-NATIONS OF THE EARTH.

 1 nd there came one of the seven angels which had intro-duced the seven vi-ruses, and talked with me, saying unto me: Come hither; I will shew unto thee the judgment of the great whore that sitteth upon many waters:

2 With whom the kings of the earth have committed fornication, and the inhabitants of the earth have been made drunk with the wine of her fornication.

3 So he carried me away to a north-ern wilderness; and I saw a woman sitting upon a red ele-phant that was full of names of blasphemy; it had seven heads and ten horns.

4 And the woman was arrayed in a tailored skirt, and decked with dangling gemstones; her eyes were encircled in clear discs; she was well put-together, in general;

5 But upon her forehead was a name written, MILFSTERY, BABBLING THE GREAT, THE MOTHER OF HARLOTS AND REFUDIA-TIONS OF THE EARTH.

⁶ And I saw the woman drunken with the blood of the saints, and with the blood of the martyrs of Jesus: and when I saw her, I wondered with great admiration.

⁷ And the angel said unto me, Wherefore didst thou marvel? I will tell thee the mystery of the woman, and of the beast that carrieth her, which hath the seven heads and ten horns.

⁸ The beast that thou sawest was, and is not; and shall ascend out of the bottomless pit, and go into perdition: and they that dwell on the earth shall wonder, whose names were not written in the book of life from the foundation of the world, when they behold the beast that was, and is not, and yet is.

⁹ And here is the mind which hath wisdom. The seven heads are seven mountains, on which the woman sitteth.

¹⁰ And there are seven kings: five are fallen, and one is, and the other is not yet come; and when he cometh, he must continue a short space.

⁶ And I saw the woman cackling, and drinking the blood of a moose, and the blood of the martyrs of Jesus: and when I saw her, I wondered with great admiration.

⁷ And the angel said unto me, Wherefore didst thou marvel? I will tell the milfstery of the woman, and of the beast that carrieth her, that hath the seven heads and ten horns.

⁸ For this beast was left by the son of Cain; he who was a rebel, but is no longer; who ascended out of a jungle pit to lead his people in the desert; though many of his legion wondered whether he was worthy to be written in the book of the Gospel, this son of Cain, who was a rebel, but now is not.

⁹ And here is the mind which hath wisdom: For the seven heads are seven rivals, on which the woman sitteth.

¹⁰ But soon the seven heads of the seven would-be kings will fall off the beast; one at a time will they fall, until only one is left; but it too shall fall, as soon as word gets out about what it did on that camping trip to those Boy Scouts.

11 And the beast that was, and is not, even he is the eighth, and is of the seven, and goeth into perdition.

12 And the ten horns which thou sawest are ten kings, which have received no kingdom as yet; but receive power as kings one hour with the beast.

13 These have one mind, and shall give their power and strength unto the beast.

14 These shall make war with the Lamb, and the Lamb shall overcome them: for he is Lord of lords, and King of kings: and they that are with him are called, and chosen, and faithful.

15 And he saith unto me, The waters which thou sawest, where the whore sitteth, are peoples, and multitudes, and nations, and tongues.

16 And the ten horns which thou sawest upon the beast, these shall hate the whore, and shall make her desolate and naked, and shall eat her flesh, and burn her with fire.

11 And when they have fallen off, the whore shall seize control of the now-headless beast and its ten horns.

12 For each of the ten horns ends in a point bearing the power to utter a single phrase; these points shall talk their phrase incessantly on behalf of the beast and the Whore;

13 For these have one mind, and give their power and strength unto the beast.

14 These shall make war with the Bieb, and the Bieb shall overcome them; for he is Lord of Lords, and Hottie of Hotties; and they that are with him are chosen, and faithful, and loyal to the point of murder.

15 And the angel saith unto me, The wilderness which thou sawest, where the whore sitteth, is a cold and wild land, full of trucking most icy, and catches most deadly, and bears most grizzly, and mountains most denali.

16 And the people of this wilderness hate the whore; and would like nothing better than to make her desolate and naked and eat her flesh; or even worse, put her back doing sports on KTUU-TV.

17 For God hath put in their hearts to fulfill his will, and to agree, and give their kingdom unto the beast, until the words of God shall be fulfilled.

18 And the woman which thou sawest is that great city, which reigneth over the kings of the earth.

17 But God hath cooled their hearts, so that they may agree to give the kingdom unto the beast and the whore, until the words of God shall be fulfilled.

18 So that the woman may for a time rule over the kings of the earth, while her husband roams the snow on loud machines that whoosheth.

REVELATIONS
(Original)

CHAPTER 18

REVELATIONS
(Revised)

 1 nd after these things I saw another angel come down from heaven, having great power; and the earth was lightened with his glory.

 1 nd after these things I saw another figure descend stiffly from heaven; he carried a gold idol and a gold medallion, and descended on butterfly wings on a scissor-lift of his own invention;

2 And he cried mightily with a strong voice, saying, Babylon the great is fallen, is fallen, and is become the habitation of devils, and the hold of every foul spirit, and a cage of every unclean and hateful bird.

2 And he cried in a deafeningly sleepy drawl, saying, Gaea the great is falling, is falling, and is become the habitation of uncleanness, and the hold of every pollution, and the radiation capital of the Milky Way.

3 For all nations have drunk of the wine of the wrath of her fornication, and the kings of the earth have committed fornication with her, and the merchants of the earth are waxed rich through the abundance of her delicacies.

3 For all nations are producing the smoke of her downfall, and the kings of the earth do nothing to limit the smoke, and the consumers of the earth wallow in the mud of their own carbon footprints.

4 And I heard another voice from heaven, saying, Come out of her, my people, that ye be not partakers of her sins, and that ye receive not of her plagues.

5 For her sins have reached unto heaven, and God hath remembered her iniquities.

6 Reward her even as she rewarded you, and double unto her double according to her works: in the cup which she hath filled fill to her double.

7 How much she hath glorified herself, and lived deliciously, so much torment and sorrow give her: for she saith in her heart, I sit a queen, and am no widow, and shall see no sorrow.

8 Therefore shall her plagues come in one day, death, and mourning, and famine; and she shall be utterly burned with fire: for strong is the Lord God who judgeth her.

9 And the kings of the earth, who have committed fornication and lived deliciously with her, shall bewail her, and lament for her,

4 And I heard another voice; like that of Michael, only more; fat and flinty; saying, You know, this used to be a great planet; a planet where if you worked hard, you could make enough money to raise your kids, maybe even send them to college.

5 But now Earth has changed, and God hath remembered her iniquities.

6 Now he's going to reward us with misery and double misery and quadruple misery, and all the bad things human beings deserve; because people are terrible people.

7 How much we have glorified ourselves, and lived selfishly; well, karma is a boomerang; now you're going to pay the price for thinking, Look at me, I'm a human being, la-di-da, I deserve to live.

8 Well, you don't; and now here comes death, and mourning, and famine, and also we're all going to be utterly burned with fire, which I'm personally looking forward to.

9 And all the bigwigs, the CEOs in their limousines who have raped the planet and exploited the seven billion little guys, shall moan and

when they shall see the smoke of her burning,

lament and bewail when they see the world ending.

¹⁰ Standing afar off for the fear of her torment, saying, Alas, alas, that great city Babylon, that mighty city! for in one hour is thy judgment come.

¹⁰ They'll be standing safely in their corporate jets, saying, Wow, it's too bad that the world is ending because we're such bastards; and I'll catch them saying that too, because I'll sneak on board posing as a stewardess.

¹¹ And the merchants of the earth shall weep and mourn over her; for no man buyeth their merchandise any more:

¹¹ And the merchants of the earth shall weep and mourn over her; for no man buyeth their merchandise any more;

¹² The merchandise of gold, and silver, and precious stones, and of pearls, and fine linen, and purple, and silk, and scarlet, and all thyine wood, and all manner vessels of ivory, and all manner vessels of most precious wood, and of brass, and iron, and marble,

¹² The merchandise of gold, and silver, and precious stones, and home furnishings, and swimwear, and loungewear, and audio components, and precision-tip tweezers, and ultrasonic dog deterrents, and all manner of printer cartridges, and all manner of personal lubricants, and shiatsu lumbar massage cushions, and *Iron Man 2* promotional Cyclone Spinning Robot Drones available only at participating Burger Kings, and Snuggies,

¹³ And cinnamon, and odours, and ointments, and frankincense, and wine, and oil, and fine flour, and wheat, and beasts, and sheep, and horses, and chariots, and slaves, and souls of men.

¹³ And Jacuzzis, and Uzis, and perfume, and pickles, and hammers, and sickles, and zippers, and zappers, and dippers, and diapers, and clippers, and clappers, and Whoppers, and wipers.

14 And the fruits that thy soul lusted after are departed from thee, and all things which were dainty and goodly are departed from thee, and thou shalt find them no more at all.

15 The merchants of these things, which were made rich by her, shall stand afar off for the fear of her torment, weeping and wailing,

16 And saying, Alas, alas, that great city, that was clothed in fine linen, and purple, and scarlet, and decked with gold, and precious stones, and pearls!

17 For in one hour so great riches is come to nought. And every shipmaster, and all the company in ships, and sailors, and as many as trade by sea, stood afar off,

18 And cried when they saw the smoke of her burning, saying, What city is like unto this great city!

19 And they cast dust on their heads, and cried, weeping and wailing, saying, Alas, alas, that great city, wherein were made rich all that had ships in the sea by reason of her costliness! for in one hour is she made desolate.

14 No more hot stone massages; no more hand-groomed emu feathers for call girls to stroke millionaires' balls with; all that stuff's gone now.

15 The merchants of these things, which were made rich by her, shall stand afar off, weeping and wailing in their fancy-schmancy mansions,

16 And saying, Alas, alas our fine planet, which once had all those nice oceans and continents and animals and plants and things.

17 For in one hour its great riches are come to naught. And every yachtmaster and his crew will also stand afar off,

18 And cry when they see the world ending—which I will also catch them doing after I ambush them after sneaking on board posing as an assistant purser—saying, Woe!

19 And they will cast margarita salt on their heads, and cry weeping and wailing, saying, Alas, alas, our fine planet, which we used to get to sail around on in these floating affronts to the notion of need! For in one hour she is made unmarketable.

20 Rejoice over her, thou heaven, and ye holy apostles and prophets; for God hath avenged you on her.

21 And a mighty angel took up a stone like a great millstone, and cast it into the sea, saying, Thus with violence shall that great city Babylon be thrown down, and shall be found no more at all.

22 And the voice of harpers, and musicians, and of pipers, and trumpeters, shall be heard no more at all in thee; and no craftsman, of whatsoever craft he be, shall be found any more in thee; and the sound of a millstone shall be heard no more at all in thee;

23 And the light of a candle shall shine no more at all in thee; and the voice of the bridegroom and of the bride shall be heard no more at all in thee: for thy merchants were the great men of the earth; for by thy sorceries were all nations deceived.

24 And in her was found the blood of prophets, and of saints, and of all that were slain upon the earth.

20 I hope you're happy, God; I hope making rich people unhappy makes you feel like a real man.

21 And a mighty-winged angel picked up a great millstone like it was a rock, and cast it into the sea, and cast himself in a family comedy, saying, Canst thou smell what the Lord is cooking?

22 For the Earth is destroyed; and the voice of musicians, and directors, and Foley artists shall be heard no more; and no craft services man, of whatsoever craft services company, shall be found any more; and worst of all, the work of The Rock shall be seen no more at all;

23 And the spotlights shall shine no more at all on me; and the voice of my agent telling me I've landed another lead despite my total lack of acting ability shall be heard no more; for thy merchants were the great men of the earth, and led it astray.

24 And you also gave supreme power to the whore; which is like knocking on God's door and saying, Hey, come kill us now.

REVELATIONS
(Original)

CHAPTER 19

REVELATIONS
(Revised)

 1 nd after these things I heard a great voice of much people in heaven, saying, Alleluia; Salvation, and glory, and honour, and power, unto the Lord our God:

 1 nd after these things I heard innumerable women singing like a choir of suburban angels, saying, Alleluia; O Salvation, and glory, and self-acceptance, and empowerment, unto the Lord our God:

2 For true and righteous are his judgments: for he hath judged the great whore, which did corrupt the earth with her fornication, and hath avenged the blood of his servants at her hand.

2 For true and righteous are her judgments; for she hath interviewed the great whore, which did corrupt the earth with her refudiation, and after an hour revealed her as disingenuous and not coming from a place of spiritual authenticity.

3 And again they said, Alleluia. And her smoke rose up for ever and ever.

3 And again they sang, Alleluia; O, may her name rise like a silent brother forever and ever.

4 And the four and twenty elders and the four beasts fell down and worshipped God that sat on the throne, saying, Amen; Alleluia.

4 And the four and twenty cherubs and seraphs and the four best buddies fell down and worshipped she that now sat on the throne, saying, It raineth men; Alleluia; it raineth men; amen.

5 And a voice came out of the throne, saying, Praise our God, all ye his servants, and ye that fear him, both small and great.

5 And then I heard one of the cherubs cry out, Praise our God, ye network of angels, and ye that keep the secret, small and great.

6 And I heard as it were the voice of a great multitude, and as the voice of many waters, and as the voice of mighty thunderings, saying, Alleluia: for the Lord God omnipotent reigneth.

7 Let us be glad and rejoice, and give honour to him: for the marriage of the Lamb is come, and his wife hath made herself ready.

8 And to her was granted that she should be arrayed in fine linen, clean and white: for the fine linen is the righteousness of saints.

9 And he saith unto me, Write, Blessed are they which are called unto the marriage supper of the Lamb. And he saith unto me, These are the true sayings of God.

10 And I fell at his feet to worship him. And he said unto me, See thou do it not: I am thy fellow servant, and of thy brethren that have the testimony of Jesus: worship God: for the testimony of Jesus is the spirit of prophecy.

11 And I saw heaven opened, and behold a white horse; and he that sat upon him was called Faithful and True, and in righteousness he doth judge and make war.

6 And again I heard the suburban choir singing a song sounding like the soft moans of fifty million working moms getting backrubs, saying, Alleluia: for the Lord God omniprahtent reigneth.

7 Let us be glad and rejoice, and give honor to her: for the marriage of the Bieb is come, and his wife hath made herself ready.

8 And to her was granted that she should be arrayed as if he were thunder and she were lightning.

9 And one watching this saith unto me, Write, Blessed are they who are invited to the marriage supper of the Bieb. And he saith unto me, Behold; I nabbed an invite.

10 And I fell at his feet to worship him. And he said unto me, See thou do it not: I am thy fellow servant; I got in only because I know an Usher. Rather worship Bieb: for his music is the music of eternity.

11 And I saw heaven opened, and behold a knight on a steel horse: and he that sat upon him was called Faithful and Clear, and in righteousness doth he set and achieve goals for himself.

12 His eyes were as a flame of fire, and on his head were many crowns; and he had a name written, that no man knew, but he himself.

13 And he was clothed with a vesture dipped in blood: and his name is called The Word of God.

14 And the armies which were in heaven followed him upon white horses, clothed in fine linen, white and clean.

15 And out of his mouth goeth a sharp sword, that with it he should smite the nations: and he shall rule them with a rod of iron: and he treadeth the winepress of the fierceness and wrath of Almighty God.

16 And he hath on his vesture and on his thigh a name written, KING OF KINGS, AND LORD OF LORDS.

17 And I saw an angel standing in the sun; and he cried with a loud voice, saying to all the fowls that fly in the midst of heaven, Come and gather yourselves together unto the supper of the great God;

12 And his eyes were closed firmly, and he rode in two kinds of thunder through a thick white sky; and he had a secret name written nowhere other than a map;

13 And he was clothed with a currency-tinted vesture: And his name is called The Word of Ron.

14 And the forces which were behind him followed him through clear water and free winds in floating boats, clothed in the emblems of a mystical navy;

15 And out of his mouth cometh a sharp laugh, that with it he should petrify the nations; and he treadeth the stairmaster of his own intensity; and he holds in his hands the truth, which he handles ably.

16 And he hath on his vesture two names written, CRIMINON and NARCONON.

17 And I saw his guardian angel standing over a volcano; and he cried with a loud voice, saying to all the sheep that herd in the clouds of heaven, Come and take ye this free personality test;

18 That ye may eat the flesh of kings, and the flesh of captains, and the flesh of mighty men, and the flesh of horses, and of them that sit on them, and the flesh of all men, both free and bond, both small and great.

19 And I saw the beast, and the kings of the earth, and their armies, gathered together to make war against him that sat on the horse, and against his army.

20 And the beast was taken, and with him the false prophet that wrought miracles before him, with which he deceived them that had received the mark of the beast, and them that worshipped his image. These both were cast alive into a lake of fire burning with brimstone.

21 And the remnant were slain with the sword of him that sat upon the horse, which sword proceeded out of his mouth: and all the fowls were filled with their flesh.

18 That ye may gain insight into your income, and your future, and your personal relationships, and your life, and the secrets to the modern science of mental health.

19 And I saw the beast, and the whore, and the peacock, and the false prophet, gathered together to make war against him that sat on the horse, and against his army.

20 And the whore was taken, and with her the beast and the fox and peacock and the false prophet, who had deceived the people with his chalk and magic underpants. They were all cast alive into a lake of fire burning with brimstone, and no cameras.

21 And their remnants were slain upon a wheatstone bridge by the hand of he who sat upon the horse: for whatever he doth, he doth all out.

CHAPTER 20

1 And I saw an angel come down from heaven, having the key of the bottomless pit and a great chain in his hand.

2 And he laid hold on the dragon, that old serpent, which is the Devil, and Satan, and bound him a thousand years,

3 And cast him into the bottomless pit, and shut him up, and set a seal upon him, that he should deceive the nations no more, till the thousand years should be fulfilled: and after that he must be loosed a little season.

4 And I saw thrones, and they sat upon them, and judgment was given unto them: and I saw the souls of them that were beheaded for the witness of Jesus, and for the word of God, and which had not worshipped the beast, neither his image, neither had received his mark upon their foreheads, or in their hands; and they lived and reigned with Christ a thousand years.

1 And I saw an angel come down as it were through the back of the crystal screen and onto the battlefield, bearing the black talisman wielded by the Bieb.

2 And he laid hold of the pouched fox, which is the Devil, and Satan, and bound him for a thousand years, which is about as old as he already looked;

3 And cast him back down under, and shut him up, and set a seal upon him, that he should not have his broadcast license renewed until a millennium should have elapsed; at which point he could apply for renewal.

4 And I saw thrones, and the new trinity of God and the Bieb and the Knight sat upon them, and rendered judgment: and I saw the souls of those whose faith in God had never wavered, even when it threatened to break into a thousand little pieces, swathed in the color purple.

5 But the rest of the dead lived not again until the thousand years were finished. This is the first resurrection.

6 Blessed and holy is he that hath part in the first resurrection: on such the second death hath no power, but they shall be priests of God and of Christ, and shall reign with him a thousand years.

7 And when the thousand years are expired, Satan shall be loosed out of his prison,

8 And shall go out to deceive the nations which are in the four quarters of the earth, Gog and Magog, to gather them together to battle: the number of whom is as the sand of the sea.

9 And they went up on the breadth of the earth, and compassed the camp of the saints about, and the beloved city: and fire came down from God out of heaven, and devoured them.

5 But the rest of the dead lived not again until the thousand years were finished. This is the first resurrection.

6 Blessed and holy are they that hath part in this first resurrection: on such the second death hath no power, but they shall be priestesses of God, and shall reign with her a thousand years, and each day God will fill them with gladness by saying, Thou gettest a car; and thou gettest a car; and thou gettest a car; yea, everybody getteth a car.

7 And when the thousand years are expired, the fox shall be loosed out of the pit,

8 And shall go out once more, this time to deceive all the droids living in the four robo-sectors of the earth, from D2 to R2, to gather them together to battle: for their number shall be as the sand of the sea.

9 But God shall send robot transformers down upon earth in spaceships, to attack the underground matrix of the mutant droids, and shatter their Holodeck; and they will fire their phasers and photon torpedoes at them until they disintegrate into the eighth dimension.

10 And the devil that deceived them was cast into the lake of fire and brimstone, where the beast and the false prophet are, and shall be tormented day and night for ever and ever.

11 And I saw a great white throne, and him that sat on it, from whose face the earth and the heaven fled away; and there was found no place for them.

12 And I saw the dead, small and great, stand before God; and the books were opened: and another book was opened, which is the book of life: and the dead were judged out of those things which were written in the books, according to their works.

13 And the sea gave up the dead which were in it; and death and hell delivered up the dead which were in them: and they were judged every man according to their works.

14 And death and hell were cast into the lake of fire. This is the second death.

15 And whosoever was not found written in the book of life was cast into the lake of fire.

10 And the fox shall be cast alongside the whore, and peacock, and bat-prophet into the hellish abyss of the triple-digits, where they shall be forever tormented between Logo and Here!

11 And now I saw the great leather La-Z-God, and her that sat on it, from whose face the earth and the heaven fled away; for she looked all business.

12 And I saw the dead, small and great, stand before God; and then did the great Googling begin: and every human soul was judged by those traces of their lives which were Googlable.

13 And the graveyards gave up their dead; and death and hell delivered up their dead: and every man and woman who had ever lived was Googled, and judged according to the results.

14 And the unworthy were cast into the lake of fire forever.

15 (And by "unworthy," I mean anything less than 20,000 hits.)

CHAPTER 21

¹ nd I saw a new heaven and a new earth: for the first heaven and the first earth were passed away; and there was no more sea.

¹ nd I saw a new heaven and a new earth: for the first heaven and the first earth had been sent back; and replaced with a new heaven, and an improved earth.

² And I John saw the holy city, new Jerusalem, coming down from God out of heaven, prepared as a bride adorned for her husband.

² And I saw the holy city, New Jerusalem, coming down from God out of heaven, prepared as a bride adorned for her husband.

³ And I heard a great voice out of heaven saying, Behold, the tabernacle of God is with men, and he will dwell with them, and they shall be his people, and God himself shall be with them, and be their God.

³ And I heard the voice of an angel descending from behind a proscenium saying, The great work begins; God will dwell with her people, and they shall be her people, and God herself shall be with them, and be their God.

⁴ And God shall wipe away all tears from their eyes; and there shall be no more death, neither sorrow, nor crying, neither shall there be any more pain: for the former things are passed away.

⁴ And God shall wipe away all tears from their eyes; and there shall be no more death, neither sorrow, nor crying, neither shall there be any more pain: for all suffering has ceased.

⁵ And he that sat upon the throne said, Behold, I make all things new. And he said unto me, Write: for these words are true and faithful.

⁵ And she that sat upon the throne said, Behold, I make all things new. And she said unto me, Write: For it is time you know why the caged bird sings.

6 And he said unto me, It is done. I am Alpha and Omega, the beginning and the end. I will give unto him that is athirst of the fountain of the water of life freely.

7 He that overcometh shall inherit all things; and I will be his God, and he shall be my son.

8 But the fearful, and unbelieving, and the abominable, and murderers, and whoremongers, and sorcerers, and idolaters, and all liars, shall have their part in the lake which burneth with fire and brimstone: which is the second death.

9 And there came unto me one of the seven angels which had the seven vials full of the seven last plagues, and talked with me, saying, Come hither, I will shew thee the bride, the Lamb's wife.

10 And he carried me away in the spirit to a great and high mountain, and shewed me that great city, the holy Jerusalem, descending out of heaven from God,

11 Having the glory of God: and her light was like unto a stone most precious, even like a jasper stone, clear as crystal;

6 And she said unto me, It is done. I am Oprah and Harpo, the beginning and the end. I will give unto him that is athirst of the fountain of the water of life freely.

7 We have overcome; and he or she that overcometh shall inherit all things; and I will be his or her God, and he/she shall be my son/daughter.

8 But the fearful, and the selfish, and the abusive, and the deceitful, and the co-dependent, and those afraid to go on that inner journey which is the only path to happiness, shall burn forever in the lake of fire and brimstone: which is the second death.

9 And there came unto me one of the seven angels who had introduced the seven viruses, now in a much better mood; saying, Hey, let's get out of here and go to the city.

10 And he carried me away in the darkness to the topmost point of a great tower, and shewed me that great city, the holy Jerusalem, descending out of heaven from God,

11 Shining all around me with the glory of God; and her lights were like unto stones most precious, and her sidewalks glittered in welcome;

¹² And had a wall great and high, and had twelve gates, and at the gates twelve angels, and names written thereon, which are the names of the twelve tribes of the children of Israel:

¹³ On the east three gates; on the north three gates; on the south three gates; and on the west three gates.

¹⁴ And the wall of the city had twelve foundations, and in them the names of the twelve apostles of the Lamb.

¹⁵ And he that talked with me had a golden reed to measure the city, and the gates thereof, and the wall thereof.

¹⁶ And the city lieth foursquare, and the length is as large as the breadth: and he measured the city with the reed, twelve thousand furlongs. The length and the breadth and the height of it are equal.

¹⁷ And he measured the wall thereof, an hundred and forty and four cubits, according to the measure of a man, that is, of the angel.

¹² And on a single street corner, I saw twelve restaurants, serving twelve different cuisines;

¹³ On the northeast, Mexican, Indian, and Thai; on the northwest, Japanese, Italian, and Greek; on the southeast, Chinese, French, and Tuscan; and on the southwest, American, Ethiopian, and a cute little tapas place.

¹⁴ And the next block over had a twelveplex, and on its marquee the names of twelve well-reviewed films, even a few documentaries.

¹⁵ And he that talked with me had a pen and clipboard to take the measure of the city, and the people thereof.

¹⁶ And the city lieth foursquare, and extends beneath as much as above: and he measured the city with the clipboard, eight million stories; this being the tally of both the city and its people.

¹⁷ And he measured the headlines of the newspapers therein, and they were one hundred and forty four points large; that they might be visible from the moon.

¹⁸ And the building of the wall of it was of jasper: and the city was pure gold, like unto clear glass.

¹⁹ And the foundations of the wall of the city were garnished with all manner of precious stones. The first foundation was jasper; the second, sapphire; the third, a chalcedony; the fourth, an emerald;

²⁰ The fifth, sardonyx; the sixth, sardius; the seventh, chrysolite; the eighth, beryl; the ninth, a topaz; the tenth, a chrysoprasus; the eleventh, a jacinth; the twelfth, an amethyst.

²¹ And the twelve gates were twelve pearls; every several gate was of one pearl: and the street of the city was pure gold, as it were transparent glass.

²² And I saw no temple therein: for the Lord God Almighty and the Lamb are the temple of it.

²³ And the city had no need of the sun, neither of the moon, to shine in it: for the glory of God did lighten it, and the Lamb is the light thereof.

²⁴ And the nations of them which are saved shall walk in the light of it: and the kings of the earth do bring their glory and honour into it.

¹⁸ And the buildings were all of glittering steel, inlaid with thousands of sheets of clear glass.

¹⁹ And the foundations of the city were built upon all manner of wretched refuse. The first foundation was limeys; the second, krauts; the third, kikes; the fourth, coons;

²⁰ The fifth, micks; the sixth, wops; the seventh, Polacks; the eighth, bohunks; the ninth, spics; the tenth, chinks; the eleventh, nips; and the twelfth, A-rabs.

²¹ But the city they made was as one pearl: and the streets of the city were paved with gold, on which members of all twelve groups drove yellow chariots.

²² And there were no temples therein: for the city and the people inside are the temple.

²³ And the city had no need of the sun, neither of the moon, to shine in it: for it was lit by its own glory.

²⁴ And the representatives of all nations gather in the light of it: and all the peoples of the earth do bring their hopes and dreams to it.

25 And the gates of it shall not be shut at all by day: for there shall be no night there.

26 And they shall bring the glory and honour of the nations into it.

27 And there shall in no wise enter into it any thing that defileth, neither whatsoever worketh abomination, or maketh a lie: but they which are written in the Lamb's book of life.

25 And the gates of it shall never be shut: for the city shall never sleep.

26 And men shall bring the hopes and dreams of all the nations into it.

27 And there shall never again enter into it anything that defileth, neither whatsoever worketh abomination, or taketh life; but only the gorgeous, come to join the mosaic.

REVELATIONS
(Original)

CHAPTER 22

REVELATIONS
(Revised)

1 And he shewed me a pure river of water of life, clear as crystal, proceeding out of the throne of God and of the Lamb.

2 In the midst of the street of it, and on either side of the river, was there the tree of life, which bare twelve manner of fruits, and yielded her fruit every month: and the leaves of the tree were for the healing of the nations.

3 And there shall be no more curse: but the throne of God and of the Lamb shall be in it; and his servants shall serve him:

1 And he shewed me a pure river or water of life, clear as crystal, proceeding out of the fountain in front of a plaza.

2 In the midst of the streets, between the two rivers, was there a great park overflowing with grass and all manner of trees: and the trees and the park were for the healing of the people.

3 And there shall be no more sadness: but the throne of God and of the Bieb shall be in it; and her minions shall serve her:

4 And they shall see his face; and his name shall be in their foreheads.

5 And there shall be no night there; and they need no candle, neither light of the sun; for the Lord God giveth them light: and they shall reign for ever and ever.

6 And he said unto me, These sayings are faithful and true: and the Lord God of the holy prophets sent his angel to shew unto his servants the things which must shortly be done.

7 Behold, I come quickly: blessed is he that keepeth the sayings of the prophecy of this book.

8 And I John saw these things, and heard them. And when I had heard and seen, I fell down to worship before the feet of the angel which shewed me these things.

9 Then saith he unto me, See thou do it not: for I am thy fellow servant, and of thy brethren the prophets, and of them which keep the sayings of this book: worship God.

10 And he saith unto me, Seal not the sayings of the prophecy of this book: for the time is at hand.

4 And her face shall be in their wristwatches.

5 And there shall be no night there; and they need no candle, neither light of the sun; for God giveth them light: and she shall reign forever and ever.

6 And the angel said unto me, These sayings are faithful and true: and the Lord God of the holy prophets sent me to shew unto you the things which must shortly be done.

7 Blessed is he that keepeth the sayings of the prophecy of this book; and blessed more is he who purchaseth a copy.

8 And I saw all these things, and heard them. And when I had heard and seen, I said to the angel, Let me ask you a question: Did somebody give me acid tonight?

9 Then did the angel chuckle and saith unto me, yea, it was me, Jesus; it was right at 1:9, when I stopped by thy home office; I slipped a tab into thy Zico.

10 Yet dismiss not the visions thou hast beheld: for the time *is* at hand.

11 He that is unjust, let him be unjust still: and he which is filthy, let him be filthy still: and he that is righteous, let him be righteous still: and he that is holy, let him be holy still.

12 And, behold, I come quickly; and my reward is with me, to give every man according as his work shall be.

13 I am Alpha and Omega, the beginning and the end, the first and the last.

14 Blessed are they that do his commandments, that they may have right to the tree of life, and may enter in through the gates into the city.

15 For without are dogs, and sorcerers, and whoremongers, and murderers, and idolaters, and whosoever loveth and maketh a lie.

16 I Jesus have sent mine angel to testify unto you these things in the churches. I am the root and the offspring of David, and the bright and morning star.

11 What thou sawest, shall come to pass; and what thou sawest not, shall not come to pass; and he who believes thee, let him believe thee; and he who believes thee not, let him suck it.

12 For behold, I must go quickly; I am due in a meth-head's trailer in ten minutes to make a cameo in a paranoid delusion.

13 I am Alpha and Omega, the beginning and the end, the Hebe and the Bieb.

14 Blessed are they that make a reasonable attempt at abiding by as many of my teachings as possible, whether or not they believe in my divinity; for they may enter the gates of New Jerusalem;

15 Unlike the murderers, and sorcerers, and whoremongers, and the entire class of people who make things more unpleasant for other people than is strictly necessary.

16 I Jesus have sent mine angel to testify unto you these things in the churches. I am the root and offspring of David; I mean King David, not *thee*, thou Jewfro'd hack.

17 And the Spirit and the bride say, Come. And let him that heareth say, Come. And let him that is athirst come. And whosoever will, let him take the water of life freely.

18 For I testify unto every man that heareth the words of the prophecy of this book, If any man shall add unto these things, God shall add unto him the plagues that are written in this book:

19 And if any man shall take away from the words of the book of this prophecy, God shall take away his part out of the book of life, and out of the holy city, and from the things which are written in this book.

20 He which testifieth these things saith, Surely I come quickly. Amen. Even so, come, Lord Jesus.

21 The grace of our Lord Jesus Christ be with you all. Amen.

17 And the Simon and the Schuster say, Buy. And let him whose mouth gives word say, Buy. And let him that revieweth books say, Buy. And whosoever will, let him take this book freely, in exchange for money.

18 But I testify unto every man that readeth the words of the prophecy of this book, If any man shall add unto these things, God shall add unto him the plagues that are written in this book:

19 And if any man shall take away from the words of the book of this prophecy, God shall take away his part out of the book of life, and out of the holy city, and from the things which are written in this book.

20 And if thou believest that, I have a stairway to heaven to sell thee.

21 The grace of our Lord Jesus Christ be with you all. Amen.

CHAPTER 23

(THE LAST CHAPTER)

1   *Thou shalt bow as I present myself; I'm a being divine and supreme.*

2   *I've been around since the dawn of time; those who say not so, do blaspheme.*

3   *I was above when Jesus Christ gave his life to save your souls.*

4   *Made damn sure apostles wrote it down on moldy scrolls.*

5   *Gaze not on me; never say my name.*

6   *But what confoundest thee is my portion of the blame.*

7   *I watched them kill St. Peter; then I watched the Second Temple fall.*

8   *Now he's just a basilica, and it's only a Wailing Wall.*

9   *I was twice-paid during each Crusade when both sides died and both sides prayed.*

10 *Gaze not on me; never say my name.*

11 *Lo, yea.*

12 *But what confoundest thee is my portion of the blame.*

13 *Lo, yea.*

14 *I stayed at rest while I saw the West pass the centuries raping colonies.*

15 *I shouted out, "Who slew Leviathan?" when after all, it was only me.*

16 *Thou shalt bow as I present myself; I'm a being divine and supreme.*

17   *I had a lapse for two World Wars, but I'm thrilled about thy football team.*

18   *Gaze not on me; never say my name; lo, yea.*

19   *But what confoundeth thee is my portion of the blame; lo, yea.*

20   *Descendeth.*

21   *Gaze not on me; never say my name; lo, yea.*

22   *But what confoundest thee is my portion of the blame.*

23   *Just as every rabbi eats bacon, and all imams drink wine,*

24   *As wrong is right, call me Merciful; for I wouldst thou fall in line.*

25   *So this Apocalypse, show humility; show some piety and some awe.*

26   *Use every kiss-ass compliment, or I'll suck thee with a straw.*

27   *Gaze not on me; never say my name; lo, yea.*

28   *But what confoundest thee is my portion of the blame.*

29   *Descendeth.*

30   *Lo, yea, get down; lo, yea; lo, yea.*

31   *Never say it; never say my name.*

32   *Never think it; never think my name.*

33   *Never say it; never say my name.*

34   *Say it one time, I'll set thy skin aflame.*

35   *Lo, lo.*

36   *Lo, lo.*

37   *Lo, lo lo.*

38   *Lo, lo lo.*

39   *Lo, yea.*

40   *Lo, yea.*

41   *Lo, yea yea.*

42   *Lo, yea yea.*

(Long, slow fadeout.)

PRE-MISINTERPRETATIONS

he Author is aware that many verses in his previous Scriptures have been wildly, and often lethally, misinterpreted over the centuries. To expedite this process, he has asked that this time the publisher include, by way of exegesis, the following pre-misinterpretations of several key verses in this text. (Note: These are not intended to be the definitive misinterpretations. Readers are encouraged to form, preach, and enforce their own wrong ideas about any lines they like, so long as they in some way diverge from the words' clear meaning.)

PRE-MISINTERPRETATIONS

Chapter/Verse	Text	Misinterpretation
Againesis 4:17	"And Adam and Steve were naked, and felt no shame; they knew each other, as often as possible."	"I dislike homosexuals."
Againesis 14:23	"I have been accused of many things in my day, and of some rightly; but I am in no way homophobic."	"I strongly dislike homosexuals."
Reduxodus 9:9	"And thou shalt make his pans to receive his ashes, and his shovels, and his basins, and his fleshhooks, and his firepans."	"I cannot even begin to tell you how much I dislike homosexuals."
Reduxodus 9:13–16	"The laws of *kashrut* . . . are . . . lacking the barest lick of common sense."	"The laws of *kashrut* . . . are a vital means of preserving cultural identity in the face of an intermarriage epidemic watering Judaism down like a carp in a bathtub."
Jewed 2:8	"If [gentiles] could found a secret organization that meets once a week in the basements of local synagogues to control every aspect of law and finance and entertainment, they *would*."	"We gentiles have the cunning, deviousness, and duplicity needed to pull this off."
Games 1:20	"I have . . . on *extremely* rare occasions, influenced the outcome of a sporting event to affect the spread."	"And every single one of those occasions adversely impacted *you*, the specific fan or gambler reading this."
Gospel According to Dad 9:28	"Throughout his youth Jesus attended synagogue, and observed the Sabbath."	"Young Jesus liked to play dress-up Jew."
Gospel According to Dad 11:19	"[The devil] doth, indeed, visit people in their time of need; and offer to grant them mortal happiness in exchange for their immortal soul."	"The first time you hear about Obamacare, it might not sound that bad."
Koranicles 1:18	"Thou shalt not find any anti-Muslim propaganda anywhere in this book."	"This book is rife with the virulent hatred of Islam shared by all loyal Americans."
Romance 3:5	"I meant marriage to be a relationship between *any* two people, and the enormous amount of shit they have to deal with on a daily basis."	"God meant marriage to be a relationship between *any* two people, with *any* italicized because it is old High Akkadian for 'differently gendered.' "

ACKNOWLEDGMENTS

[1] nlike the universe, a book like this is not the kind of project one can throw together by oneself in under a week.

[2] No; a book like this is a journey through the forest of the mind, and the text is the trail of words left behind on that journey.

[3] But as it happens, my mind is an infinite forest; and since the information it holds is also infinite, putting it on paper would require chopping down every tree in that forest.

[4] (Plus it would have made for an ∞-page memoir; which the publishers felt, probably rightly, would make it a tough sell.)

[5] Thus a memoir like this requires skillful editing by a brilliant, strong-minded editor, with the confidence to offer frank editorial guidance to a writer who could reduce her down to cinders in a trillionth of a second.

[6] Fortunately such an editor was mine; so thank thee, Sarah Knight, for thy gift for language, thy good cheer, and thy deft emotional handling of an Author I admit could at times be quite temperamental.

[7] And sorry again about smiting that intern; although in my defense the coffee *was* cold.

[8] To Jonathan Karp, the head of Simon & Schuster, thanks for taking a chance—both creative and financial—on this project.

[9] I know the advance was steep; but given the sales of my previous books, it was fair.

[10] Fear not, Jon: After the first 300 million copies, the rest shall be pure profit!

[11] I would also like to thank my literary agent, Daniel Greenberg.

[12] This is thy triumph, too, Danny; thou went to bat for me; thou stuck with me e'en in the bad times; thou never lost faith in my work;

¹³ Yea, even after losing faith in my existence.

¹⁴ And Jessica Abell in Marketing and Kelly Welsh in Publicity: You were me-sends!

¹⁵ The human help I received in writing these Scriptures was vital; but in many ways, the real angels in this process were my angels.

¹⁶ There are so many I could thank, for their count is as numerous as the stars in heaven; but here I will mention only my four "Kids in the Halo": Uriel, Raphael, Michael, and Gabriel.

¹⁷ Ur, Raf, Mike, Gabe: you are my boon companions forever; I love you guys.

¹⁸ Above all, I would like to thank my wonderful family.

¹⁹ Sweetheart, I love thee more than ever.

²⁰ And kids: the three of you are *truly* my greatest accomplishments.

²¹ Lastly, a brief mention of my earthly amanuensis, David Javerbaum.

²² DJ, thou takest a mean dictation.

PHOTO CREDITS

18 Page 12: Ham, Brand X Pictures/Getty Images. Additional design by James Iacobelli.

19 Page 13: Map, © The Print Collector/Heritage-Images/Imagestate. Additional design by James Iacobelli.

20 Page 14: Portrait of Marthin Luther King Jr., AP Photo/Jim Bourdier.

21 Page 14: Portrait of Martin Luther, the Granger Collection, New York.

22 Page 14: Portrait of James Madison, the Granger Collection, New York.

23 Page 14: Portrait of Charles Darwin, the Granger Collection, New York.

24 Page 15: Photo of the Rat Pack, Warner Bros. Pictures/Photofest. Additional design by James Iacobelli.

25 Page 16: Photo of God in suit, © Michael Cogliantry.

INDEX